Cascading Style Sheets (Third Edition)

Georgina Evangeline
Abhilash Pillai

Cascading Style Sheets (Third Edition)

Part Number: 085568
Course Edition: 1.01

Acknowledgments

Project Team

Project Lead: Ravindran V • **Media Instructional Designers:** Georgina Evangeline and Abhilash Pillai • **Content Manager:** Adrian B K • **Content Editor:** Tayub Refai • **Material Editor:** Babu Subramanian • **Quality Assurance Analyst:** Padmanaban R • **Graphic Designer:** Manoj Pampady • **Art and Media Producer:** Muthuraman R

NOTICES

CASCADING STYLE SHEETS (THIRD EDITION)

LESSON 1: CONTROLLING COLOR AND TYPOGRAPHY

Contents

Lesson 2: Designing with the Cascade

Lesson 3: Designing Content Sections

LESSON 4: CONTROLLING LAYOUT WITH POSITIONING

LESSON 5: ENHANCING AN EXISTING DESIGN

Contents

ABOUT THIS COURSE

You are familiar with using HTML to design web pages. You have used HTML style-oriented tags and attributes to stylize and design your pages. Cascading Style Sheets, or CSS, is integrated into HTML 4.01 and forms an important component of successful web design. CSS offers great flexibility and ease in designing web pages without code heavy HTML documents. In this course, you will work with properties and styles related to colors, typography, page layouts, customized cursors, links, and forms available in CSS to build an effective web page.

As a web developer, you would have encountered the term CSS or *Cascading Style Sheets*. CSS significantly broadens the designer's palette and provides several advantages. Without CSS, it is time-consuming to create or update a web document. CSS provides web designers several design, usability and accessibility features. Also, web pages designed without CSS require a lot more code, resulting in bulkier documents that take longer to load.

Course Description

Target Student

Cascading Style Sheets (Third Edition) is intended for the student who is an experienced developer of web pages and has some experience with HTML. Students should be comfortable creating web pages, writing HTML code, and in using Internet Explorer or Netscape Navigator.

Course Prerequisites

To ensure your success, we recommend you first take the following Element K courses or have equivalent knowledge:

- *HTML 4.01: Web Authoring, Level 1 (Second Edition)*
- *HTML 4.01: Web Authoring, Level 2 (Second Edition)*

How to Use This Book

As a Learning Guide

Each lesson covers one broad topic or set of related topics. Lessons are arranged in order of increasing proficiency with *CSS*; skills you acquire in one lesson are used and developed in subsequent lessons. For this reason, you should work through the lessons in sequence.

We organized each lesson into results-oriented topics. Topics include all the relevant and supporting information you need to master *CSS*, and activities allow you to apply this information to practical hands-on examples.

You get to try out each new skill on a specially prepared sample file. This saves you typing time and allows you to concentrate on the skill at hand. Through the use of sample files, hands-on activities, illustrations that give you feedback at crucial steps, and supporting background information, this book provides you with the foundation and structure to learn *CSS* quickly and easily.

As a Review Tool

Any method of instruction is only as effective as the time and effort you are willing to invest in it. In addition, some of the information that you learn in class may not be important to you immediately, but it may become important later on. For this reason, we encourage you to spend some time reviewing the topics and activities after the course. For additional challenge when reviewing activities, try the "What You Do" column before looking at the "How You Do It" column.

As a Reference

The organization and layout of the book make it easy to use as a learning tool and as an after-class reference. You can use this book as a first source for definitions of terms, background information on given topics, and summaries of procedures.

Course Objectives

In this course, you will use cascading style sheets to design and develop efficient and effective websites.

You will:

- control color and typography.
- create style sheets that cascade according to established guidelines.
- design content sections using box properties.
- control your page layouts with CSS positioning.
- enhance an existing design.
- create alternate style sheets, and link your pages to them to enhance the accessibility and functionality of your websites.

Course Requirements

Hardware

PC

- A Pentium-class machine with a minimum processor speed of 233 MHz.
- At least 32 MB RAM (64 MB recommended).
- An 800 x 600 or higher resolution monitor set to High Color (16-Bit) or higher. A resolution of 1024 x 768 is strongly recommended (a higher resolution will provide more screen space to work).
- A working connection to the Internet (recommended).
- A networked or standalone printer.

Mac

- A PowerPC, G3, or G4 with a minimum processor speed of 266 MHz.
- At least 32 MB RAM (64 MB recommended).
- An 800 x 600 or higher resolution monitor set to High Color (16-Bit) or higher. A resolution of 1024 x 768 is strongly recommended (a higher resolution will provide more screen space to work).
- A working connection to the Internet (recommended).
- A networked or standalone printer.

Software

PC

- Windows 95, 98, 2000, Me, or XP.
- Netscape 7.1 (or higher) installed with default settings. You can download this browser for free at **http://www.netscape.com**.
- Microsoft Internet Explorer 6.0 (or higher) installed with default settings. You can download this browser for free at **http://www.microsoft.com**.

Mac

- Mac OS 8.6, 8.6.1, 9.x, or X.
- Netscape 7.1 (or higher) installed with default settings. You can download this browser for free at **http://www.netscape.com**.
- Microsoft Internet Explorer 6 (or higher) installed with default settings. You can download this browser for free at **http://www.microsoft.com**.

Class Setup

If your book did not come with a CD, please go to **http://www.elementk.com/courseware-file-downloads** *to download the data files.*

1. Install the course data files from the CD-ROM:
   — **Windows:** On the course CD-ROM, run the 085568dd.exe self-extracting file located within. This will install a folder named 085568Data on your C drive. This folder contains all the data files that you will use to complete this course. Solution files are also provided in this folder. These files may help you find a possible solution if you get stuck at any point during the course. If you would like to view the final output or solution of an activity, navigate to the respective lesson\activity\solution folder.
2. If you are using a Windows-based machine, in Windows Explorer, make sure that the File Extensions option is enabled.
3. If your computer does not have core fonts installed, such as Verdana, Arial, or Trebuchet MS, you should download them from **http://www.microsoft.com/typography/**. These basic fonts are available free-of-charge.
4. Connect to a standalone or networked printer.
5. If you are using a Windows-based machine, in Internet Explorer, make sure the Edit With Windows Notepad button is available on the toolbar. If it's not, choose View→Toolbars, and select Customize. In the Customize Toolbar dialog box, select the Edit button and click Add. Click Close to apply the change.
6. In addition to the specific setup procedures needed for this class to run properly, you should also check the Element K Press product support website **http://support.elementkcourseware.com** for more information. Any updates about this course will be posted there.

List of Additional Files

Printed with each activity is a list of files students open to complete that activity. Many activities also require additional files that students do not open, but are needed to support the file(s) students are working with. These supporting files are included with the student data files on the course CD-ROM or data disk. Do not delete these files.

LESSON 1
Controlling Color and Typography

Lesson Time
2 hour(s), 30 minutes

Lesson Objectives:

In this lesson, you will control color and typography.

You will:

- Create an embedded style sheet.
- Apply color.
- Create CSS comments.
- Apply text properties to control the alignment, spacing, casing, and indentation of text.
- Apply font styles to control typography.
- Create a style sheet and link multiple documents to it.

Introduction

You are already familiar with HTML and its use in designing web pages. A Cascading Style Sheet, or CSS, offers great flexibility and ease in designing effective web pages. CSS styles are considered *safe* styles as they are well supported by a majority of browsers and do not affect the usability of your documents when viewed in browsers that don't support these styles. In this lesson, you'll design web pages using CSS to apply color and typography styles.

When working on a large document with HTML tags and attributes you will have to spend hours checking every element or attribute to edit its color and text style settings. The size and style of text influences the height and width of content sections, which requires you to go back and make changes to the established layout. Establishing the typographical styles before deciding on the layout provides you with a good idea of what you're working on, in terms of available page space, and it also reduces rework to a great extent.

TOPIC A

Create an Embedded Style Sheet

You are familiar with using HTML to design web pages. You can apply color and text styles to web pages more effectively using CSS. However, before applying color and typographical styles to a document, you need to define a style sheet. In this topic, you will create embedded style sheets and add simple rules to control and style them.

Embedded style sheets allow you to control all aspects of a page's design from a central location in the document. This allows you to develop the page faster and to easily update your styles. CSS provides the flexibility to implement designs that are not possible with HTML alone.

Cascading Style Sheet (CSS)

Cascading Style Sheet, or CSS, is a core technology of dynamic HTML (*DHTML*), which also includes HTML, the document object model (DOM), and scripting languages like JavaScript. Together, these technologies allow for the manipulation of web content and the creation of dynamic and interactive pages. You will learn how CSS interacts with scripts in later lessons.

Though there are other *style sheet* languages, CSS is the standard presentational markup language for the web. With CSS, you can modify a document's appearance by changing the formatting of page elements, just like a word processor template. CSS is an elegantly designed specification that is easy to learn and use. With its powerful, common sense approach to page layout and design, several websites use CSS to control all presentational attributes such as the colors, fonts, and positioning.

CSS Specifications

CSS Level One (CSS-1) is the first specification of Cascading Style Sheets. It is partially supported by Netscape Navigator 4.x and Microsoft Internet Explorer 4.x, and is fully supported in Navigator 7.1, Internet Explorer 6 (PC) and 5 (Macintosh).

CSS Level Two (CSS-2) has several new features, many of which are also supported in Navigator 7.1, Internet Explorer 6 for Macintosh and Windows, as well as in lesser known browsers like Opera and Konqueror. CSS-2 expands on CSS-1 and includes all of Level One's features, except for some minor modifications in terminology and functionality.

Benefits of CSS

CSS adds flexibility and ease to designing effective web pages. With CSS, you can:

- Separate style from basic document structure.

  With a single text document, the layout and design of an entire website can be controlled. This translates into greater efficiency than you could achieve with style-related HTML elements and attributes. Preserving document structure also enables Internet search engines to index documents more efficiently. Separation of style and structure makes HTML documents more efficient. As the amount of HTML code needed to design a page is greatly reduced, pages load faster and are far easier to update.

- Create clean, standards-compliant code.

  Websites using CSS will be standards-compliant. This means that websites can be viewed in a variety of emerging client devices.

- Improve the accessibility of websites.

  With the separation of style and structure, users with alternative browsers like screen readers and Braille devices can effectively scan web documents. CSS also includes several powerful techniques that allow you to enhance the accessibility and usability of your websites in ways that cannot be done by using HTML alone.

- Develop and maintain websites quickly and easily.

  Authoring with CSS speeds up development time by precluding the need to insert style information into every element in a document. From a single document, you can change the presentation of an entire website without having to modify any HTML code.

Style Sheet Types

There are four types of Cascading Style Sheets: inline, embedded, linked, and imported.

Style Sheet Type	Description
Inline	Inline styles only affect the HTML element that they're directly inserted into.
Embedded	Embedded style sheets control the styles for the page in which they are embedded.
Linked	Linked style sheets can control the design of multiple documents.
Imported	Imported style sheets can also control the design of multiple documents and are typically used for purposes of modularity.

LESSON 1

Style Sheet Rules

Style sheets establish *rules* that declare how certain elements are rendered on a page or throughout a site. Style sheet rules apply specific style commands that effect the elements in a document. Every style sheet rule contains four components:

- A *selector*, which selects the element you want to style.
- A *declaration*, which applies the style to the selected element.
- One or more properties within the declaration.
- And, a *value* for each *property*.

Properties are predefined terms that define the action taken on an element. For example, the `color` property applies a color specification to an element. All properties have a value, an exact specification of the property. The selector always precedes the declaration, which consists of everything inside the declaration's braces.

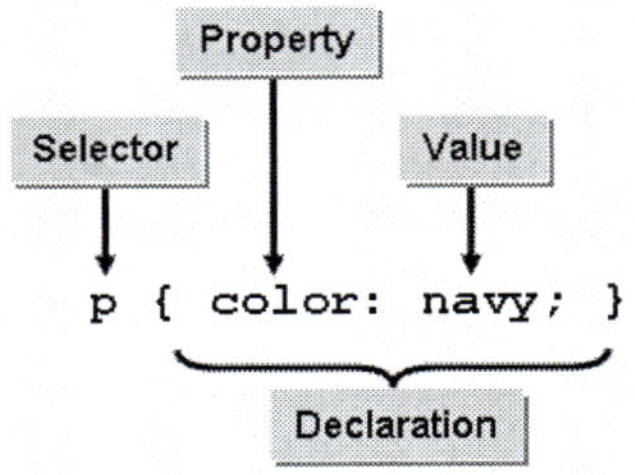

Grouping Properties

You can declare one or more properties for a rule. For example, if you want all paragraphs to have navy text and a silver background, you can group the properties together within a rule by separating each property with a semicolon.

```
p { color: blue; background-color: silver; }
```

Type Selectors

You can use any valid HTML element as a selector for your style rules. The <p>, <div>, or <td> tags are *type selectors* that attach a style to a particular HTML element. When you use a type selector, every instance of that HTML element picks up the style. Most type selectors are not case-sensitive, so it doesn't matter if your HTML markup is uppercase and your type selectors are lowercase, or vice versa. Type selectors were previously referred to as *element selectors*.

There are many kinds of selectors, but type selectors are the most basic.

Grouping Selectors

You can group selectors if you want to apply the same styles to more than one element. By grouping multiple selectors into one rule, you can make your style sheets more economical and avoid redundant statements. For example, if you want three elements to share the same style characteristics, it would be very tedious to declare each style separately, like this:

```
td  { color: orange; }
p   { color: orange; }
div { color: orange; }
```

Spaces are optional
rember ;

Using CSS you can group the three selectors into one rule by separating each selector with a comma:

```
td, p, div { color: orange; }
```

Embedded Style Sheets

Embedded style sheets control the design of the document in which they are embedded. They allow you to separate all your style information from the document's structure or the elements that make up the HTML document. Embedded style sheets are defined by the `<style>` element, which contains your style sheet rules.

The <style> Element

Embedded style sheets are the only style sheet type that uses the HTML `<style>` element to contain its rules. The `<style>` element must be placed inside a document's head section or the `<head>` element. The `<style>` element uses the type attribute to declare the content type for the style sheet. Web style sheets are defined with the content type `text/css`.

```
<html>
<head><title>Sample Page</title>
<style type="text/css">
<!--
body { background-color: #eee;
font-size: 12px; }
h1 { color: navy; }
p { color: #333; }
-->
</style>
</head>
<body>
<h1>Welcome!</h1>
<p>This is a sample paragraph for demonstration.</p>
</body>
</html>
```

Characteristics of the <style> Element

Style rules are enclosed in an HTML comment tag. This is required as older browsers like Netscape Navigator 2.0, Internet Explorer 2.0, and older AOL browsers do not support style sheets. Though, there aren't many of these in use anymore, it's possible that your site will be visited by a user with one of these older browsers. It's important to ensure that the site content is still usable by all.

When one of these older browsers encounters a `<style>` container, it doesn't understand the `<style>` element, so the element itself is ignored but its contents are not. Any rules you have inside your `<style>` element will display as text, which will be confusing and meaningless to users. By enclosing your embedded style sheet rules within an HTML comment tag, you can prevent the rules from being displayed as text in older browsers.

How to Create an Embedded Style Sheet

Procedure Reference: Create an Embedded Style Sheet

To create an embedded style sheet:

1. Obtain a valid HTML document with at least the basic structural elements `<html>`, `<head>`, and `<body>`.

   It's vital that you always start with a valid HTML document. If you have nesting errors, missing closing tags, or any other kind of syntax error in your HTML code, your styles might not work as you expect. This will inevitably lead to frustration and the assumption that your CSS is the problem. Always validate your HTML code before or during CSS development.

2. Inside the document's `<head>` section, insert a `<style>` container with the `type="text/css"` attribute and value.
3. Add an HTML comment delimiter inside the `<style>` container.
4. Inside the HTML comment, add the desired style rules.
5. Save the changes, and reload the page to verify the result of the style rules.

Adding White Space

The amount of space you insert between the opening brace, rules, and the closing brace is a matter of preference. It's generally a good idea to make sure that your styles can be easily read. For example, you can keep all properties on their own lines, as follows:

```
p {
color: blue;
background-color: silver; }
```

It's always a good idea to insert a semicolon after every property value—even if it's the last property in a rule. This way, it's easier to add styles later, and you don't have to worry about forgetting them.

OPTIONAL ACTIVITY 1-1

Reviewing a CSS-Based Design

Data Files:

- index.html

Scenario:

You're just getting started with CSS-based web development, so you decide to explore an existing CSS-based design to get a handle on the kind of design control you will have for future projects. Someone on your team gives you the files for the NewsParrot website, which is designed with Cascading Style Sheets. You need to evaluate it to determine if CSS will allow you to create the designs, layouts, and unique effects that are impossible with straight HTML. Starting with the index.html file (the home page for the NewsParrot website), you need to observe the color, typography, layout, and other design effects in use to reinforce your interest in moving forward with CSS-based designs.

What You Do	How You Do It
1. **Navigate through the NewsParrot site.**	a. **Navigate to the C:\085568Data\color and typography\Activity 1\Starter\Instructor Demo folder and open index.html.** b. In the Main navigation box, **click through the links.**
2. **Observe how color, typography, and layout have been applied.**	a. **Notice that the site has a clear and consistent color scheme across all pages. The content sections that use color for emphasis are consistent and provide effective visual cues.** b. **Notice that the typographical styles are consistent throughout the site pages. The text and font styles used throughout the site are consistently applied, and the style choices make the text easy to read.** c. **Notice that the layout scheme provides for clear delineation between content sections. The layout consists of separate content sections that are clearly distinguished with borders and ample white space.** d. **Close the Internet Explorer window.**

ACTIVITY 1-2

Creating an Embedded Style Sheet and Adding Rules

Activity Time:

10 minutes

Data Files:

- info.html

Scenario:

You're just getting started on a new design project for the Illuminati publishing company. The HTML coding is complete, and you want to begin adding styles to modify the design. The page you're working on has no color other than the client's logo image. To get started, you need to create an embedded style sheet in which you can add rules to control the page's design. In particular, you need to add color to the paragraph text and both headings in the document.

What You Do	How You Do It
1. **Open the info.html file and view the source code.** The page is fairly simple and is arranged using an HTML table to provide a typical layout to which you can add CSS styles.	a. On the desktop, **double-click the Internet Explorer icon.** b. **Choose File→Open.** c. In the Open dialog box, **click Browse.** d. **Navigate to the C:\085568Data\color and typography\Activity 2\Starter\Illuminati folder and double-click the info.html file.** e. **Click OK.** f. **Choose View→Source** to open the source code for the page.

2. **Insert an embedded style sheet container and view the result.**

   a. In the Info.html - Notepad window, **click after the `</title>` element and press Enter.**

   b. In the Head section, under the `<title>` element, **insert an embedded style sheet container for the info.html file.**

      See Code Sample 1.

   c. **Choose File→Save** to save the changes.

   d. **Minimize the Info.html - Notepad window.**

   e. In the Internet Explorer window, **click the Refresh button** to reload the page.

   f. **Notice that there will be no changes to the document because the embedded style sheet does not yet contain any style rules.**

Code Sample 1

```
<style type="text/css">
<!--
-->
</style>
```

---

3. **Change the color of the level-one heading.**

   a. **Restore the Info.html - Notepad window.**

   b. In the `<style>` container, **click after `<!--` and press Enter.**

   c. **Type `h1 { color: teal; }` and press Enter.**

   d. **Choose File→Save.**

   e. **Minimize the Info.html - Notepad window.**

   f. In the Internet Explorer window, **click the Refresh button.** The style rule changes the default color of the heading text to teal.

---

4. **Change the color of all paragraphs in the document.**

   a. **Restore the Info.html - Notepad window.**

   b. **Type `p { color: navy; }`**

   c. **Choose File→Save.**

   d. **Minimize the Info.html - Notepad window.**

   e. In the Internet Explorer window, **click the Refresh button.** The paragraph text will be displayed in navy blue.

---

5. **Change the color of the level-two heading without creating a new rule.**

   a. **Restore the Info.html - Notepad window.**

   b. **Click after `h1` and type `, h2`**

   c. **Choose File→Save.**

   d. **Close the Info.html - Notepad window.**

   e. In the Internet Explorer window, **click the Refresh button.**

   f. **Close the Internet Explorer window.**

---

6. **Would the embedded styles have influence over other pages on the site?**

TOPIC B

Apply Color

You have created an embedded style sheet and inserted simple style elements to control and style a document. Every web page has a color scheme that helps create its distinctive character and atmosphere. With CSS, applying and controlling colors in web documents is easy and flexible. In this topic, you will learn how to apply color in more detail to achieve the effect you desire.

Color enhances the look and appeal of a web document and forms a critical element of any web page. Typically, an organization's logo or *corporate colors* dictate the palette you will have to use. Using CSS to apply and control colors in web documents is far more powerful, flexible and easy. Remember, it is very time-consuming to change the color settings of a large web document with several HTML color-specific tags and attributes like `bgcolor`, or the `color` attribute of the `<font>` tag. With CSS, you can effectively apply and edit colors in your web pages and easily establish consistency across pages using style sheets.

Color Methods

Color methods in CSS allow you to declare the color of an element. There are three color methods in CSS—color names, RGB values, and hexadecimal values.

Color Names

Color names are predefined keywords in CSS that represent a specific color. There are 16 color name keywords in the CSS specification that are considered as *safe colors*, for they appear similar in different browsers and operating systems. These colors are:

black	maroon
white	purple
silver	fuchsia
gray	teal
blue	green
navy	lime
aqua	yellow
red	olive

There are hundreds of additional color names that are not part of the official HTML or CSS specifications. If you validate your CSS code or HTML markup, you might get an error message regarding a color name that's not recognized as one of the 16 safe colors in the official specifications.

RGB Format

The RGB format is a method of specifying gradations of red, green, and blue that combine to create a specific color in the visible spectrum. Specifying color in the RGB format is a more powerful and flexible method than using color names, because there are more than 16 million colors available in the full color palette. There are 256 possible gradations for each red, green, and blue value—256 x 256 x 256 = 16,777,216 colors.

When you specify a color in the RGB format, the value must begin with `rgb`, followed by parentheses that enclose the red, green, and blue values. Red is always the first pair, green the second, and blue the third pair. You can specify the values as an integer value within 0-255 or as a percentage within 0-100%. You can apply colors in the RGB format in two different ways.

```
div { color: rgb(100,50,55); }
td  { color: rgb(40%,12%,67%); }
```

You can also combine the two methods in one syntax:

```
p { color: rgb(53%,114,21%); }
```

The above rule states that the paragraph text will have 53% red, 114% green, and 21% blue; it will be displayed in a brownish-green color. The greater the percentage value or number, the greater the intensity of that specific color.

You can create shades of gray by specifying equal values of red, green, and blue in either hexadecimal or RGB format. For example, `rgb(190,190,190)` is a light shade of gray. The exceptions to this are black (where all the values are 0) and white (where all the values are 255).

Hexadecimal Values

Hexadecimal values, or *hex* values as they are commonly called, are the most commonly applied color method on the web. Hexadecimal values are equivalent to RGB values, but use a different syntax.

Hexadecimal values consist of a pound sign (#), followed by any combination of the integers 0-9 and the letters A through F. There are three pairs of these value combinations; one for each red, green and blue value. They are expressed as `#RRGGBB`. The value `00` gives no color value, while `FF` gives a full red, green, or blue value.

For example, when the rule defined by the <body> element gives no color value for red, green, or blue, the page background will be rendered black—the absence of any color.

```
body { color: #000000; }
```

If the red, green, and blue values are defined in full strength, the page background will be rendered white, which typically marks the presence of all colors.

```
body { color: #ffffff; }
```

The 216 *safe* colors in the hexadecimal palette are those colors that are represented by combinations of the following six values: 00, 33, 66, 99, CC, and FF. Since there are six possible values for each of the three red, green, and blue variables, 6 x 6 x 6 = 216 possible permutations exist. These colors display consistently across different browsers and operating systems. Hexadecimal values are not case-sensitive.

Shorthand Hex Values

A shorthand notation can be used to represent your hexadecimal values: you can use the `#RGB` format instead of the full `#RRGGBB` notation. With the shorthand method, a single color value represents a red, green, or blue value pair. For example, the two rules declare the same color:

```
h1 { color: #336699; }
h1 { color: #369; }
```

However, this means that the shorthand method can't access all colors in the hexadecimal palette because you have to use a color with RGB pairs, such as `#ccff33`. The shorthand method cannot be used to declare the hex color `#ac3fde`. Mostly, shorthand hex values are used by developers to ensure that their chosen colors are within the 216 *safe* colors, since RGB pairs are required in the shorthand method. You can still specify a color using the hex shorthand that's not among the *safe* 216 colors, such as `#3d9` or `#0ef`.

Foreground and Background Colors

An element's foreground color is simply its text color. Foreground color has no effect for non-text elements like images. An element's background color is displayed behind the text. Color is controlled by two CSS properties: `color` and `background-color`.

The color Property

The `color` property controls an element's foreground color. The default foreground color for any text element, usually black, depends on the browser. But if you want the text elements of all your paragraphs to be blue, you may write:

```
p { color: blue; }
```

The background-color Property

The `background-color` property controls an element's background color. For example, if you want all the elements in the paragraph to have a silver background, you may write:

```
p { background-color: silver; }
```

In the following figure, the background color fills the entire area of every <p> element. By default, when you apply a background color to a block-level element, the background color fills the element's entire containment area, which is defined by the width of the browser window; this includes any margins that might be present, the width of the element's parent element, or the width of the element itself.

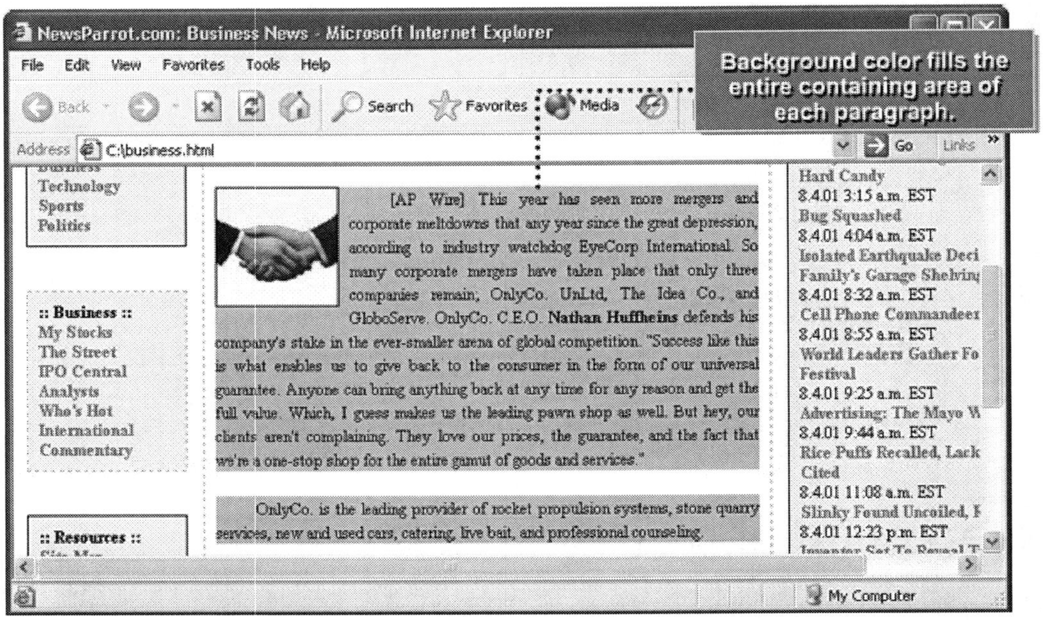

If you apply a background color to an inline-level element like <span> or <i>, the background color will extend only to the length of the element's text as shown in the following figure.

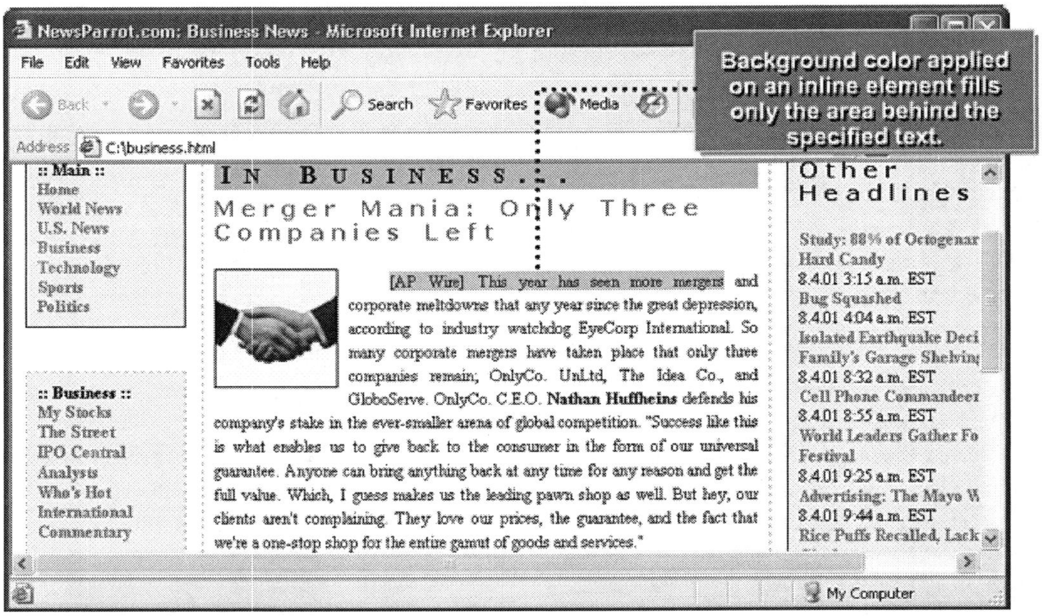

Inheritance

Inheritance is a mechanism in CSS whereby elements pick up the styles of their parent elements. The CSS properties `color` and `background-color` inherit styles from parent elements.

Applying the Rule of Inheritance

The law of inheritance ensures continuity of styles. As a result of the law of inheritance, all the child elements nested within a paragraph also pick up an applied style. For example, if you set the color for the following paragraph:

```
<p>To apply by mail, send your application to <address>
RandomFolks, P.O. Box 1, Thisldo, NY, 14141. </address></p>
```

Then, the `<address>` element nested within the paragraph will also pick up the applied color style.

This makes perfect sense as you wouldn't want to break up a section of text with different styles every time it contains one or more child elements.

The default values of the `color` and `background-color` properties enforce this rule of inheritance. For the `color` property, `inherit` is the default value; `transparent` is the default value of the `background-color` property. Both of these values literally mean, use the parent element's color or background color.

These values are important because you should always declare a background color when you specify text color, and vice-versa. Some users set their own color choices in their browser preferences, and these colors will apply to your site if you don't explicitly declare them. For example, if you specify navy text but do not declare a background color, and a user has navy set as the default background color, the text on the pages will not be visible. You can ensure that this does not happen if you use the `inherit` and `transparent` values; you don't need to change an element's inherited text or background color.

The property of inheritance is not limited to color. All CSS properties that accept the keyword value `inherit` can be inherited by child elements.

How to Apply Color

Color is not necessarily a *requirement* of web design, but you won't find many well-designed sites that consist only of black text on a white background. Good designers know that there is more to choosing colors than arbitrary matters of taste. Effective application of color on your website will establish the overall look and feel of your design and enhance your site's appeal, readability, and usability.

Guidelines

To apply color effectively:

- Use color consistently across your site pages.
- Use color to create emphasis where necessary.
- Use color to highlight areas that deserve focus.
- Use color to provide a *path* for the eye to follow.
- Ensure there's sufficient contrast between your background and foreground colors.
- Create clear delineations between headings and related content.

There's a way to approach these things, of course. It all depends on the project at hand, the target audience, and a variety of other factors. But if you choose your colors with these guidelines in mind, you are likely to find creative ways to improve your site's use of color.

Example:

For example, the web pages color1.html and color2.html (both of which are found in the Instructor Demo folder) show a page with poor use of color and another with more effective use of color.

In color2.html, the colors have purpose—to reinforce the relationships between content sections, draw the user's eye toward specific text, and generally help users navigate through the site's sections to locate important material. Thinking critically about how you use color in your pages will help you produce more effective designs.

ACTIVITY 1-3

Adding Color with Hexadecimal and RGB Values

Activity Time:

5 minutes

Data Files:

- info.html

Before You Begin:

From the C:\085568Data\color and typography\Activity 3\Starter\Illuminati folder, open the info.html file in Internet Explorer and its source file in Notepad.

Scenario:

You're ready to establish the color scheme for the Illuminati website. Your client has asked you to use colors that complement the colors in their logo. You need to apply color values that meet this request, which will likely require either RGB or hexadecimal values so that you can access a larger palette of colors than color name keywords provide.

You need to apply color to several elements on the page, including the link text, the `<h1>` element, all paragraphs, and the `<i>` and `<address>` elements.

You can use the color_swatches.html page as a resource. This page contains a table of many colors and their associated hexadecimal and RGB codes. The color_swatches.html file is in the C:\085568Data\instructor demo folder.

You can also refer to the following list as a resource for suitable colors and their suggested elements:

use w/ hex

- `#99CCB3` or `rgb(153,204,179)` for heading background color.
- `#FFF` or `rgb(255,255,255)` for address text color.
- `#699` or `rgb(102,153,153)` for address background color.
- `#006` or `rgb(0,0,102)` for paragraph and link text color.
- `transparent` for paragraph background color.
- `inherit` for italic text color.
- `#FFC` or `rgb(255,255,204)` for background color of italic text.

What You Do	How You Do It
1. **Change the color of all link text.**	a. In the Info.html - Notepad window, **click after `h1, h2 { color: teal; }` and press Enter.**
	b. **Type `a { color: #006; }` and press Enter.**
	c. **Choose File→Save.**
	d. **Minimize the Info.html - Notepad window.**
	e. In the Internet Explorer window, **click the Refresh button.** All links will be displayed in dark blue.
2. **Change the foreground and background colors of the page elements using the details given in the scenario as a guide.**	a. **Restore the Info.html - Notepad window.**
	b. In the embedded style sheet, **click after `<!--` and press Enter.**
	c. In the style sheet, **insert the code** to define the foreground and background colors of the page elements. *See Code Sample 1.*
	d. **Choose File→Save** to save the changes.
	e. **Minimize the Info.html - Notepad window.**
	f. In the Internet Explorer window, **click the Refresh button** to reload the page. The colors will now more precisely complement the colors in the company logo.
	g. **Close both the Internet Explorer and the Info.html - Notepad windows.**

Code Sample 1

```
h1, h2 {color: teal;background-color: #99CCB3;}
address { color: #FFF;background-color: #699; }
p { color: navy;background-color: transparent;}
i { color: inherit;background-color: #FFC; }
a { color: #006; }
```

3. **Of all the colors listed in the scenario, which color cannot be expressed with a short-hand hexadecimal value, and why?**

ACTIVITY 1-4

Applying Colors for Effective Design

Activity Time:

10 minutes

Data Files:

- index.html

Before You Begin:

From the C:\085568Data\color and typography\Activity 4\Starter\NewsParrot folder, open the index.html file in Internet Explorer and its source file in Notepad.

Scenario:

You've been asked to develop a color scheme for NewsParrot's home page that reinforces the colors in the client's logo. To help you get started, they've provided you with a mock-up of their home page content, index.html, and their logo. The colors in the logo establish a basic palette from which you've been asked to choose colors. You need to apply complementary colors to the page, and make color choices that provide clear delineation and emphasis for each content section. You need to decide which elements or content sections to style, which colors to choose, and then apply them to the page for review by the client.

You can use the color_swatches.html page, in the C:\085568Data\instructor demo folder, as a resource for your color choices.

You can also use the following colors, which lists several complementary color choices and also provides a reference of the content sections in the index.html file.

The following lists the hex value, RGB value, and color description of complementary colors:

- `#668099`; `102,128,153`—Gray-blue
- `#CCC`; `204,204,204`—Light gray
- `#FA9B17`; `250,155,23`—Orange
- `#99B3CC`; `153,179,204`—Light blue
- `#FFF`; `255,255,255`—White

The following lists the elements that can be used as selectors:

- `div`: Contains the navigation links along the top.
- `h1`: Contains the text Top Story.
- `h2`: Elements contain the text Nothing New and Other News.
- `p`: Elements contain all the body text.

- `address`: Contains the page's copyright statement and address.
- `a`: Elements (link tags) define the document's links.

What You Do	How You Do It
1. In the index.html file, **determine which elements you want to style and the colors you want to apply.** Base your decision on the colors in the image.	a. **Determine the background color to apply on the page.** b. **Determine the heading text and the background colors to apply.** c. **Determine the link text and the background color to apply.** d. **Determine the paragraph color to apply.** e. **Determine the color to apply for the copyright statement and the address.**
2. **Match the background color to the company logo's outer color.**	a. In the embedded style sheet, **click after `<!--` and press Enter.** b. **Type `body { background-color:#99B3CC; }`** c. **Choose File→Save.** d. **Minimize the Index.html - Notepad window.** e. In the Internet Explorer window, **click the Refresh button.**

3. **Add style sheet rules to change colors by using hexadecimal shorthand values, and also to group two properties and selectors for a rule.**

   a. **Restore the Index.html - Notepad window.**

   b. **Press Enter.**

   c. In the style sheet, **insert the code** to change the colors of headings, link text, and copyright statement by using hexadecimal shorthand values, and to group two properties and selectors for a rule.

      See Code Sample 1.

   d. **Choose File→Save.**

   e. **Close the Index.html - Notepad window.**

   f. In the Internet Explorer window, **click the Refresh button.**

Code Sample 1

```
h1 { color: #FA9B17; background-color: #668099; }
h2 { color: black; background-color: #CCC; }
a, address { color: #FFF; }
```

---

4. **Verify your results against the guidelines in the scenario.**

   a. Do the colors strain your eyes, or are they complementary?

   b. Does your use of background color effectively draw your eye to different areas of content and provide clear delineation between content sections?

   c. Do your color choices provide effective visual emphasis for content that might require it?

   d. Is it easy to quickly identify different content sections?

   e. Is the text easy to read against every background color?

   f. **Modify the color styles until you're satisfied with the results.**

   g. **Close the Internet Explorer Window.**

TOPIC C

Comment Your Code

You applied color to enhance the overall look and usability of your web pages. Sometimes, it may not be clear why the rules in the style sheets were created. In this topic, you will learn how to add appropriate CSS comments to clearly document the role of particular rules in your style sheets.

When creating large HTML documents, you will apply several CSS rules to these documents. Sometimes these rules are not self-explanatory, so it will be harder for you and other developers to understand and update your style sheet rules later. Adding comments to your code allows you to record information about your rules. For example, if you add a comment next to a hexadecimal or RGB color value that indicates the declared color, you won't have to remember or look up the color code. This will also help other developers who might need to modify the code at some point.

CSS Comments

CSS comments are statements in the CSS code that provide meta-information about a particular rule, group of rules, or the style sheet itself. Just as in HTML comments, you can write anything that will be helpful to you or another developer, without affecting the code that controls the design. Adding comments next to a particular style, rule, or group of rules enables the user of the style sheet to easily parse the code and determine the effect that each style has on the page. Like all other code comments, CSS comments are not displayed to the end user in the browser.

Inserting CSS Comments

CSS comments are denoted with the forward slash (/) and asterisk (*) characters, as follows:

```
/* Your comment here */
```

A typical application of a style sheet comment might look like this:

```
selector { property: value; } /* Relevant comment */
```

Or, you can even put comments inside rules, like this:

```
selector { property: value; /* Relevant comment */
property: value; /* Another comment */ }
```

How to Comment Your Code

Inserting effective comments can help you and other developers to read and understand the purpose of certain style sheet rules, thus making it easier to revise the rules when required.

Guidelines

To create effective comments:

- Use them when the purpose of a particular style or rule is not immediately clear or self-explanatory.
- Describe your declared color when you apply RGB or hexadecimal color values.
- Write your comment text clearly and succinctly.

- Use them to group rules that are related in one way or other.
- Use them to provide meta-information about the style sheet itself, if required by your organization or client.

Example:

For example, it isn't always easy to discern the actual color you're dealing with when you look at a hexadecimal value, especially when you get into the nether region of the 16 million RGB color values. For this reason, it's a good idea to include CSS comments that describe the color you're using.

You can also use comments to insert meta-information about the style sheet itself, including the author name, the date the style sheet was created, the date it was last modified, and so on. This can help you track revisions and keep you or your project team informed of changes.

ACTIVITY 1-5

Commenting Code

Activity Time:

5 minutes

Data Files:

- index.html

Before You Begin:

From the C:\085568Data\color and typography\Activity 5\Starter\NewsParrot folder, open the index.html file in Internet Explorer and its source file in Notepad.

Scenario:

You have set the colors for NewsParrot's index.html page, but you and your development team agree to write comments next to any rules or values that are not self-explanatory, or may require meta-information to make the style sheets easier to read and understand.

What You Do	How You Do It
1. **Write CSS comments for each rule that closely indicates the colors.**	a. In the embedded style sheet, **click after <!-- and press Enter.**
	b. **Insert the code** to write CSS comments for the color choices you have made. *See Code Sample 1.* You can enter CSS comments inside or outside the declaration braces.
	c. **Choose File→Save.**
	d. **Close the Index.html - Notepad window.**
	e. In the Internet Explorer window, **click the Refresh button.**
	f. **Notice that there are no changes to the document displayed because CSS comments are not rendered in the browser.**
	g. **Close the Internet Explorer window.**

Code Sample 1

```
body{background-color:#99B3CC;/*light blue*/ }
h1{color: #FA9B17; background-color: #668099;/*gray-blue*/}
h2{color: black; background-color: #CCC;/*light gray*/}
a, address { color: #FFF; /*white text*/ }
```

2. **Which of these codes represent valid usage of comments?**
   a) selector { property: value; } /* comment */
   b) selector { property: value; } */ comment /*
   c) selector { property: value; /* Relevant comment */ property: value; /* Another comment */ }
   d) selector { property: value; /* Relevant comment */ property: value; /* Another comment }*/
   e) selector /* { property: value; } comment /*

3. **How do your comments add to the effectiveness of the code?**

TOPIC D

Modify Text Styles

You have applied color styles and added CSS comments to certain rules in the style sheet. Text is a critical component of an effective web page. The appearance of text plays an important role in web design because it enhances the general usability of your site pages and establishes the overall look and feel of your site. In this topic, you will explore the text styles needed to control the alignment, spacing, casing, and indentation of your text content.

As a web designer, your primary goal is to communicate your message effectively through your web page. It is vital to control the manner in which text is displayed in a web page. HTML offers very limited control over text styles. CSS text properties allow you to control the readability of text, which is vital to the success of any textual content.

Text Styles

Typography generally refers to font faces, font sizing, and the alignment and spacing of type. CSS *text styles* are intended to control the appearance of text, and are not designed to influence images or content layout. You can use several typographical properties to enhance the readability and appearance of content on your web page. Some of these properties aren't supported in older browsers such as Internet Explorer 4.x and Netscape Navigator 4.x, but the more standards-compliant browsers support them consistently.

The ability to control typographical styles is unique to CSS. In HTML, there is no mechanism that can achieve true typographical control other than alignments.

CSS text properties allow you to control various aspects of text in your document.

Property	Description
`text-align`	Controls the horizontal alignment of text content.
`vertical-align`	Controls the vertical alignment of text content. This property is not supported in Netscape Navigator 4.x, and is only partially supported in Internet Explorer 4.x.
`text-indent`	Applies an indent of any specified length to the first line of text in a paragraph or other element containing text.
`letter-spacing`	Modifies the amount of space between the letters of any given text element. This is known as *kerning*. This property is not supported in Netscape Navigator 4.x.
`word-spacing`	Modifies the amount of space between the words of any given text element. This property is only supported in Netscape Navigator 6 and above, Internet Explorer 6, and Opera 3.

Property	Description
line-height	Controls the spacing between adjacent lines of text. This is known as *leading,* pronounced as ledding. This property is supported well by most browsers, except for Netscape Navigator 4.x, which has only partial support for it.
text-decoration	Creates underline, overline, and line-through effects on any given text element.
text-transform	Controls the casing of text—either uppercase, lowercase, or initial capitalized letters. This property is important for enforcing a site's style guide with regard to text casing.

The `text-indent` property is the only text property that does not inherit child elements.

Horizontal Text Alignment

You can set the horizontal alignment of text to `left`, `center`, `right`, and `justify`. These values are common in word processing and all other software programs that deal with text. These alignments can be controlled with the `text-align` property.

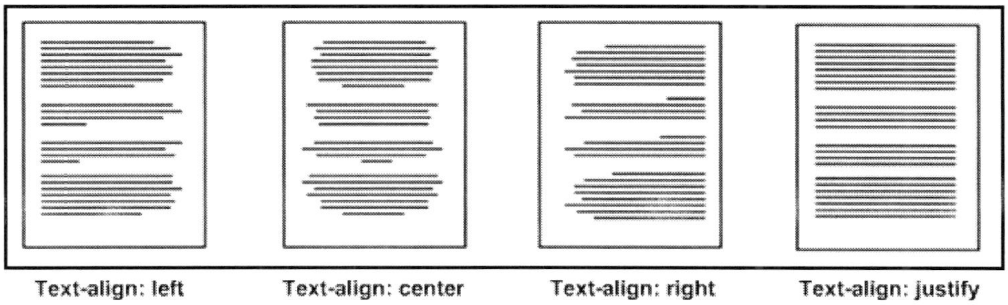

Values of text-align property

Vertical Text Alignment

The `vertical-align` property controls the vertical alignment of text, and is only valid on inline-level elements such as <span>, <b>, or <i>. This is because the property acts upon text relative to its parent text. You can set the vertical alignment of text to `sub` to create subscript text, and `super` to create superscript text.

The values `super` and `sub` replace the HTML elements <sup> and <sub> respectively.

Text Indentation

With the `text-indent` property, you can precisely control the amount of indentation for the first line of text in a block-level element, similar to what you might commonly find in books, correspondence, and other forms of print communication. You can set the value of the `text-indent` property in either absolute or relative units of measurement. For example, the following figure shows two paragraphs, each with indent values of 10 percent.

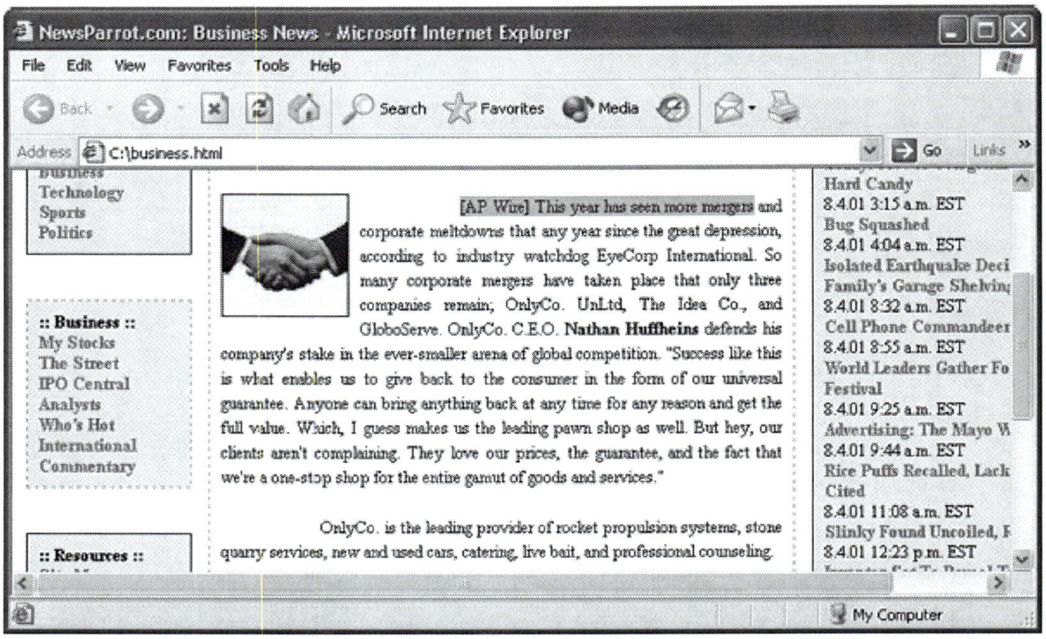

Paragraphs with 10 percent indent applied

The `text-indent` property is valid for only block-level elements like `<p>`, `<div>`, and `<blockquote>`.

Text Spacing

There are three CSS properties which control different aspects of text spacing: `letter-spacing`, `word-spacing`, and `line-height`. With the `letter-spacing` property, you can control kerning, the spacing between individual letters. With this style you can create text effects for headings, titles, links, or just about anything else. For example, if you want to give the letters in a heading extra spacing, you could declare it as: `h2 { letter-spacing: 8px; }`

This would produce the effect as shown in the following figure.

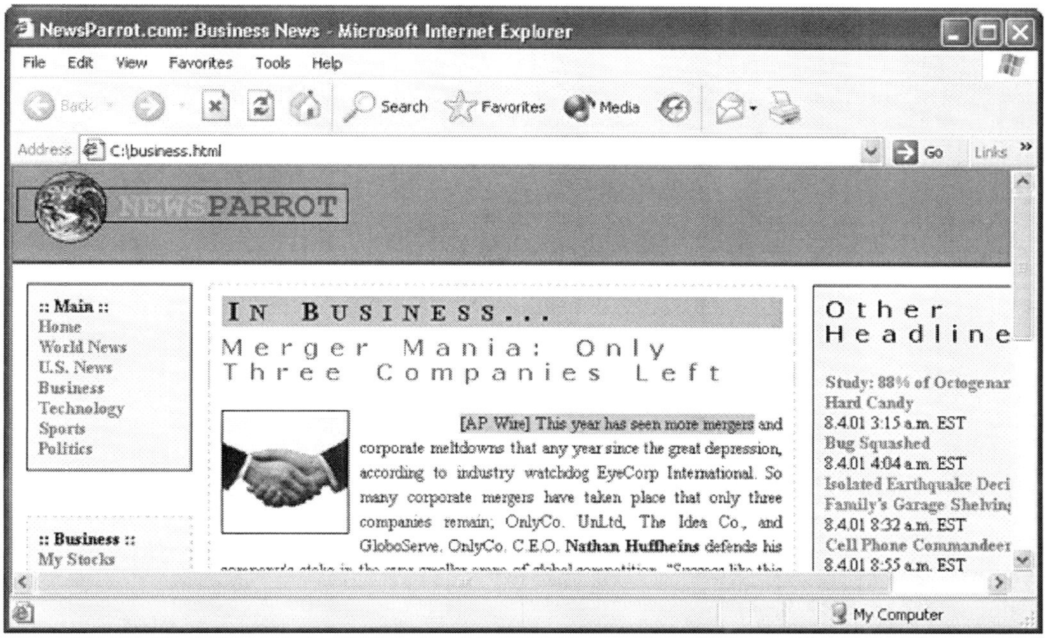

Heading with 8-pixel letter-spacing

To use a relative unit of measurement that adjusts the spacing according to the size of the font in use, you could declare as: `h2 { letter-spacing: .8em; }`. This will use the default size of an <h2> element as shown in the following figure.

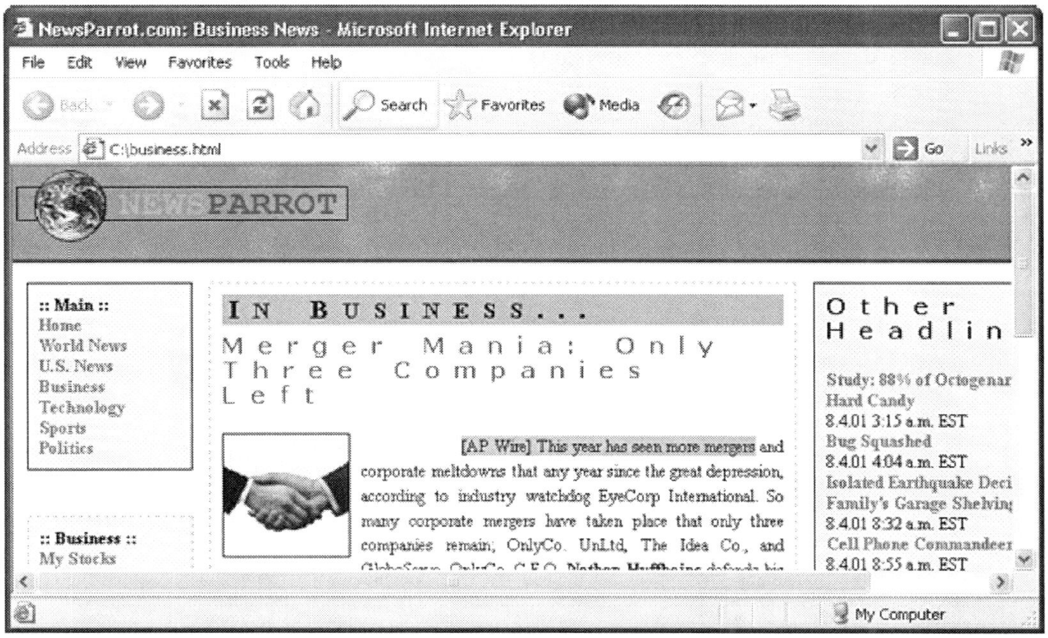

Heading with .8 ems letter-spacing

A negative value can be applied to push letters closer together. You can declare it as:

```
h2 { letter-spacing: -2px; }
```

This would produce the effect as shown in the following figure.

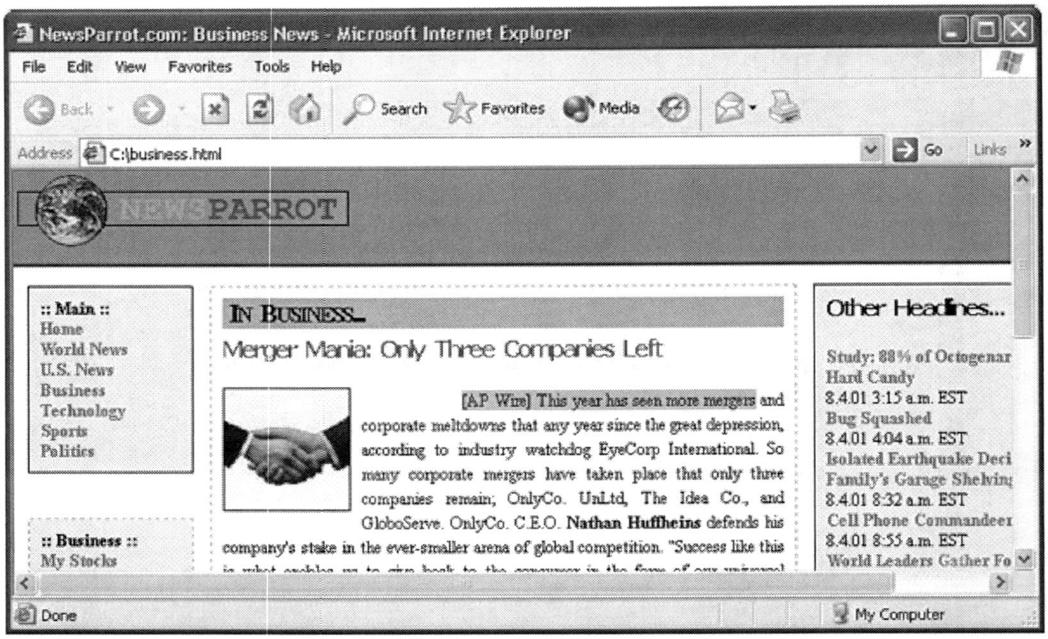

Heading with -2 pixels letter-spacing

The `letter-spacing` property is supported in Netscape 6+, Internet Explorer 4+, and Opera 3+.

The `word-spacing` property is similar to `letter-spacing`, except that instead of controlling the spacing between individual letters, it controls the spacing between whole words. For example, if you want to increase the amount of spacing between words in a heading, you could declare as: `h2 { word-spacing: 10px; }` to produce the effect as shown in the following figure.

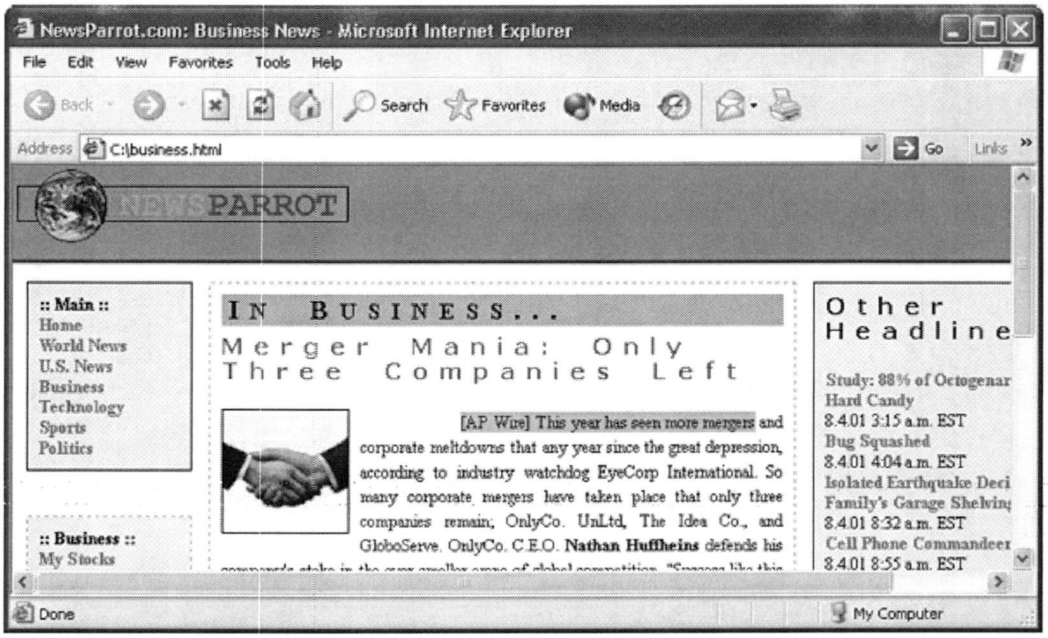

Heading with 10-pixel word-spacing

You could also, of course, use any relative unit of measurement, or a negative value to push the words closer together.

The `word-spacing` property is supported in Netscape 6+, Internet Explorer 6+ for PCs and Internet Explorer 4+ for Macintosh, and Opera 3+.

The `line-height` property enables you to control the amount of space between adjacent lines of text, which is called leading. Different fonts have their own default line height, which can vary significantly. With the line-height property, you can override a font's default line height, and increase or decrease the amount of space between adjacent lines. Line height is measured by the distance between the baselines of two adjacent lines of text, and can be expressed with any unit of measurement. The following figure demonstrates how `line-height` is measured.

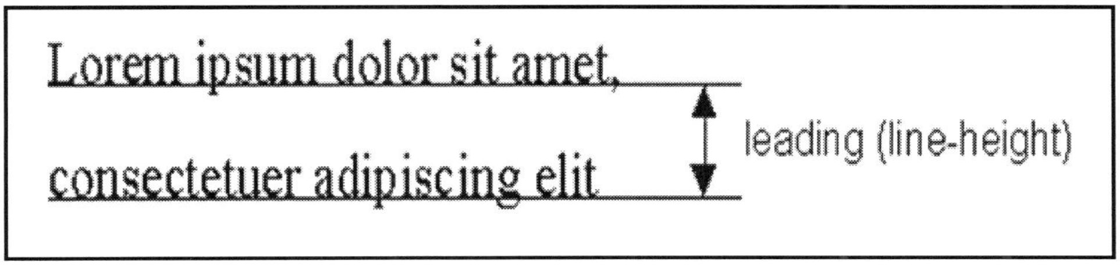

The `line-height` property also accepts integer values with no explicit unit of measurement, such as 2, 1.5, or 1.2. For example, if you want to double-space your text, you can declare as: `p { line-height: 2; }`. This sets the leading to twice the default size for that element and produces an effect as shown in the following figure.

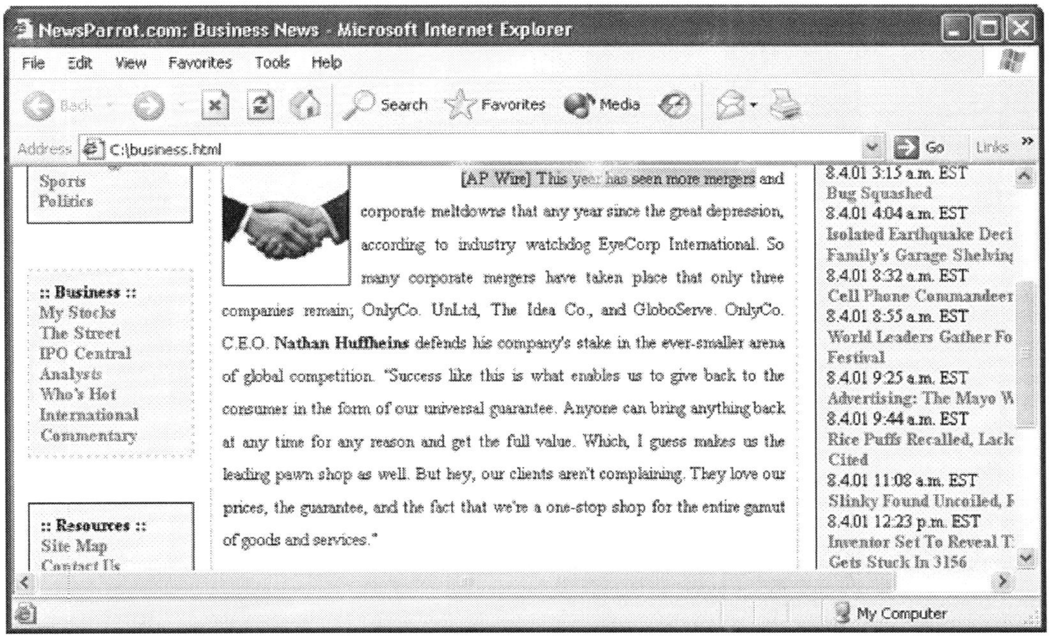

Paragraph with double-space applied

With the `line-height` property, negative values are not valid. To decrease the leading of text, you have to use a relative unit of measurement that's less than the default amount for the current font. For example, you can declare as: `p { line-height: 75%; }`

Certain fonts have more built-in leading than others. Some fonts appear double-spaced by default, including Trebuchet MS.

Text Casing

With the `text-transform` property, you can control the casing of text no matter how it's entered in a document. You can create basic text qualities like initial-letter capitalization, and upper or lowercase text.

The `capitalize` value capitalizes the first letter of each word in a paragraph or phrase. The `uppercase` value styles the text in uppercase letters; the `lowercase` value styles the text in lowercase letters. The `normal` value is the default, and can be used to override an inherited value.

You might think that you can enter your text with all necessary capitals, uppercase text, and so on. But imagine you are working on a large site with headings of one sort or another on every page that feature normal capitalization, and you are suddenly asked to change headings in all pages to all caps. In such cases the `text-transform` property becomes a powerful and valuable tool.

Editing all the pages of a large web document can be time consuming because you will have to go into every page of the document and manually change the text. But with the `text-transform` property, you can update the site with a single line of code. If the content on a web page is authored with incorrect capitalization and casing, the `text-transform` property can be used to enforce your website's style guide in accordance with your site's established style conventions.

Text Decoration

The `text-decoration` property draws a line under, over, or through the text. This property accepts five keywords: `underline`, `overline`, `line-through`, `blink`, and `none`. The `underline` value draws a line under the text. Underlining is typically used for links, but can also be used for emphasis or reference. The `overline` value draws a line above the text, and the `line-through` value draws a line through the middle of text. The `blink` value makes text blink at a browser-defined interval that cannot be controlled.

Of all the values of the `text-decoration` property, the `none` value is most commonly used to disable the default underlining of links. The `underline` and `line-through` values replace the deprecated HTML elements `<u>` and `<strike>`, respectively. But, remember, blinking text is considered distracting to the user, so you use it discreetly.

Units of Measurement

Some CSS properties don't have their own keyword values and instead rely on units of measurement, while some accept both units of measurement and their own keywords. Any CSS property that accepts a unit of measurement as its value can be specified with a variety of different absolute and relative units of measurement. *Absolute units* specify a precise length measurement, such as pixels or inches, while *relative units* of measurement specify a length value that is relative to an inherited or a default value. Absolute units of measurement can be used if you want your length values to remain constant.

The following table lists the different absolute units of measurement used in CSS.

Unit of Measurement	Description
pixels (`px`)	A standard screen measurement. One pixel equals one physical pixel on a computer screen, but it varies with screen resolution. So, pixels are sometimes considered to be a relative unit of measurement.
inches (`in`)	A standard English measurement. One inch is equal to 2.54 centimeters.
centimeters (`cm`)	A standard metric measurement. One centimeter is equal to almost 2/5th of an inch.
millimeters (`mm`)	A standard metric measurement. Ten millimeters are equal to one centimeter.
points (`pt`)	A standard print measurement. One point is equal to 1/72 of an inch. But, point values are not this precise on the web, and vary according to the font face in use.
picas (`pc`)	A standard print measurement. One pica is equal to 12 points.

For any CSS property, pixels are the most reliable absolute unit of measurement across different browsers and operating systems. Points and picas, for example, are units of print measurement that have no real meaning on a computer screen.

If you want your length values to scale from user to user and from one output device to the next, use relative units of measurement.

The following table lists the relative units of measurement in CSS.

Unit of Measurement	Description
ems (`em`)	A standard print measurement. Ems are relative to the width of the uppercase M character of the parent element's font, or the inherited font size when applied to the `font-size` property.
x-height (`ex`)	A standard print measurement. The x-height is defined by the size of the lowercase x character of the parent element's font, or the size of the x character of the inherited font size when applied to the `font-size` property.
percent (`%`)	A fraction value based on the computed value of an inherited length.

Ems and percentage values are the most reliable if you intend to use relative units of measurement, for x-height values aren't as consistently applied among different browsers.

Property values that require units of measurement consist of an integer or decimal, followed *directly* by the unit, such as `14px` or `50%`. Your style won't work if you add space between the property value and the unit of measurement.

Both absolute and relative units of measurement can be applied to any CSS property that accepts units of measurement.

How to Modify Text Styles

Text styles need to be applied appropriately and effectively to make your web documents readable and usable.

Guidelines

To apply text styles effectively:

- Keep your text styles consistent, both within each page and across all site pages.
- Keep your text styles simple and elegant, and avoid overuse of text styles.
- Make sure that the spacing between the lines of text is sufficient.
- Use text styles to help enforce your client's or organization's established style conventions.
- Use text alignments that enhance readability, not detract from it.
- Keep your text alignment consistent and avoid using different alignments, both within a page or across all pages.
- Make use of white space to provide clear delineation between content sections.

Example:

In the example, you can see images of two versions of the same page. The first image contains text styles that get in the user's way because there's not enough space between text, and the centering of the paragraphs is not appropriate to the design.

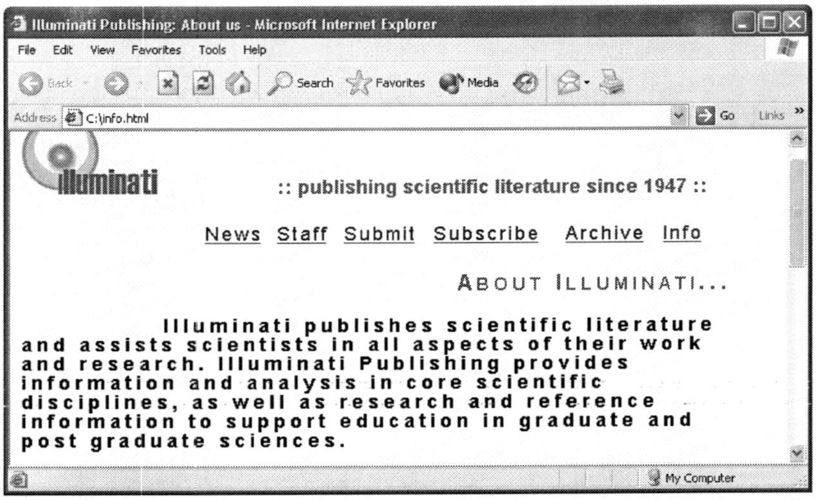

Web page with ineffective text styles

With added spacing between the text and consistent alignments, the second version of the page is more usable and readable.

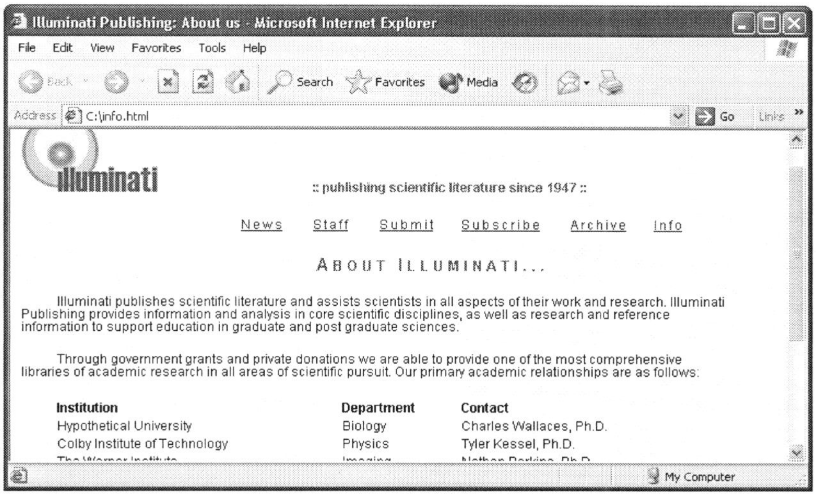

Web page with effective text styles

Effective Usage of CSS Text Styles

CSS text styles offer designers the power and flexibility to achieve any text-based design. When designing a web page, it's vital to put yourself in the mindset of your site visitors who seek information. If the web pages are difficult to read due to excessive text styles, users might not be able to access the information they need, and the success of your site will suffer. The more simple and elegant your text styles, the more readable and effective your pages are likely to be.

How to Modify an Element's Text Styles

Procedure Reference: Modify an Element's Text Styles

To modify an element's text styles:

1. Based on the text style guidelines, determine the text style(s) you want to apply to a given element.
2. In the style sheet, create a rule that declares your desired text styles for the element.
3. Repeat steps 1 and 2 for applying text styles to other elements.
4. Save and view the changes to verify that the expected result is achieved.

ACTIVITY 1-6

Controlling the Alignment and Indentation of Text

Activity Time:

5 minutes

Data Files:

- info.html

Before You Begin:

From the C:\085568Data\color and typography\Activity 6\Starter\Illuminati folder, open the info.html file in Internet Explorer and its source file in Notepad.

Scenario:

The Illuminati project team has determined that the text in the info.html page needs more distinct styles. You decide to enhance the appearance of the text by modifying the alignment and indentation. In particular, you need to align the copyright statement to the center to distinguish it from other text, and justify the paragraphs to create an even appearance along the left and right edges of the text. You also need to offset the first line of text in each paragraph.

What You Do	How You Do It
1. **Align the copyright statement to the center.** 	a. In the `address` rule, **click after** **`background-color:#699;`** **and type** **`text-align:center;`**
	b. **Choose File→Save.**
	c. **Minimize the Info.html - Notepad window.**
	d. In the Internet Explorer window, **scroll down** to view the copyright symbol.
	e. In the Internet Explorer window, **click the Refresh button.**

2. **Justify the paragraphs.**

> Illuminati publishes scientific literature and assists scientists in all aspects of their work and research. Illuminati Publishing provides information and analysis in core scientific disciplines, as well as research and reference information to support education in graduate and post graduate sciences.
>
> Through government grants and private donations we are able to provide one of the most comprehensive libraries of academic research in all areas of scientific pursuit. Our primary academic relationships are as follows:

a. **Restore the Info.html - Notepad window.**

b. In the first `p` rule, **click after `background-color: transparent;` and type `text-align:justify;`**

c. **Choose File→Save.**

d. **Minimize the Info.html - Notepad window.**

e. In the Internet Explorer window, **scroll up and click the Refresh button.**

---

3. **Indent the paragraphs.**

> Illuminati publishes scientific literature and assists scientists in all aspects of their work and research. Illuminati Publishing provides information and analysis in core scientific disciplines, as well as research and reference information to support education in graduate and post graduate sciences.
>
> Through government grants and private donations we are able to provide one of the most comprehensive libraries of academic research in all areas of scientific pursuit. Our primary academic relationships are as follows:

a. **Restore Info.html - Notepad window.**

b. **Type `text-indent:15px;`**

c. **Choose File→Save.**

d. **Close the Info.html - Notepad window.**

e. In the Internet Explorer window, **click the Refresh button.**

f. **Close the Internet Explorer window.**

ACTIVITY 1-7

Modifying the Text Spacing

Activity Time:

5 minutes

Data Files:

- info.html

Before You Begin:

From the C:\085568Data\color and typography\Activity 7\Starter\Illuminati folder, open the info.html file in Internet Explorer and its source file in Notepad.

Scenario:

You decide to improve the general readability of text in the info.html page by increasing the leading of paragraph text and the space between them.

You also note that the heading text, links, and copyright statement need to be more catchy. You decide to increase the white space between letters in the headings and links, and between the words in the copyright statement by adjusting the space between the letters and words in these elements to distinguish them from other text on the page.

Your project team has no set specifications for the exact amount of spacing to apply to these elements, and has left it to you to create styles that are effective.

What You Do | **How You Do It**

1. **Modify the line height of the paragraphs to enhance their readability.**

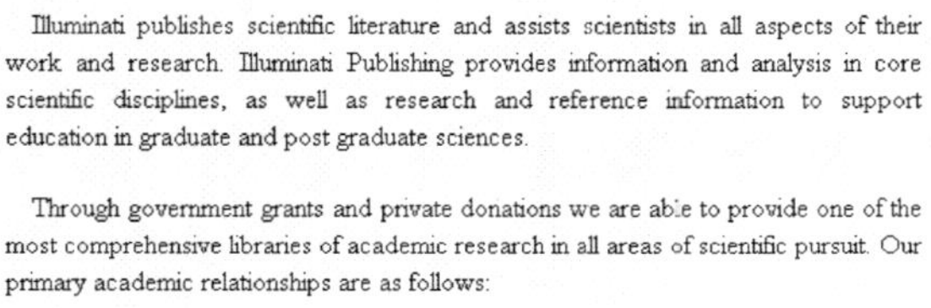

Illuminati publishes scientific literature and assists scientists in all aspects of their work and research. Illuminati Publishing provides information and analysis in core scientific disciplines, as well as research and reference information to support education in graduate and post graduate sciences.

Through government grants and private donations we are able to provide one of the most comprehensive libraries of academic research in all areas of scientific pursuit. Our primary academic relationships are as follows:

a. In the Info.html - Notepad window, in the first `p` rule, **click after `text-indent:15px;` and type `line-height:1.4;`**

b. **Choose File→Save.**

c. **Minimize the Info.html - Notepad window.**

d. In the Internet Explorer window, **click the Refresh button** to view the space between lines being increased, making the text a bit easier to read.

2. **Modify the line height of the text in the table.**

Institution	Department	Contact
Hypothetical University	Biology	Charles Wallaces, Ph.D.
Colby Institute of Technology	Physics	Tyler Kessel, Ph.D.
The Warner Institute	Imaging	Nathan Perkins, Ph.D.
National Astronomical Society	Cosmology	Ed Brodie, Ph.D.
Billings Institute	Medicine	Rachel Vincent, M.D.

a. **Restore the Info.html - Notepad window.**

b. **Click after the first `p` rule and press Enter.**

c. **Type `td { line-height: 1.5em; }`**

d. **Choose File→Save.**

e. **Minimize the Info.html - Notepad window.**

f. In the Internet Explorer window, **click the Refresh button** to view the space between the text being increased, even though the text is in a table.

---

3. **If you specify the line height in relative units of measurement like EM units or percentages, will the amount of space change if the browser window is resized?**

---

4. **Modify the kerning of both headings.**

about illuminati...

Illuminati publishes scientific literature and assists scientists in all aspects of their work and research. Illuminati Publishing provides information and analysis in core scientific disciplines, as well as research and reference information to support education in graduate and post graduate sciences.

Through government grants and private donations we are able to provide one of the most comprehensive libraries of academic research in all areas of scientific pursuit. Our primary academic relationships are as follows:

Institution	Department	Contact
Hypothetical University	Biology	Charles Wallaces, Ph.D.
Colby Institute of Technology	Physics	Tyler Kessel, Ph.D.
The Warner Institute	Imaging	Nathan Perkins, Ph.D.
National Astronomical Society	Cosmology	Ed Brodie, Ph.D.
Billings Institute	Medicine	Rachel Vincent, M.D.

partnerships...

a. **Restore the Info.html - Notepad window.**

b. In the `h1, h2` rule, **click after `background-color: #99CCB3;` and type `letter-spacing: 5px;`**

c. **Choose File→Save.**

d. **Minimize the Info.html - Notepad window.**

e. In the Internet Explorer window, **click the Refresh button** to view the extra kern distinguishing the headings from the other text on the page.

5. **Modify the kerning of the link text to distinguish it.**

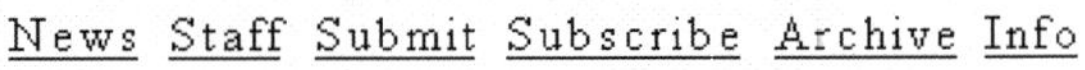

a. **Restore the Info.html - Notepad window.**

b. In the first `a` rule, **click after `color: #006;` and type `letter-spacing: 2px;`**

c. **Choose File→Save.**

d. **Minimize the Info.html - Notepad window.**

e. In the Internet Explorer window, **click the Refresh button** to view an increase in the kerning of the link text, enhancing its visibility.

---

6. **Modify the spacing between the words in the copyright statement.**

a. **Restore the Info.html - Notepad window.**

b. In the `address` rule, **click after `text-align:center;` and type `word-spacing: 5px;`**

c. **Choose File→Save.**

d. **Close the Info.html - Notepad window.**

e. In the Internet Explorer window, **scroll down to view the copyright statement, and then click the Refresh button.**

f. **Close the Internet Explorer window.**

ACTIVITY 1-8

Controlling Text Casing and Underlining

Activity Time:

5 minutes

Data Files:

- info.html

Before You Begin:

From the C:\085568Data\color and typography\Activity 8\Starter\Illuminati folder, open the info.html file in Internet Explorer and its source file in Notepad.

Scenario:

Your team has created a style guide for the Illuminati project. It was decided that all headings should be capitalized, and all links be lowercase and not underlined. The team supposed that you'll have to go into every HTML page and manually change the casing of the text. Fortunately, you know better. You can simply enforce the new style guide using CSS, starting with the info.html page.

What You Do	How You Do It
1. **Capitalize the words in both headings.**	a. In the style sheet, **click after `<!--` and press Enter.** b. In the style sheet, **insert the code** to capitalize the heading text in the info.html file. *See Code Sample 1.* c. **Choose File→Save.** d. **Minimize the Info.html - Notepad window.** e. In the Internet Explorer window, **scroll down and click the Refresh button.** The `text-transform` property will override the actual casing of the document's heading text.

Code Sample 1

```
h1, h2 {
  color: teal;
  background-color: #99CCB3;
  letter-spacing: 5px;
  text-transform: capitalize; }
```

2. Change all link text to lowercase. *and not underlined*

a. **Restore the Info.html - Notepad window.**

b. **Press Enter.**

c. In the style sheet, **insert the code** to lowercase all link text in the info.html file.

See Code Sample 2.

d. **Choose File→Save.**

e. **Close the Info.html - Notepad window.**

f. In the Internet Explorer window, **click the Refresh button.**

g. **Close the Internet Explorer window.**

Code Sample 2

```
a {
  color: #006;
  letter-spacing: 2px;
  text-transform: lowercase; }
```

TOPIC E

Modify Font Styles

You have applied text styles, modified text spacing, and controlled text casing and formatting. But text styles are only half of the typographical picture; you also need to control your fonts and font styles to enhance the readability of your web page. In this topic, you will declare fonts, font sizes, and font-related styles.

Fonts and font styles help establish the overall text presentation in your web page. Precise control of your fonts and font styles allows you to:

- Ensure that your content is legible and easy to read.
- Emphasize important words, phrases, or content sections when needed.
- And, establish a consistent overall look and feel.

When font styles are applied wisely, your content will be accessible and readable to the users.

Font Styles

Font styles relate directly to fonts and their variations. But most of the browsers apply their own default fonts and font sizes. With CSS, you can override these default styles and control all aspects of your text design. All fonts have built-in variations, such as different weights or degrees of boldness, sizes, and styles. The font properties, together with text properties, complete the palette of CSS typographical styles.

There are five font properties and an additional shorthand property that enables you to set all font properties.

Property	Description
`font-family`	Allows you to declare the font face for any text element.
`font-style`	Allows you to create or disable italic text.
`font-variant`	Allows you to create or disable small-caps.
`font-weight`	Allows you to make text bold in varying degrees, depending on the font in use.
`font-size`	Allows you to declare a specific font size using a variety of keywords and units of measurement.
`font`	A shorthand property that allows you to declare all font properties at once.

Need for Font Styles

The correct usage of CSS font styles ensures the effective presentation of textual content in your web page. Font styles are important because:

- If users have trouble reading your content, your site will not be effective enough.
- Web users scan text rather than read as they would a book or magazine. Therefore, you should use the appropriate fonts and font styles to draw attention to important words, phrases, or content sections.
- Typography in design is as important as the physical layout of content sections and the colors you choose.

If you don't apply font styles wisely, your content will not be as accessible and readable to your users as it should be. The following web page illustrates poor use of font styles. The difference in font sizes between the headings and paragraphs is excessive, the title text is too small for readers, and all the bold and italic fonts makes the text even more difficult to read. Therefore, these styles, instead of enhancing the web page, result in ugly and obtrusive design.

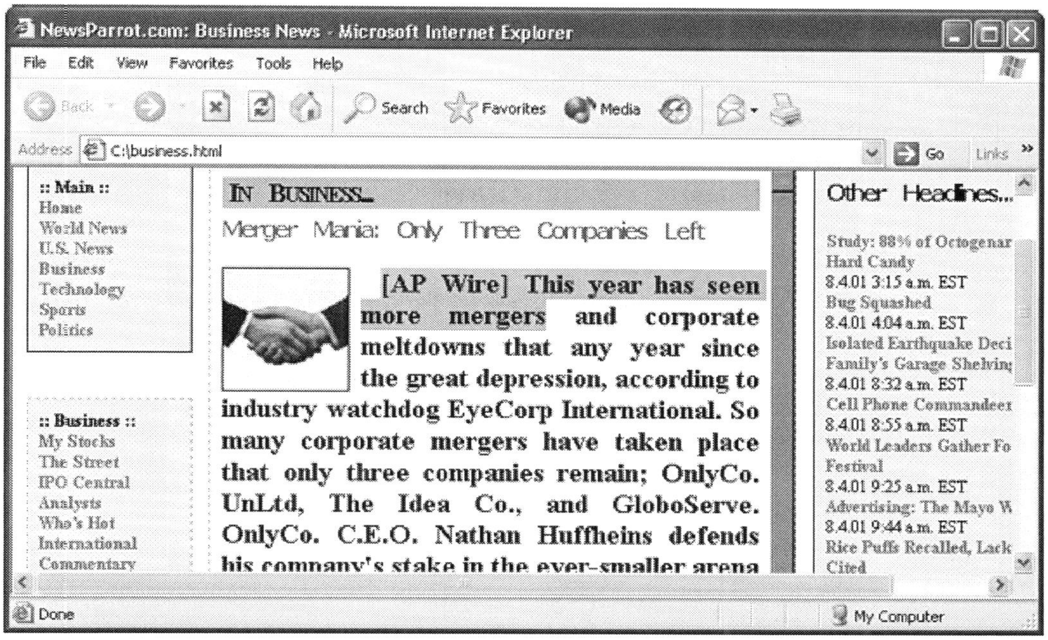

Web page with ineffective font styles

In the following illustration, the same page is styled more simply and logically. The headings are larger than the body text, but not excessively so. The paragraph text is moderately sized for easy reading, and there are no unnecessary bold or italic styles. The headings are also rendered with small-caps to further distinguish them. Therefore, the overall appearance of the page is more effective.

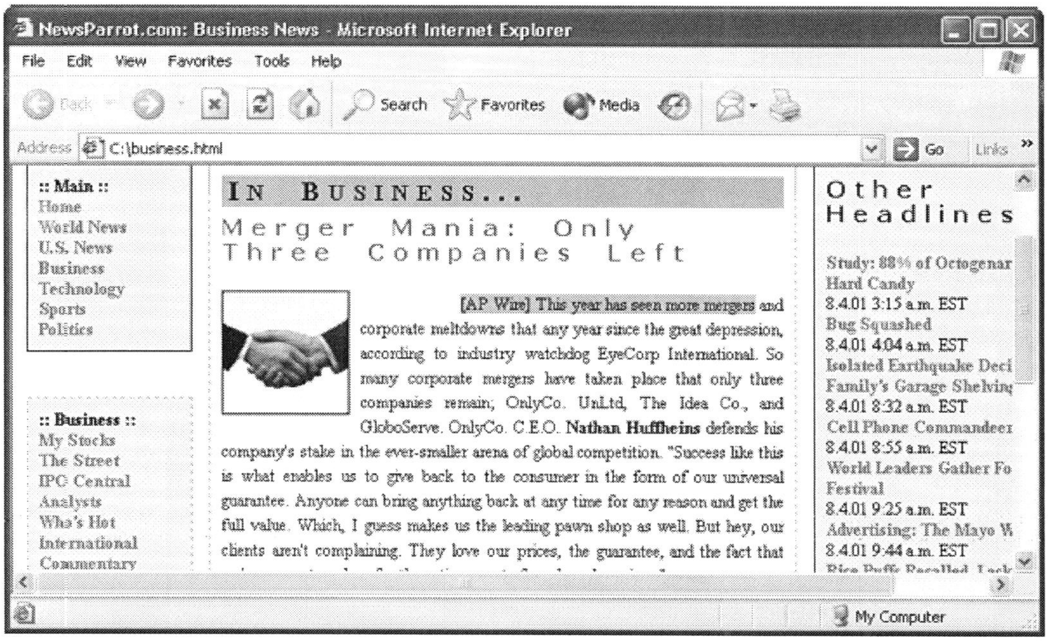

Web page with effective font styles

Font Faces

The `font-family` property can be used to set the font face for any text element. The `font-family` property can be used as follows:

```
p {font-family:Arial;}
```

The preceding rule would make all the paragraphs display with the font Arial, which is one of the many popular font families.

Font family is the name of a specific font, such as Times New Roman or Arial, and all of its variations such as bold, italic, etc. You can also declare a *generic family*, which describes a type of font, rather than a specific font face. You can declare five generic font families with the `font-family` property.

The following table lists the generic font families with a brief description of each.

Generic Family	Description
Monospace	Fonts with uniformly spaced characters, such as Courier or Courier New. Each character takes up the same amount of space, regardless of the width of the individual character.
Serif	Fonts with letters having *decorations*, which are also called flourishes, that help to distinguish a letter. Serifs are usually applied to the ends of a letter. Times New Roman and Garamond are examples of serif fonts.
Sans-serif	Fonts without serifs or decorations. Helvetica, Arial, and Verdana are examples of sans-serif fonts.
Cursive	Fonts that look similar to handwriting.
Fantasy	Typically, browsers will display an unusual or exotic font face. Generally, this isn't a good choice as a final declaration because browsers apply different font faces depending on the platform and version. Fantasy font faces also vary in appearance.

To achieve a consistent appearance for all potential viewers, it's important to include a generic font family at the end of your font declaration. If the user's browser can't access your preferred font, it will by default shift to a similar font face. For example, the font face Verdana is a sans-serif Windows font widely used on the web because it was designed specifically for the screen. Non-PC users, however, might not have Verdana installed on their systems.

You can start the font declaration with font family list and your preferred font face, followed by a second or even third option, and finally, end it with a generic family name, typically serif or sans-serif. Each font name must be separated by a comma. This syntax is unique to the `font-family` property and can be declared as follows:

```
body { font-family: Verdana, Arial, sans-serif; }
```

Some font faces consist of multiple words, such as Comic Sans, Trebuchet MS, Times New Roman, and Courier New. In instances when you need to specify font faces with multiple words, you have to enclose them in quotation marks as follows:

```
p { font-family: "Trebuchet MS", sans-serif; }
```

When specifying font names, the font name must be spelled exactly as displayed on the user's system. For example, *Comic Sans* on the Macintosh is *Comic Sans MS* on PCs. Without the *MS*, a PC browser will ignore the font declaration and move on to the next font in the list.

Setting Font Size

With CSS you can precisely control the size of your text with the `font-size` property. You can specify a font's size with absolute or relative units of measurement or keywords.

The absolute keyword values are as follows:

- `xx-small`
- `x-small`
- `small`
- `medium`
- `large`
- `x-large`
- `xx-large`

The relative keyword values are as follows:

- `smaller`
- `larger`

The following table lists the units of measurement that can be used for font sizing.

Unit of Measurement	Description
pixels (`px`)	Pixel values are the most commonly applied unit of measurement for font sizes, mainly because it's the most logical unit of measurement for the screen. It also provides the most reliable degree of consistency across different platforms.

Unit of Measurement	Description
percentages (%)	Percentage values establish font sizes that are relative to the font size of the element's parent. So, if the body element is the parent of all paragraphs, and the body element is set to 16px which is the default font size in both Internet Explorer for the PC and Netscape, then a value of 80% for the paragraphs will be 80% of 16 pixels, which computes to 12 pixels.
ems (em)	Ems is a relative unit of measurement, and is relative to the size of the text's inherited value, or the size that the text would normally be. Using the same scenario as the percentage values, paragraphs specified with the value .8em will have the same effect as the percentage value 80%.
points (pt)	Points are an absolute unit of measurement that's native to print, and while many web developers use this unit of measurement, it's not a logical choice of measurement for the screen as it results in less consistent results across different platforms.
picas (pc)	Picas are another absolute unit of measurement native to print. Picas aren't commonly used on the web because most browsers have buggy, unreliable support for this unit of measurement.
ex-height (ex)	The ex-height of a font refers to the height of the current font's lowercase x character. This unit of measurement is also rarely used because of spotty support among different browsers.

Font sizes for the web are most commonly expressed in pixels, the unit of measurement specific to the screen. It's important to note that fonts appear to display at different font sizes depending on the font face in use. For example, text displayed with the font Times New Roman at 14 pixels will appear smaller than Arial at 14 pixels. This is simply because some font families are larger than others and has nothing to do with font size values.

In most browsers, text sized with absolute units of measurement remains as specified, even if users choose to expand the size of text in their browser preferences. However, Netscape 6 allows users to increase or decrease the size of text even if the text is expressed in absolute units of measurement. In the future, it might not be as critical to use relative units of measurement if you want to allow users to modify your site's text size, as most browsers will allow users to alter text size to suit their convenience.

Font Weight

Boldness of text is referred to as a font's *weight*. Using the `font-weight` property, you can assign different degrees of boldness to your fonts. The `font-weight` property accepts four keywords: `bold`, `bolder`, `lighter`, and `normal`. The `bolder` and `lighter` are relative keywords, which means they will render the font either bolder or lighter than a default or inherited weight.

The `font-weight` property also accepts the numerical values 100, 200, 300, 400, 500, 600, 700, 800, and 900. Each numerical value represents a specific weight, or degree of boldness—the least bold being 100 and the most bold being 900. However, not all font families accept all nine numerical values. If the font family does not have all degrees of boldness, then only the `700` and `900` values will have an effect.

The value `400` is equal to the keyword `normal`, both of which are the default value. The value `700` is equal to the keyword `bold`. The following rules provide an example of `font-weight` values and their equivalent:

```
body { font-weight: 400 } /* normal */
h1 { font-weight: 900 } /* bolder */
h2 { font-weight: 400 } /* lighter */
```

In the first rule, the font weight is set to the default value of 400, which is the same as the value `normal`. In the second rule, the font weight is set to 900, which is the highest degree of font weight and is the same as the value `bolder`. In the third rule, the value 400 is the same as `lighter`.

Italicizing Text

To italicize text, use the `font-style` property:

```
span { font-style: italic; }
```

The `font-style` property accepts three keyword values: `italic`, `oblique`, and `normal`. The default value is `normal`, and it overrides an inherited style or a native italic element such as <i> or <em>. The value `italic` uses a font family's italic variant, while the value `oblique` is meant to take any normal font and slant it forward to simulate italics. The `oblique` value is not supported by most browsers and a font's italic variant is just applied when `oblique` is specified. So it is better to use the `italic` value to ensure that your style is supported.

Setting Small-Caps

With the `font-variant` property, you can set any text element to be displayed in small-caps. Small-caps is a font style that capitalizes all letters, and makes all the initial caps slightly larger, as shown in the following figure.

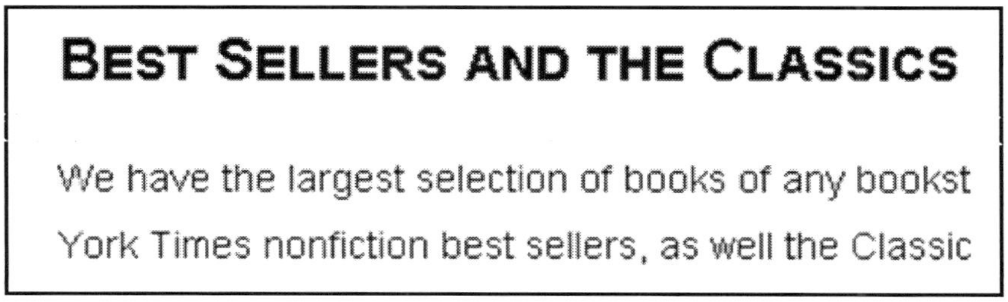

A heading with small-caps style

The `font-variant` property accepts only two keyword values: `small-caps` and `normal`. The `normal` value can be used to override an inherited small-caps style.

Small-caps is a popular heading style in print, and is often overlooked on web, mainly due to lack of support in the 4.x browsers. But it's well supported in the 5.x and 6.x versions of Internet Explorer and Netscape.

How to Modify Font Styles

The readability of text and the overall look and feel of your site can be enhanced by applying font styles effectively.

Guidelines

To choose effective font styles:

- Always declare multiple, similar font faces when specifying a font face, to ensure that users who don't have your first font choice will at least see a similar one thus preserving your intended design.
- Use simple and elegant font styles.
- Use font weight adjustments for headings or only where you need to provide visual emphasis.
- Use font sizes that are just large enough for most users to comfortably read.
- Use consistent units of measurement for your font sizes. In particular, don't mix absolute and relative values unless a special circumstance calls for it.
- Use italics only when it calls for references, distinguishing words or phrases, or where you need to imply spoken emphasis.

Users can adjust the size of text when it's specified with relative units, so mixing the units of measurement values can result in comparative sizes that don't match your design intentions.

Example:

For example, in the displayed web page a few font styles are used. The font face is easy to read, the heading text is larger than the body text without being excessively large, and the names of individuals are bold to distinguish them and draw the user's eye. These styles are simple but effective.

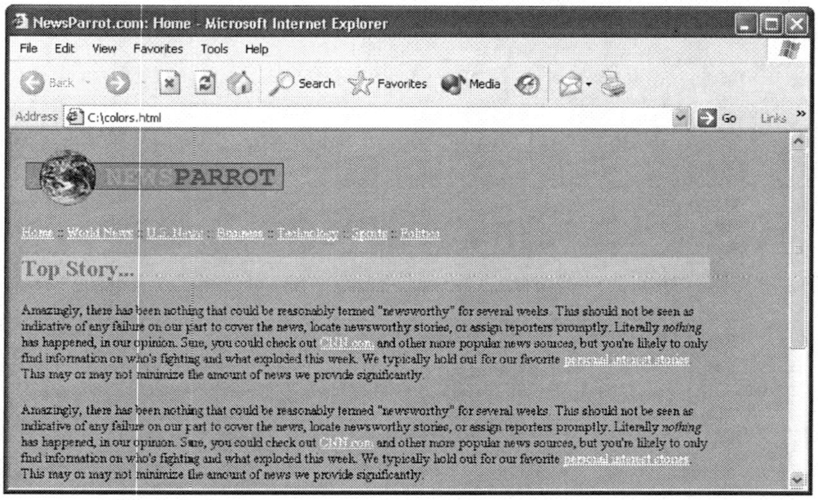

Web page with minimal usage of font styles

How to Modify an Element's Font Styles

Procedure Reference: Modify an Element's Font Styles

To modify an element's font styles:

1. Based on the font style guidelines, determine the font style you need to apply to a given text element.
2. In the style sheet, create a rule that declares one or more font styles for the target element(s).
3. Repeat steps 1 and 2 to apply font styles to other elements as needed.
4. Save and view the changes to verify that the expected result is achieved.

The font Shorthand Property

With the `font` shorthand property, you can declare all font properties at once. You can declare `font-style`, `font-weight`, `font-size`, `font-variant`, `font-family`, and even `line-height` without having to specify each property individually, as shown in the following example:

```
p { font: italic bold .8em/2em Arial, sans-serif; }
```

The preceding rule is the same as declaring the following:

```
p { font-style: italic;
    font-weight: bold;
    font-size: .8em;
    line-height: 2em;
    font-family: Arial, sans-serif; }
```

Note the unique syntax for the font size and line height. The values for `font-size` and `line-height` are grouped together and separated by a forward slash, with `font-size` to the left of the slash, and `line-height` to the right. Also note that all properties are separated by a space, and multiple values of the `font-family` property are separated by commas, as usual.

With the `font` shorthand property, each property is implicit in its value. If any property is left out, its default value is applied—even if it would otherwise inherit that style from its parent element.

⚠ To make the `font` shorthand property work for users with Navigator 4.x, the rule must begin with either the `font-style` or `font-weight` values, and `font-family` must be listed last, even if the element already inherits a desired value.

ACTIVITY 1-9

Specifying Fonts and Font Sizes

Activity Time:

5 minutes

Data Files:

- info.html

Before You Begin:

From the C:\085568Data\color and typography\Activity 9\Starter\Illuminati folder, open the info.html file in Internet Explorer and its source file in Notepad.

Scenario:

You're ready to put the final touches on the info.html page—the sample page you're designing for the Illuminati project. The client has no font face or size directives for you, except that they do not want to use the default font face and size. The web project team has left it up to you to choose font styles that work with the existing theme. You need to apply font faces and sizes that further enhance the design.

What You Do	How You Do It
1. **Declare Arial, Helvetica, and sans-serif as the fonts to be used.**	a. **Click after the first a rule and press Enter.**
	b. **Type `body { font-family: Arial, Helvetica, sans-serif; }`**
	c. **Choose File→Save.**
	d. **Minimize the Info.html - Notepad window.**
	e. In the Internet Explorer window, **click the Refresh button** to display all the text in Arial font.

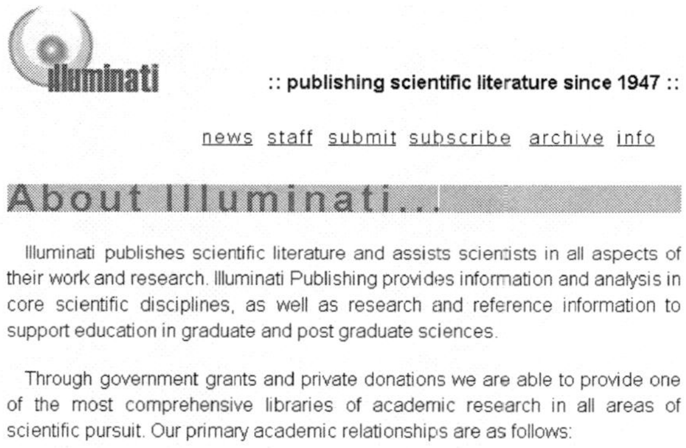

2. **Decrease the font size for all page elements.**

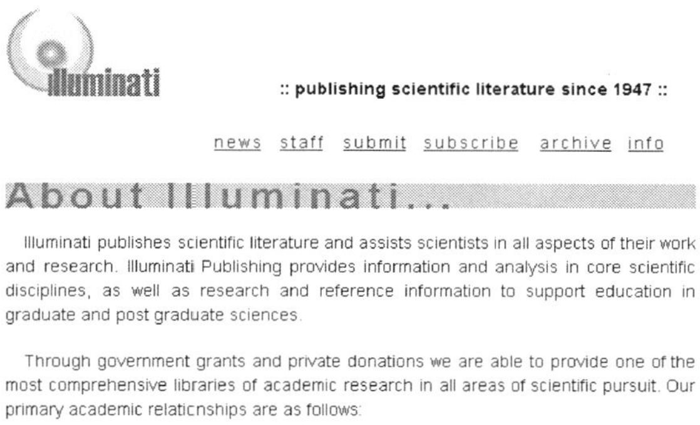

a. **Restore the Info.html - Notepad window.**

b. In the `body` rule, **click after** **`sans-serif;`** **and type** **`font-size:14px;`**

c. **Choose File→Save.**

d. **Minimize the Info.html - Notepad window.**

e. In the Internet Explorer window, **click the Refresh button.**

---

3. **Make the text of both headings smaller.**

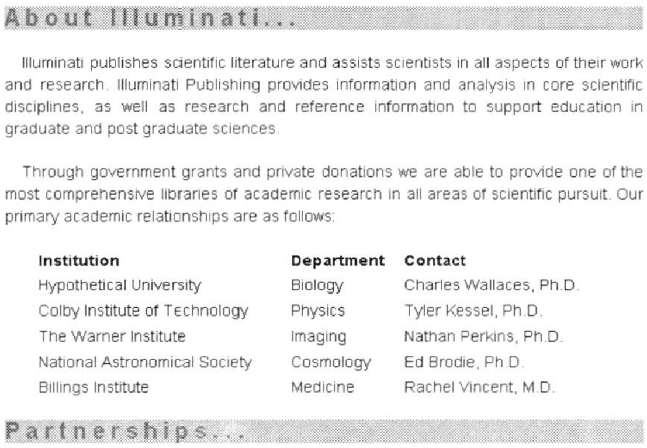

a. **Restore the Info.html - Notepad window.**

b. In the first `h1, h2` rule, **click after** **`text-transform: capitalize;`** **and type** **`font-size: 20px;`**

c. **Choose File→Save.**

d. **Close the Info.html - Notepad window.**

e. In the Internet Explorer window, **click the Refresh button.**

f. **Notice that the heading font sizes have changed.**

g. **Close the Internet Explorer window.**

OPTIONAL ACTIVITY 1-10

Controlling Font Size with Relative Units

Data Files:

- info.html

Before You Begin:

From the C:\085568Data\color and typography\Activity 10\Starter\Illuminati folder, open the info.html file in Internet Explorer and its source file in Notepad.

Scenario:

Your project team has had a change of heart. They like the font face and sizes you have chosen for Illuminati's info.html page, but they want all font sizes to be specified with relative values to ensure that users can adjust the text size in their browser.

What You Do	How You Do It
1. **Use the View menu in the Internet Explorer to change the display of the font size.**	a. If necessary, **minimize the Info.html - Notepad window.**
	b. **Choose View→Text Size→Largest.**
	c. **Verify that the text size does not change.** This is because the font sizes are expressed in an absolute value—pixels.
	d. **Choose View→Text Size→Medium.**
	Netscape Navigator 6 allows users to change text size even if absolute values are used. They literally *zoom in* on the text, rather than use the document's unit of measurement as a source. It's possible that future versions of Internet Explorer will implement the same feature. As of version Internet Explorer 6.0, this feature does not exist, and users can only change a page's font size if relative units of measurement are used.

2. **Apply the existing font size to the body and heading elements using a relative unit of measurement.**	a. **Restore the Info.html - Notepad window.** b. In the `body` rule, **select `font-size:14px;`** c. **Choose Edit→Delete.** d. **Type `font-size: .9em;`** e. **Choose File→Save.** f. **Minimize the Info.html - Notepad window.** g. In the Internet Explorer window, **click the Refresh button.** The font size either does not change or changes slightly.
3. **Apply the existing or similar font size to the headings using a relative unit of measurement.**	a. **Restore the Info.html - Notepad window.** b. In the first `h1, h2` rule, **select `font-size: 20px;` and choose Edit→ Delete.** c. **Type `font-size: 1.4em;`** d. **Choose File→Save.** e. **Minimize the Info.html - Notepad window.** f. In the Internet Explorer window, **click the Refresh button.** The font size either does not change or changes slightly.
4. **Change the display of font size in the Internet Explorer.**	a. **Choose View→Text Size→Largest.** The text size changes according to the selection. b. **Choose View→Text Size→Medium.** The text size changes to the original size. c. **Close the Internet Explorer and the Info.html - Notepad window.**

ACTIVITY 1-11

Controlling Font Weight and Style

Activity Time:

10 minutes

Data Files:

- info.html

Before You Begin:

From the C:\085568Data\color and typography\Activity 11\Starter\Illuminati folder, open the info.html file in Internet Explorer and its source file in Notepad.

Scenario:

Your design of the info.html page is taking shape—you've applied many styles, but you still need to establish some emphasis for certain words, phrases, and content sections. In particular, your client wanted the two headings to be more distinguished from each other in terms of font styles. The client wanted the level-one heading to be extra bold and the level-two heading to be less bold than it currently is. Also, both headings need to be displayed in small-caps, and the copyright statement should be bold rather than italic.

What You Do	How You Do It
1. **Make the text of the level-one heading bolder.** 	a. **Click after <!-- and press Enter.** b. **Type `h1 { font-weight: 900; }`** c. **Choose File→Save.** d. **Minimize the Info.html - Notepad window.** e. In the Internet Explorer window, **click the Refresh button.** The heading text is bolder than it is by default. Headings, by default, are already bold. Applying the bold value would have no effect because it's essentially redundant.

2. **Make the level-two heading less bold.**

   a. **Restore the Info.html - Notepad window.**
   b. **Press Enter.**
   c. **Type `h2 { font-weight: 400; }`**
   d. **Choose File→Save.**
   e. **Minimize the Info.html - Notepad window.**
   f. In the Internet Explorer window, **click the Refresh button.**

---

3. **Bold the copyright statement.**

   a. **Restore the Info.html - Notepad window.**
   b. In the `address` rule, **click after `word-spacing: 5px;` and type `font-weight: bold;`**
   c. **Choose File→Save.**
   d. **Minimize the Info.html - Notepad window.**
   e. In the Internet Explorer window, **scroll down to view the copyright statement and click the Refresh button.**

---

4. **Disable the `<address>` element's default italicization.**

   a. **Restore the Info.html - Notepad window.**
   b. **Type `font-style: normal;`**
   c. **Choose File→Save.**
   d. **Minimize the Info.html - Notepad window.**
   e. In the Internet Explorer window, **click the Refresh button** to view the font style change to normal.

---

5. **Convert both headings to small-caps.**

ABOUT ILLUMINATI...

Illuminati publishes scientific literature and assists scientists in all aspects of their work and research. Illuminati Publishing provides information and analysis in core scientific disciplines, as well as research and reference information to support education in graduate and post graduate sciences.

Through government grants and private donations we are able to provide one of the most comprehensive libraries of academic research in all areas of scientific pursuit. Our primary academic relationships are as follows:

Institution	Department	Contact
Hypothetical University	Biology	Charles Wallaces, Ph.D.
Colby Institute of Technology	Physics	Tyler Kessel, Ph.D.
The Warner Institute	Imaging	Nathan Perkins, Ph.D.
National Astronomical Society	Cosmology	Ed Brodie, Ph.D.
Billings Institute	Medicine	Rachel Vincent, M.D.

PARTNERSHIPS...

a. **Restore the Info.html - Notepad window.**

b. In the first `h1, h2` rule, **click after `font-size: 1.4em;` and type `font-variant: small-caps;`**

c. **Choose File→Save.**

d. **Close the Info.html - Notepad window.**

e. In the Internet Explorer window, **click the Refresh button.**

f. **Close the Internet Explorer window.**

ACTIVITY 1-12

Modifying Font Styles

Activity Time:

5 minutes

Data Files:

- index.html

Before You Begin:

From the C:\085568Data\color and typography\Activity 12\Starter\NewsParrot folder, open the index.html file in Internet Explorer and its source file in Notepad.

Scenario:

Your client, the NewsParrot news service, has asked you to modify the font styles for the index.html design proof. They have also asked that you do whatever you can to keep the file size of the page as small as possible. You decide to use the `font` shorthand property to apply all required font styles, in order to condense and streamline your style sheet. Your client has given you the freedom to explore font styles as you see fit, but they do have a few particular style requirements.

For paragraphs:

- Use the Georgia font face.
- Specify a reasonable font size with an emphasis on readability.
- Give the paragraphs extra line height.

For both headings:

- Use the Arial font face.

- Convert the text to small-caps.
- Set the text size of level-one heading to 18px, level-two heading 16px.
- Decrease the degree of boldness.

To ensure that your font styles help establish the overall look and feel of the site and enhance the readability of the site's content, follow these guidelines:

- After the preferred font face is specified, declare one or more similar font faces—especially a generic font family—to ensure that users who don't have your first font choice will have a similar one.
- Reserve font weight adjustments for headings or where you need to provide visual emphasis.
- Use font sizes that are large enough for most users to read but not so large that page space is needlessly consumed.
- Use consistent units of measurement for your font sizes.

What You Do	How You Do It
1. **Modify the paragraphs by using the `font` shorthand.**	a. **Click after `<!--` and press Enter.**
	b. **Type `p { text-indent: 12px; text-align: justify;}`**
	c. **Choose File→Save.**
	d. **Minimize the Index.html - Notepad window.**
	e. In the Internet Explorer window, **click the Refresh button.**

2. **Modify the headings by using the `font` shorthand.**

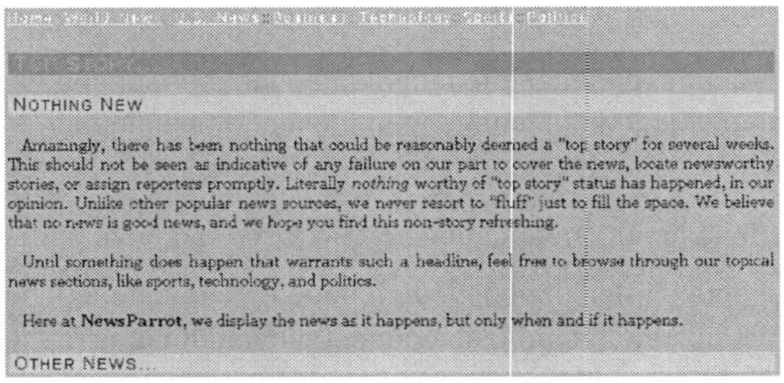

a. **Restore the Index.html - Notepad window.**

b. In the first `h1` rule, **click after `background-color: #668099; /*gray-blue*/` and type `font: 400 small-caps 18px Arial, sans-serif;`**

c. In the first `h2` rule, **click after `background-color: #CCC; /*light gray*/` and type `font: 400 small-caps 16px Arial, sans-serif;`**

d. **Choose File→Save.**

e. **Close the Index.html - Notepad window.**

f. In the Internet Explorer window, **click the Refresh button.**

g. **Close the Internet Explorer window.**

TOPIC F

Create a Linked Style Sheet

You have created and modified font styles that effect the textual content of your site, and you have created rules in an embedded style sheet that control the color and typography of a single page in your site. All well-designed sites should have consistent color and typography styles across most pages. In this topic, you will learn how to create an external style sheet and link documents to it, which will allow you to share color and typographical styles across multiple pages in the site.

Linked style sheets present the real advantage of CSS. You can redesign a large website by simply modifying a single style sheet using the linked style sheets concept. For example, if you want all the styles that you applied to individual pages to carry over to the other pages in the site, you will have to apply duplicate styles on each page's embedded style sheet. But with linked style sheets, you can modify and control all the color and typographical styles for as many pages as necessary from a single style sheet.

Linked Style Sheets

Linked style sheets are text files with a .css extension that contain only CSS rules. Linked style sheets are the most powerful and frequently used style sheet type because you can link multiple documents to it and control styles of any number of pages from a central location. There's no need for the `<style>` container that enables embedded style sheets. HTML elements are also prohibited in the linked style sheet.

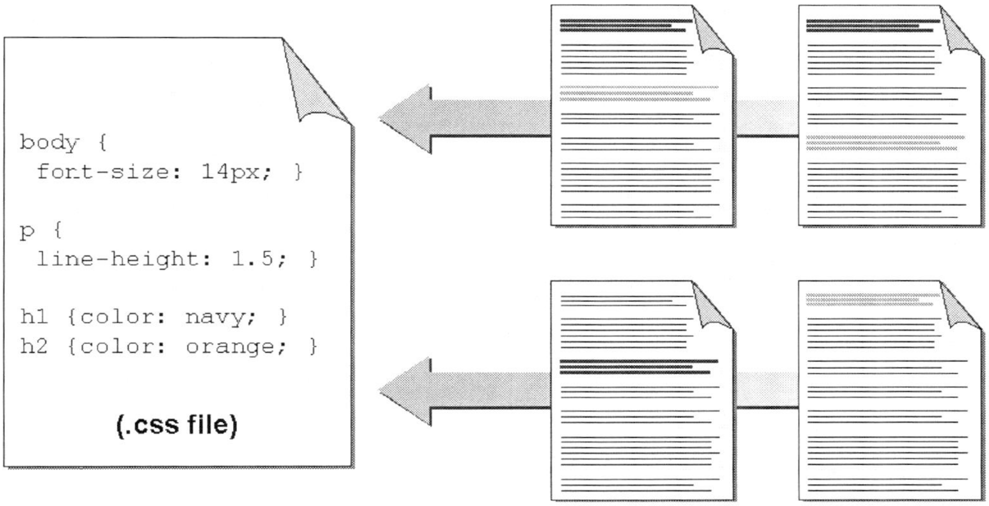

Documents link to an external style sheet via the <link> tag

The <link> Tag

You can link multiple documents to a .css file it with the `<link>` tag. The `<link>` tag creates a relationship between a document and a style sheet. The `<link>` tag does not require a closing tag, but requires several attributes such as rel, type, and href when you link to an external style sheet.

The following table lists the attributes and their description.

Attribute	Description
`rel`	Specifies the relationship of the referenced file to the current document; `rel="stylesheet"` indicates that the current document's link relationship is a style sheet.
`type`	Specifies the type of style sheet used in the document. All linked and embedded style sheets should include this attribute with the value `"text/css"`.
`href`	Declares the URL or file name of the external style sheet you are linking to.
`title`	An optional attribute you can use to indicate the style sheet's name.

To create a link between a document and a style sheet, you may write as:

Use closing slash />

```
<link rel="stylesheet" type="text/css" href="MyStyles.css">
```

How to Create a Linked Style Sheet

Procedure Reference: Create a Linked Style Sheet

To create a linked style sheet:

1. Open a new file in any text editor.
2. Enter the style sheet rules you want to share among multiple web pages.
3. Save the file with a .css extension.
4. Link all pages that you want styled with the external style sheet by using the `<link>` element and required attributes.
5. Save all linked pages.
6. Verify that the styles are applied to all linked pages.

ACTIVITY 1-13

Creating a Linked Style Sheet

Activity Time:

10 minutes

Data Files:

- info.html

Before You Begin:

From the C:\085568Data\color and typography\Activity 13\Starter\Illuminati folder, open the info.html file in Internet Explorer and its source file in Notepad.

Scenario:

You have created several style rules that control the color and typography of individual pages. You're beyond the proof stage now, and you need your styles to apply to all pages on the Illuminati site. You need to move all the styles that are currently in the embedded style sheet within info.html to an external style sheet and then link it to all pages on the site.

What You Do	How You Do It
1. **Verify that the other pages in the Illuminati site don't pick up the styles you have created.**	a. If necessary, **minimize the Info.html - Notepad window.** b. **Click the links in the Navigation bar** to open their respective pages. c. **Observe the content and style of the other pages.** The other pages do not pick the styles created for the Info page.
2. **Why don't the other pages on the site pick up the styles in info.html?**	
3. **How can you make the styles in info.html apply to all pages on the site?**	
4. **Create a new external style sheet named styles.css.**	a. **Choose Start→Run.** b. In the Open text box, **type Notepad and click OK.** c. **Choose File→Save.** d. **Navigate to the C:\085568Data\color and typography\Activity 13\Starter\Illuminati folder.** e. **Click in the File Name text box, type styles.css and click Save.** f. **Minimize the Styles.css - Notepad window.**

5. **Move all styles from the embedded style sheet to the external style sheet.**

   a. If necessary, in the navigation section, **click the Info link** to open the Info page.

   b. **Restore the Info.html - Notepad window.**

   c. **Click before the opening `<style>` tag.**

   d. **Hold down Shift and click at the end of the `</style>` tag.**

   e. **Choose Edit→Cut.**

   f. **Save and minimize the Info.html - Notepad window.**

   g. **Restore the Styles.css - Notepad window.**

   h. **Choose Edit→Paste.**

   i. **Save and close the Styles.css - Notepad window.**

6.	Link all documents in the site to the styles.css style sheet.	a. **Restore the Info.html - Notepad window.** b. **Type `<link rel="stylesheet" type="text/css" href= "styles.css">`** c. **Select the `<link rel="stylesheet" type="text/css" href= "styles.css">` tag and choose Edit→ Copy.** d. **Save and close the Info.html - Notepad window.** e. In the info.html file, **click the News link.** f. **Choose View→Source.** g. **Click below the `</title>` tag and choose Edit→Paste** to paste the `<link>` tag. h. **Save and close the News.html - Notepad window.** i. In the remaining four documents, **paste the `<link>` tag in the same location.** j. **Save and close each file.**
7.	Observe the styles in the other pages of the site.	a. **Navigate through the site links again.** b. **Verify that all pages have the same style.** c. **Close the Internet Explorer window.**

8. What are some advantages of moving the styles to an external style sheet?

Lesson 1 Follow-up

In this lesson, you created embedded style sheets, applied color and typographical styles to control and modify text and font properties, and created linked style sheets to control multiple web pages from a central location.

1. **How does a poor choice of color and typography styles contribute to the ineffectiveness of a website?**

2. **Do you think a linked style sheet is the core advantage of CSS? Why?**

LESSON 2

Designing with the Cascade

Lesson Time
1 hour(s), 45 minutes

Lesson Objectives:

In this lesson, you will create style sheets that cascade according to established guidelines.

You will:

- Create element classes and independent classes.
- Create ID styles.
- Create styles with contextual selectors to take advantage of a document's parent-child structure.
- Target styles to elements that have specific attributes.
- Create style sheets that cascade from general to specific and from external to local.
- Import a style sheet from another style sheet.
- Apply styles to single element instances.

Introduction

You created embedded style sheets, applied color [illegible] sheets to control multiple web pages from a cent[illegible] tors that target a particular HTML element. Type [illegible] to style all instances of a particular element, but [illegible] an element, you can isolate an instance of a parti[illegible] lesson, you will explore several methods for isol[illegible] will also learn how to share specific styles amon[illegible] sheet type that suits a particular rule.

When working on several pages of a website, yo[illegible] design effectiveness if you use only type selector[illegible] to apply more specific rules that target particular [illegible] that best fit your style needs, you can reduce the [illegible] pages, resulting in faster, more efficient style sheets. Further, by placing each style rule in its most appropriate style sheet type, your styles will interact, or cascade, thereby organizing your styles logically and reducing redundancies in code.

TOPIC A

Create Class Styles

You are familiar with creating embedded style sheets and applying color and typographical styles. With the type selectors you have used you cannot distinguish an element from another instance of the same element. In this topic, you will learn how to distinguish elements from other like elements by using classes.

The ability to distinguish an element from other like elements adds flexibility and effectiveness to most design projects. For example, if you have a document with four paragraphs, or `<p>` elements, and you want only the first paragraph to be in bold, you can't use a type selector because all the `<p>` elements will pick up the style. Instead, if you want only the first paragraph to pick up a particular style, you can create and name your own paragraph class, and apply the styles to it. This prevents other paragraphs from picking up the style, and will also allow you to identify the style according to how it's used in the style sheet.

Class Selectors

Definition:

Class selectors, or classes, are selectors that target styles more specifically than type selectors. Classes are vital components of style sheets because they allow you to name your elements logically, distinguish an element from other like elements, or share styles among different elements. A class selector is defined with a period (.), followed by a name of your choice, without any space between them.

Example:

A class element can be declared as: `Element.ClassName { your styles }`.

CSS h1. main {color: teal:
}
Html
<h1 class="main">
Hello </h1>

Naming Classes

By naming classes logically, according to how they are used, you can make your style sheets easier to understand and modify. It is easier to understand the purpose of classes than a series of type selectors because they are logically named according to how they are used in a document.

```
div.header { styles, etc. }
div.content { styles, etc. }
div.links { styles, etc. }
div.footer { styles, etc. }
```

Element Classes

Element classes are associated with a specific HTML element. The selector begins with the element, followed by the period, and its class name. This allows you to distinguish one or more elements from other like elements. For example, you can't use a type selector if you have a `<div>` element that contains navigation links, and you need to distinguish it from other `<div>` elements on a page or across all pages in a site. Instead, you can create a class of that element and apply the style to only those elements of that class.

To do this, you need to use the `class` attribute of HTML to give the element a class name, and then attach the style to that element using a class selector, as:

```
<div class="links">
```

To attach a style to this element, your style sheet rule can be declared as:

```
div.links { property: value; }
```

Independent Classes

Independent classes are not associated with any particular HTML element and can, therefore, be shared among different elements.

```
.author { color: navy;
font-style: italic; }
```

For example, in the above rule, there is no HTML element associated with the selector, so you used `class= "author"` to classify all elements in the document or site. This is even more flexible than element classes, although both methods have their specific advantages.

The Cascading Mechanism

The *cascading* mechanism, in Cascading Style Sheets, is the method by which different styles interact when conflicts arise. All styles cascade from general to specific. The more specific a style, the higher its level of importance. For example, if you have a rule in your style sheet that declares all paragraphs should have blue text, but one of your paragraphs is attached to a class that declares that text in that `<p>` element should be green, then the specific green style overrides the blue text style.

Specificity

The term *specificity* denotes the *weight* of a given style or the level of importance that a rule has over other rules that might conflict with it. A rule's specificity is determined by its selector. The greater the specificity of the selector, the greater *weight*, or importance, the rule has. The following table lists the specificity values of type selectors and class selectors.

CSS cascade assigns weight specific to each style rule. When several rules are applied, the one with the largest weight takes precedence.

Selector	Specificity Value	Description and Example
Type selectors	1	All type selector rules are worth 1 specificity point per element. The following rule has a specificity of 1: `p { color: blue }`
Element class selectors	11	Classes with an associated element have a specificity of 11 for the element, and 10 for the class. For example: `p.nav { color: gray }`
Independent class selectors	10	Classes that are not associated with a particular element have a specificity of 10. For example: `.nav { color: green }`

Specificity is the most important aspect of the cascade. By creating conflicts using the rules of specificity, you can reduce redundancies in your code.

For example:

```
div { color: gray; background-color: white }

.nav { color: white; background-color: silver }
```

In the above rules, any plain `<div>` element will be rendered with gray text and a white background. But if one or more `<div>` elements contain a `class="nav"` attribute and value, then that `<div>` will be rendered with white text and a silver background. Even though all `<div>` elements are supposed to have gray text and a white background in accordance with the first rule, the `.nav` rule wins the style conflict because it has a greater specificity.

Specificity in Grouped Selectors

In cases where you have a rule that groups different selector types, each element's specificity is calculated separately. For example:

```
p.div, blockquote, .nav { color: blue }
```

In the above rule, the `p.div`, the `blockquote`, and the `.nav` elements are all calculated separately. The `p.div` style has a specificity of 11, the `blockquote` style has a specificity of 1, and the `.nav` style has a specificity of 10.

How to Create Class Styles

Procedure Reference: Create Class Styles

To create a class style:

1. If necessary, determine the element class or independent class to achieve the desired style.
2. Add the *`class="MyClass"`* attribute to the element or elements you want to style, using a logical name that describes how the style is used.
3. Create a new rule in the style sheet using either the element class or independent class as the selector for your desired styles.
4. Save the changes and verify that only those elements with the *`class="YourClassName"`* attribute pick up the style(s).

OPTIONAL DISCOVERY ACTIVITY 2-1

Determining How Styles Cascade

Scenario:

Your site styles are not displaying as you had expected. You need to determine which conflicting styles are taking precedence in a series of conflicting rules. The page you're working on contains the following elements:

- Three paragraphs. One paragraph has a `class="nav"` attribute.
- Two divisions, both with a `class="main"` attribute.
- A table with two rows, one of which has a `class="head"` attribute.

The document is linked to a style sheet with the following rules:

```
p { background-color: silver; }
div { background-color: white; }
tr  { background-color: silver; }
.nav { background-color: gray; }
.main { background-color: silver; }
.head { background-color: gray; }
p.nav, div.main { background-color: orange; }
```

1. **You expected all paragraphs to display with a silver background. Why does one of them display with an orange background color?**

2. **What is the *overriding* specificity value for the paragraph with orange background?**

3. **You expected the <div> elements to display with a silver background color. Why are both of them orange?**

---

4. **You expected both table rows to have a silver background color. Why is one of them a dark gray?**

ACTIVITY 2-2

Applying Class Styles

Activity Time:

10 minutes

Data Files:

- index.html

Before You Begin:

From the C:\085568Data\the cascade\Activity 2\Starter\NewsParrot folder, open the index.html file in Internet Explorer and its source file in Notepad.

Scenario:

Your client likes how the design of the NewsParrot home page (index.html) is coming along, and has asked for a few additional modifications. The style requirement and the suggested style modifications are as follows:

- Remove the background color for the subheading under the level-one headings: use the same color as the page background, or use the value `transparent`.
- Give the text a color that stands out against the page background: use `#FFF` or `#000`.

You need to use the parrot.css style sheet to distinguish the subheadings under each h1 heading from the Other News subheading—without changing the latter's style.

Also, the articles in some of the news pages have bold (<b>) elements to emphasize names relevant to each story. But there are also two instances of the name NewsParrot, which are also defined by the <b> element and must be, by convention, in orange. You need to find a way to style all instances of the text NewsParrot in these articles without changing the default black, bold style of the names of individuals.

What You Do	How You Do It
1. **Observe the heading styles used in the site.**	a. If necessary, **minimize the Index.html - Notepadwindow.**
	b. In the Internet Explorer window, **click through each link in the navigation section.** Notice that the styles for the Top Story, Nothing New, and Other News headings remain the same across every page.
	c. **Click the Home link.**

2. **Why are the styles the same for both subheadings?**

3. **How can you change the styles for the first `h2` heading (Nothing New) without affecting the styles for the Other News heading?**

pseudo-class - for links

Link
visited
hover
active

Specificity values
inheritance = 0
type = 1
ind. class = 10
element class = 11
ind. ID = 100
element ID = 101
descendant = add up
pseudo class = 11
inline styles = 1000

4. **Create a new style for the first heading.**

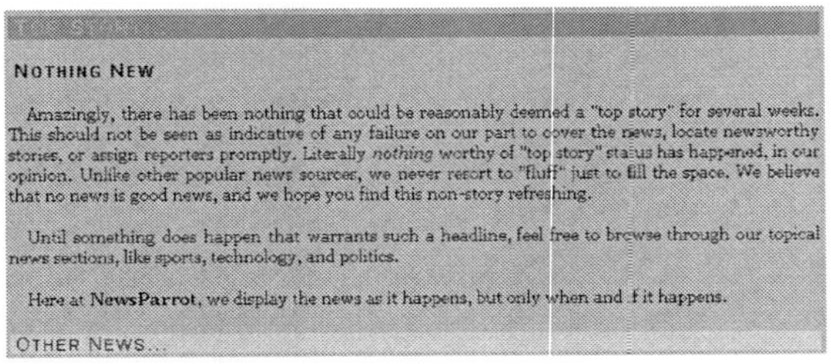

In later browsers, classes are case-sensitive.

a. **Navigate to the My Computer\C:\085568Data\the cascade\Activity 2\Starter\NewsParrot folder and open `parrot.css`.**

b. In the Parrot.css - Notepad window, **click after the `address` rule and press Enter.**

c. **Type `h2.lead { color: #000; background-color: transparent; font-weight: bold; }`**

d. **Choose File→Save.**

e. **Minimize the Parrot.css - Notepad window.**

f. **Restore the Index.html - Notepad window.**

g. In the Index.html - Notepad window, **scroll down** to view `<h2>Nothing new </h2>`.

h. **Click after `<h2` and press Spacebar.**

i. **Type `class="lead"`**

j. **Choose File→Save.**

k. **Minimize the Index.html - Notepad window.**

l. In the Internet Explorer window, **click the Refresh button.**

m. **Notice that the `<h2>` style has changed.**

n. **Insert the `class="lead"` attribute** to the World News, U.S. News, Business, Technology, Sports, and Politics web pages and then save and close the files.

o. **Click the Home page link.**

---

5. **Are the two subheadings displaying with different styles?**

---

6. Create a new rule that distinguishes all instances of the text NewsParrot without affecting the other elements.

   a. Restore the Parrot.css - Notepad window.

   b. Press Enter and type `.parrot { color: #FC0; }`

   c. Choose File→Save.

   d. Close the Parrot.css - Notepad window.

   e. Restore the Index.html - Notepad window.

   f. In the text Newsparrot, within the <b> tags, click after `<b` and press Spacebar.

   g. Type `class="parrot"`

   h. Choose File→Save.

   i. Close the Index.html - Notepad window.

   j. In the Internet Explorer window, scroll down and click the Refresh button.

   k. Close the Internet Explorer window.

---

7. Why the NewsParrot text is displayed in orange when there's an existing rule for the <b> element that declares black as the color for text?

---

8. Why don't the individual names in each story also display in orange?

TOPIC B

Create ID Styles

You have created and applied class selectors to target styles to specific element instances. With CSS, you can also create rules that target unique instances of an element. In this topic, you will learn to apply ID styles that are to be applied only to a single element on a page.

Using CSS you can attach specific elements to a class, or you can share a class among multiple different elements. Sometimes, classes aren't the best solution, and you may want to isolate a specific style to declare it as unique to a page.

ID Selectors

ID selectors are similar to class selectors because you can give your elements logical names and distinguish an element from other like elements. But, unlike classes, styles declared with an ID selector must be unique to a page, and the ID cannot be shared with other elements in a document. IDs have a specificity of 100, so the styles applied with an ID selector will override any conflicts. ID selectors are written with a pound sign (#).

ID selectors are written as: `#MyID { My Styles }`

ID selectors must be written with alphanumeric characters and an optional hyphen. They cannot start with a number, and special characters such as underscores are also not allowed. However, you can use a number after an alphanumeric character, for example, `#footer1`.

You can also combine an ID and a class in a single element, for example,`<div id="nav" class="leftnav">`

With this you can apply unique styles as well as shared styles for a given element. As your style sheets become more complex, you will encounter scenarios where this sort of construct is helpful. Like classes, you can also create element IDs and independent IDs.

Element IDs

To create an ID selector associated with a particular element, simply begin the selector with your element, followed by the pound sign, and then your ID name, as follows:

```
div#logo { My Styles }
```

This rule selects a `<div>` that contains an `id="logo"` attribute. It has a specificity of 101—100 for the ID and 1 for the type selector.

Independent IDs

For a particular ID style to be accessible to different elements throughout multiple pages in a site, you can create an ID selector that's not associated with any HTML element, as follows:

```
#MyID { My Styles }
```

For example, the rule `#nav { My Styles }` selects the single element on a page that has an `id="nav"` attribute. On one page, you can apply this ID to a `<div>` element, and to a `<td>` element on another page.

As always, the rules you create should be dictated by need. For example, if you have an element that you use for navigation and you know that you will use a `<div>` element in every case, you might want to use `div#nav` as your selector so that other elements cannot access the ID.

How to Create ID Styles

Procedure Reference: Create ID Styles

To create an ID style:

1. If necessary, determine if you need an ID to achieve the desired style.
2. If necessary, determine if you need an element ID or independent ID to achieve the desired style.
3. Add the `id="`*`MyID`*`"` attribute, using a logical name, to the element to which you want to apply the style.
4. Create a new rule in the style sheet using either the element ID or independent ID as the selector for your desired styles.
5. Save your changes and verify that only the single element using the ID picks up the style(s).

ACTIVITY 2-3

Styling with ID Selectors

Activity Time:

5 minutes

Data Files:

- index.html

Before You Begin:

From the C:\085568Data\the cascade\Activity 3\Starter\NewsParrot folder, open the index.html file in Internet Explorer and its source file in Notepad.

Scenario:

Your project team has decided that the copyright section in all the NewsParrot site pages should be uniquely identified to establish consistency. Because there is only one footer per document and they're all the same, you decide to use an ID selector to give the footers on each page a unique style—a style that is not meant to be shared among other elements on each page. The property and value of the styles you need to apply to the parrot.css style sheet are listed below.

- Property—`color`, value—`#FFF`
- Property—`background-color`, value—`transparent`
- Property—`letter-spacing`, value—`2px`
- Property—`font-size`, value—`10px`

- Property—`font-weight`, value—`bold`

The footers on the NewsParrot site pages consist of a `<div>` tag that contains an `<address>` element for the copyright text.

What You Do	How You Do It
1. **Assign an ID style to the `div` element containing the copyright statement.**	a. In the Index.html - Notepad window, **scroll down** to view the `FOOTER` comment in the code.
As with classes, IDs are case-sensitive in the newer browsers.	b. Below the `FOOTER` comment, **click after `<div` and press Spacebar.**
	c. **Type `id="footer"`**
	d. **Choose File→Save and close the Index.html - Notepad window.**
	e. **Open the site's other six pages in Notepad.**
	f. In each `<div>` element, under the FOOTER comment, **insert the `id= "footer"` attribute and value.**
	You can also copy and paste the `<div id= "footer">` element from the index.html file into each file, replacing the existing `<div>` elements.
	g. **Save and close the files.**

2. **Create an ID style for the footer element.**

a. **Navigate to the My Computer\C:\085568Data\the cascade\Activity 3\Starter\NewsParrot folder and open `parrot.css`.**

b. **Click after `.parrot { color: #FC0; }` and press Enter.**

c. **Type `div#footer { color: #FFF; background-color: transparent; letter-spacing: 2px; font-size: 10px; font-weight: bold; }`**

d. **Choose File→Save and close the Parrot.css - Notepad window.**

e. In the Internet Explorer window, **scroll down to view the footer and click the Refresh button.**

f. **Notice that the footer displays the changed style.**

g. **Click through the links on the Index.html page.** Notice that the footers on all pages have the same style.

h. **Close the Internet Explorer window.**

In this case, it doesn't matter if you use `#footer` or `div#footer` as your selector, since only one element per page can access the ID style and all footers on the site are defined by the `<div>` element.

TOPIC C

Create Contextual Styles

You have used ID selectors to target styles to specific element instances and distinguish them from other like elements. You can also apply specific styles without having to modify any HTML code. In this topic, you will target styles to specific element instances by taking advantage of the parent-child relationships that already exist in your HTML.

Consider a scenario where you have to style only certain specific elements in different HTML pages. Instead of adding more HTML code, you can use the document's existing parent-child structures to apply the styles you need. By doing that you can make both your style sheets and your HTML documents leaner and more efficient. It also makes your styles easier to update.

Contextual Selectors

Contextual selectors are also referred to as *descendant selectors*. These selectors allow you to target your styles to elements within a specified parent-child structure. The parent-child relationship defines the context of your elements. Contextual selectors are simply two or more selectors separated by a space. For example, in the rule, parent child { your styles }, the leftmost selector is the highest-level parent element and the rightmost selector is the target element.

Using Contextual Selector

There's no limit to the number of parent elements you can use in a contextual selector. In the example shown there's a <span> element that's nested inside a <div id="footer"> element. If you want to target styles for only those <span> elements that are nested inside an element that has the ID footer, without influencing other <span> elements in other contexts on the page, you can simply apply the style contextually.

```
<div id="footer">
Contents & copy; 2000-2004
<span>OnlyCo,</span>
</div>
```

```
#footer span {
    color: navy;
    font-weight: bold; }
```

The following is a more complex example:

```
div#content p.top em { color: gray; background-color: white }
```

This rule declares that all <em> elements nested inside a paragraph of the class "top," and those that are nested inside a <div> with the ID "content," should be rendered gray with a white background.

How to Create Contextual Styles

Procedure Reference: Create Contextual Styles

To create contextual styles:

1. Evaluate the document structure to establish what your contextual selector will be.
2. Check whether the other elements do not pick up the style.
3. Apply your style with a contextual selector, making sure that the rightmost element is the one that picks up the style, and the element or elements to its left represent its parent structure.
4. Save the changes and verify that your target element(s) are the only elements that pick up the styles.

ACTIVITY 2-4

Creating Contextual Styles

Activity Time:

5 minutes

Data Files:

- info.html

Before You Begin:

From the C:\085568Data\the cascade\Activity 4\Starter\Illuminati folder, open the info.html file in Internet Explorer.

Scenario:

The Illuminati project team would like you to modify two styles in the styles.css style sheet. The team wants a new background color applied to the internal content tables. They suggest that you apply a color from the logo image. They also want all links that are not part of the navigation section at the top of each page to have normal letter spacing. There is also an emphasis on keeping the documents and style sheets as lean as possible.

What You Do	How You Do It
1. **Apply a background color to the table listing the institutions without using a class or an ID style and without affecting the outer table.**	a. **Navigate to the C:\085568Data\the cascade\Activity 4\Starter\Illuminati folder and open styles.css.** b. **Type `div table { background-color: #99CCB3; }` and press Enter.** c. **Choose File→Save and minimize the Styles.css - Notepad window.** d. In the Internet Explorer window, **click the Refresh button**. The table will have a light green background color that does not affect the background color of the outer table.

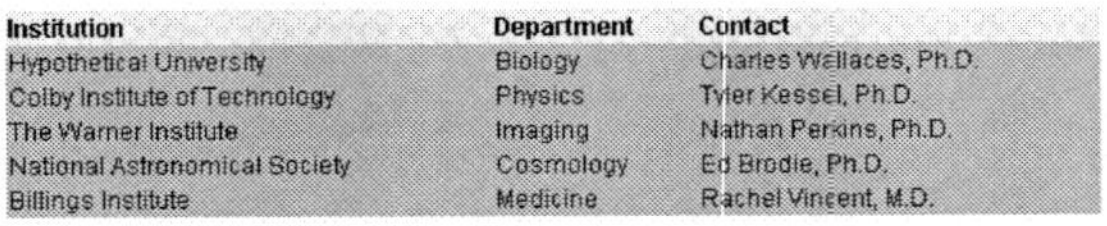

Institution	Department	Contact
Hypothetical University	Biology	Charles Wallaces, Ph.D.
Colby Institute of Technology	Physics	Tyler Kessel, Ph.D.
The Warner Institute	Imaging	Nathan Perkins, Ph.D.
National Astronomical Society	Cosmology	Ed Brodie, Ph.D.
Billings Institute	Medicine	Rachel Vincent, M.D.

What You Do	How You Do It
2. **Verify that the style is applied to the other pages in the site.**	a. **Navigate through the other pages on the site.** b. **Verify that the other content tables pick up the style.** There are several other tables that have the same parent structure. c. If necessary, **click the Info link.**
3. **Reset the default letter spacing of the links in the paragraphs without affecting the letter spacing of the links in the navigation section.**	a. **Restore the Styles.css - Notepad window.** b. **Type `p a { letter-spacing: normal; }` and press Enter.** c. **Choose File→Save and close the Styles.css - Notepad window.** d. In the Internet Explorer window, **click the Refresh button.** e. **Close the Internet Explorer window.**

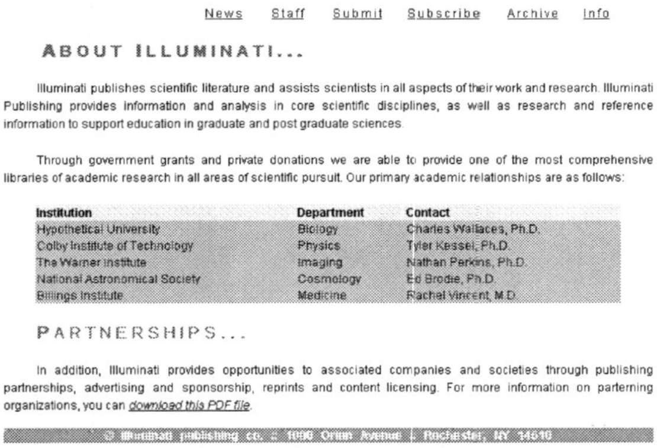

News Staff Submit Subscribe Archive Info

ABOUT ILLUMINATI...

Illuminati publishes scientific literature and assists scientists in all aspects of their work and research. Illuminati Publishing provides information and analysis in core scientific disciplines, as well as research and reference information to support education in graduate and post graduate sciences.

Through government grants and private donations we are able to provide one of the most comprehensive libraries of academic research in all areas of scientific pursuit. Our primary academic relationships are as follows:

Institution	Department	Contact
Hypothetical University	Biology	Charles Wallaces, Ph.D.
Colby Institute of Technology	Physics	Tyler Kessel, Ph.D.
The Warner Institute	Imaging	Nathan Perkins, Ph.D.
National Astronomical Society	Cosmology	Ed Brodie, Ph.D.
Billings Institute	Medicine	Rachel Vincent, M.D.

PARTNERSHIPS...

In addition, Illuminati provides opportunities to associated companies and societies through publishing partnerships, advertising and sponsorship, reprints and content licensing. For more information on parterning organizations, you can *download this PDF file*.

4. **Can you think of any advantages to using contextual styles over classes?**

---

5. **How would you make your contextual styles easier to follow when reading or updating a style sheet?**

TOPIC D

Target Styles to Elements with Specific Attributes

You have applied contextual selectors to create rules and target your styles on elements within a specified parent-child structure. But there may be instances when it's easier to use an element's existing attributes to distinguish its styles. In this topic, you will apply styles to only those elements that contain certain attributes, or specific attribute values.

Using an element's existing attribute or attribute value to pinpoint your styles is another method that can help keep your documents as lean as possible. You don't need to add any HTML code. This makes your documents more efficient, saves time, and makes your style sheets easier to update.

Attribute Selectors

Attribute selectors attach styles to an element that has specific attributes or attribute values. Like contextual selectors, attribute selectors enable you to use your existing HTML code to target specific elements. To create a rule using an attribute selector, you specify the element, followed by brackets that contain the selected attribute.

For example: `abhelement[attribute] { property: value; }`

You can use any valid HTML attribute to create a match. Even attributes such as `alt`, `title`, or `lang` that have no affect on presentation can be used. For example, in the rule `div[align] { background-color: #eee; }`, all <div> elements that have an `align` attribute are selected, giving them a light gray background color.

You can also use attribute selectors to help establish consistency in your design between Internet Explorer and Netscape 6. Even though the 5.0 and 6.0 generation of browsers support CSS equally in most cases, there may be situations where rendering differences between the two major browsers create a problem for your intended design. You can use attribute selectors to *tweak* your styles in Netscape 6 to establish consistency between the two browsers.

Rule with an Attribute Selector

The following example shows a rule built with an attribute selector. The rule selects only those `<td>` elements that have a `width="100"` attribute and value.

```
<table>
<tr>
<td width="100">Cell content</td>
<td>Cell content</td>
<td>Cell content</td>
</tr>
</table>
```

```
td[width="100']{
     font-weight: bold;
     letter-spacing: 2px; }
```

Like class and ID selectors, an independent attribute can also be used as your selector. For example, in the following rule, any element that has a `title` attribute will pick up the style:

```
[title] { font-weight: bold; }
```

How to Target Styles to Elements with Specific Attributes

Procedure Reference: Target Styles to Elements with Specific Attributes

To create rules with attribute selectors:

1. If necessary, check to see if the element you want to style contains attributes.
2. Determine if an attribute selector is the best way to achieve the desired style.
3. If necessary, ensure that the style isn't picked up by other elements that you don't want to style.
4. Apply your style with an attribute selector by placing the attribute name or *`attribute="value"`* pair within brackets.
5. Save the changes and verify that the target element(s) are the only elements that pick up the styles.

ACTIVITY 2-5

Attaching Styles to Elements with Specific Attributes and Values

Activity Time:

5 minutes

Data Files:

- info.html

Before You Begin:

From the C:\085568Data\the cascade\Activity 5\Starter\Illuminati folder, open the info.html file in Netscape Navigator.

Ensure that you use Netscape 7.1. It is anticipated that Internet Explorer 7 will soon support attribute selectors.

Scenario:

Your project team would like to add a few distinguishing styles to the Illuminati site pages without modifying the HTML documents. You need to add the following styles to the styles.css style sheet:

- Give the table cells holding the navigation links a light gray background color.
- In the table that holds the contact names, change the font face to Georgia (or Serif).

You decide to select these elements using their existing attributes and values.

What You Do	How You Do It
1. In the source code for the info.html file, **observe the two elements mentioned in the scenario.** **What attributes or attribute values do these elements have that other like elements in the document do not have?**	

2. **Change the inner table's font.**

Institution	Department	Contact
Hypothetical University	Biology	Charles Wallaces, Ph.D.
Colby Institute of Technology	Physics	Tyler Kessel, Ph.D.
The Warner Institute	Imaging	Nathan Perkins, Ph.D.
National Astronomical Society	Cosmology	Ed Brodie, Ph.D.
Billings Institute	Medicine	Rachel Vincent, M.D.

a. **Navigate to the C:\085568Data\the cascade\Activity 5\Starter\Illuminati folder and open styles.css.**

b. In the styles.css style sheet, **click after the `a` rule and press Enter.**

c. **Type `table[align] { font-family: georgia, serif; }`**

d. **Choose File→Save and minimize the Styles.css - Notepad window.**

e. In the Netscape Navigator window, **click the Reload button.**

---

3. **Apply a light gray background color to the table cells containing the navigation links.**

a. **Restore the Styles.css - Notepad window.**

b. **Press Enter.**

c. **Type `td[height="25"] { background-color: #eee; }`**

d. **Choose File→Save and close the Styles.css - Notepad window.**

e. In the Netscape Navigator window, **click the Reload button.**

f. **Notice that the table cells containing the links have picked up the style.**

---

4. **Verify that all pages in the site are updated.**

a. **Navigate through the other pages in the site.**

b. **Verify that the other table cells containing the links pick up the style.**

c. **Close the Netscape window.**

---

5. **What are the advantages of this approach to creating styles?**

TOPIC E

Create Style Sheets that Cascade

You used attribute selectors to attach styles to elements with specific attributes and values. You have applied styles using both embedded and linked style sheets, but your style sheets have not yet interacted with each other. Sometimes you may want rules in different style sheets to interact and style your pages. In this topic, you will create style sheets that interact to establish your site's design.

With style sheets that interact, you can set all *global* styles that are shared across multiple documents in a linked style sheet. With interacting style sheets you can ensure a consistent style across all pages, make global style changes from a central location, and also eliminate redundancies in your style sheet code. This keeps your style definitions out of your HTML pages and reduces the amount of code in your document, resulting in a document that downloads faster.

The Origin of Rules

The *cascading* part in Cascading Style Sheets refers to the hierarchical order in which different style sheet types interact, and how style conflicts are resolved. In the cascade, each style sheet type is prioritized. Rules cascade from general to specific and from external to local, so the more local style sheet has a higher priority than a less local style sheet. The four style sheet types have the following order of priority:

1. Inline styles
2. Embedded style sheets
3. Linked style sheets
4. And, imported style sheets

Consider a scenario where a linked style sheet declares that all level-one headings be displayed in navy text, and three of the HTML documents linked to this style sheet contain embedded styles that declare all level-one headings should be in gray. In this situation, the rules in the embedded style sheets take precedence over the rule in the linked style sheet because they're more local. The level-one headings would display with gray text on those pages with the embedded rule.

Page Specific Styles

Embedded style sheets can also be used to apply styles that are specific to each page. This allows you to:

- Keep your linked style sheets as small as possible.
- Override conflicting styles from a linked style sheet to establish page-specific style needs.

If you have a shared style in a linked style sheet, but you need the selected element to display differently on one page than it does on others, you can put the style in an embedded style sheet to ensure that your required style is displayed the way you need it to be on one page, without affecting the style on other pages.

Modularity

Cascade allows you to make your styles *modular*, which means that several different style sheets can interact to establish your site's design, with each style rule placed in the most appropriate location. This helps to logically organize your styles and prevent style rules not used by a particular document from downloading needlessly.

For example, the following figure demonstrates a series of style sheets that cascade. Styles that apply to all pages reside in the linked style sheet, and document-specific styles reside in each embedded style sheet. If conflicts arise between styles in the linked and embedded style sheets, the embedded styles will win because they're more local.

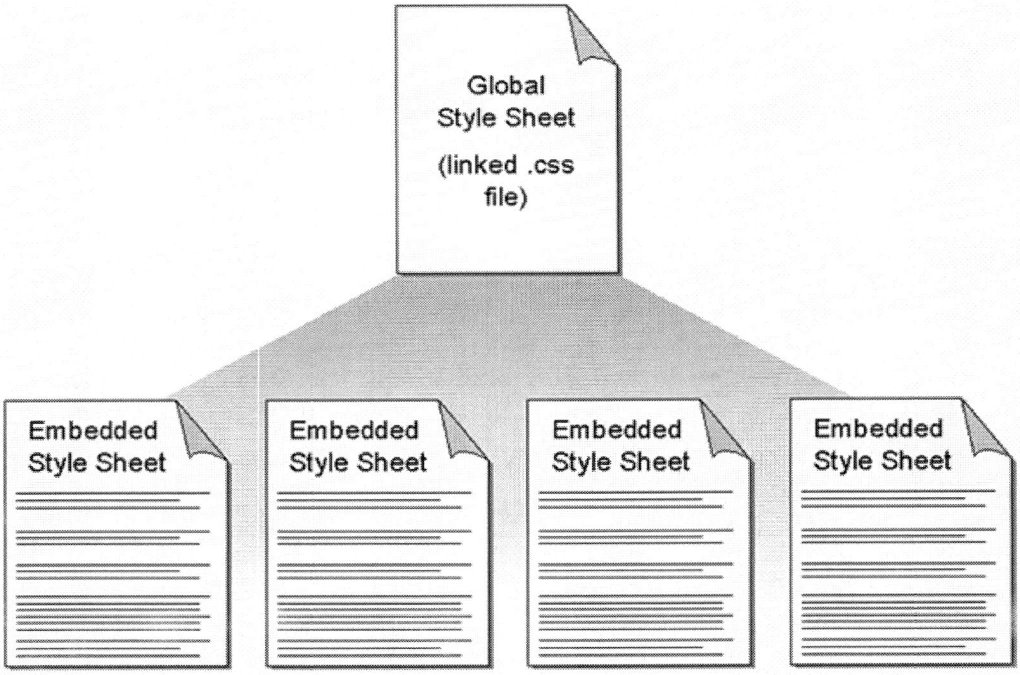

Documents are linked to a style sheet for shared styles

Order of Appearance

In cases where a property is declared for an element more than once in the same style sheet, preference is given to the style declared last—provided the two rules have the same specificity. For example, if you need to toggle between two styles often, instead of deleting the style you want to *switch off*, you can simply reverse the order of the two rules as needed.

For example, in the rule `p { font-family: arial, sans-serif; } p { font-family: verdana, sans-serif; }`, all paragraphs will be displayed in the Verdana font, as that's the last rule declared.

There is, however, an exception to this rule. For example, assume that a paragraph contains an <em> element, which, in turn, contains a <b> element that directly contains the paragraph text.

Next, assume you have set up the following rules:

```
b { color: navy; }
em { color: gray; }
```

In this, the text would be rendered navy because the <b> element is closest to the actual text content, even though the rule for em, which indirectly contains the text, is declared last in the style sheet.

How to Create Style Sheets that Cascade

Procedure Reference: Create Style Sheets that Cascade

To create style sheets that cascade:

1. Determine which style sheet type is most appropriate for a given style requirement.
2. Place all site-wide (global) styles in a linked style sheet.
3. Place all document-specific styles in embedded style sheets.
4. Verify that all your styles are working as intended.

ACTIVITY 2-6

Creating Modular Styles

Activity Time:

5 minutes

Data Files:

- staff.html

Before You Begin:

From the C:\085568Data\the cascade\Activity 6\Starter\Illuminati folder, open the staff.html file in Internet Explorer and its source file in Notepad.

Scenario:

The Illuminati project team has determined that a few styles need to be added to the site. The style requirements are as follows:

1. The staff.html page contains a table of staff images and associated text captions that need to be aligned to the center of the table, without affecting any other content.
2. The captions under the staff pictures should be made bold, without affecting any other content.
3. The text "Publishing scientific literature since 1947" should have more letter spacing on all pages. On the news.html page, this text should also have the light yellow background color `#FFC`.

The project team has also placed an emphasis on modularity, which means you need to apply styles in their most logical location—either a page-specific embedded style sheet, or the global, linked style sheet.

What You Do	How You Do It

1. **For the first requirement given in the scenario, should you use the external style sheet or create rules in one or more embedded style sheets?**

---

2. **Center the content of the Staff table without influencing the tables on other pages.**

a. In the Staff.html - Notepad window, **click after the `</title>` element and press Enter.**

b. **Insert the code** to define an embedded style sheet and center the content of the Staff table without influencing the tables on other pages.

See Code Sample 1.

c. **Choose File→Save and minimize the Staff.html - Notepad window.**

d. In the Internet Explorer window, **click the Refresh button.**

e. **Notice that the content of the Staff table is repositioned towards the center of the page.**

Code Sample 1

```
<style type="text/css">
<!--
div table { text-align: center; }
-->
</style>
```

---

3. **For the second requirement in the scenario, should you use the external style sheet or create rules in one or more embedded style sheets?**

---

4. **Bold the captions of the staff pictures.**

a. **Restore the Staff.html - Notepad window.**

b. **Click after `div table {` `text-align: center;` and type `font-weight: bold;`**

c. **Choose File→Save and close the Staff.html - Notepad window.**

d. In the Internet Explorer window, **click the Refresh button.**

e. **Notice that the captions of the staff pictures have become bold.**

---

5. **For the third style requirement in the scenario, should you use the embedded style sheet, the linked style sheet, or both?**

---

6. **Increase the letter spacing of the subtitle across all pages. In addition, on the news.html page, apply a light yellow background color to the subtitle.**

:: publishing scientific literature since 1947 ::

a. **Navigate to the My Computer\C:\085568Data\the cascade\Activity 6\Starter\Illuminati folder and open `styles.css`.**

b. In the `strong` rule, **click after `background-color: #fff;`** and type **`letter-spacing:2px;`**

c. **Choose File→Save and close the Styles.css - Notepad window.**

d. In the Internet Explorer window, **click the Refresh button.**

e. In the navigation section, **click the News link.**

f. **Choose View→Source.**

g. **Click after `<link rel="stylesheet" type="text/css" href="styles.css">` and press Enter.**

h. In the ~~body~~ head section, **insert the code** to create a new rule that uses `strong` as the selector and applies the background color #FFC to the text "publishing scientific literature since 1947."

See Code Sample 2.

i. **Choose File→Save and close the News.html - Notepad window.**

j. In the Internet Explorer window, **click the Refresh button.**

k. **Close the Internet Explorer window.**

Code Sample 2

```
<style type="text/css">
<!--
strong {background-color:#FFC;}
-->
</style>
```

TOPIC F

Import Style Sheets

You have applied modular styles in both linked and embedded style sheets. In instances where you need to apply styles to specific document groups in a site, you can create linked style sheets and import additional style sheets. In this topic, you will learn how to import style sheets from within embedded and linked style sheets.

Importing styles can enhance the organization and efficiency of your style sheets. You can create a linked style sheet that applies to all pages in a site, and then import additional style sheets to address specific document groups in the site that may require their own styles. For example, consider a site that is divided into separate *departments*. If each department requires its own shared styles in addition to the global styles, department-specific style sheets can be imported from within an embedded style sheet for each page in that department. These styles will cascade with the other style sheets in the site to create a higher level of modularity. By importing shared *departmental* styles from within embedded style sheets in each department page, consistency can be ensured across all your document groups, redundancies in code can be eliminated, and further, separate styles from HTML pages.

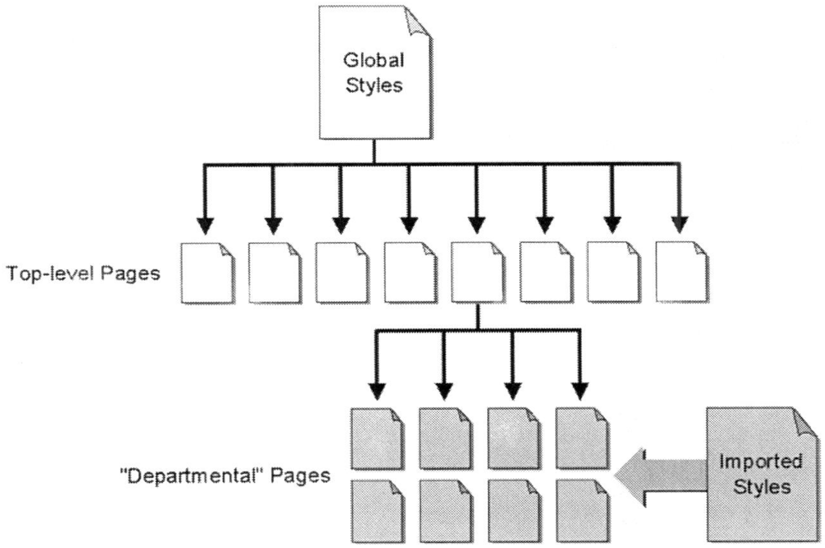

The departmental style sheet is imported so that the "department" documents can share additional styles

Imported Style Sheets

Imported style sheets are simply external style sheets that are imported from within another style sheet. It is the same as a linked style sheet, and it's simply a text file with a .css extension that contains CSS rules. Instead of the HTML document linking to the external style sheet, the style sheet that's either embedded in the document or linked to the document imports the style sheet using the `@ import` rule.

There are two methods of importing style sheets:

- `@import url(styles/stylesheet.css);`
- And, `@import "styles/stylesheet.css";`

An `@import` rule must be the first rule in a style sheet. For this reason, you always include the semicolon at the end of the `@import` rule. Netscape and Internet Explorer will ignore an `@import` rule that does not end with a semicolon, and all rules that follow it will not be read, in accordance with the syntactical requirements of CSS.

You can also use imported style sheets to *hide* styles from particular browsers. Netscape Navigator 4.x does not support imported style sheets, so you can insert *problem styles* or styles that harm your design in Navigator 4 in an imported style sheet. Navigator 4 will ignore those styles, while they are successfully applied in more standards-compliant browsers.

The Origin of Import

The origin of an imported style sheet and its priority in the cascade can vary. An imported style sheet takes on the same origin as the style sheet that imports it. For example, if a style sheet is imported from within an embedded style sheet, that style sheet's origin is the embedding document. If there are any style conflicts between this style sheet and a linked style sheet, styles in the imported style sheet will prevail, because they're considered more local.

How to Import Style Sheets

Procedure Reference: Import Style Sheets

To import style sheets:

1. Determine the need for an imported style sheet and how it will benefit your website in terms of modularity (organization and efficiency).
2. Determine the best location to import the style sheet from—either an embedded or linked style sheet.
3. Insert the *`@import`* rule at the very top of the importing style sheet, making sure that it's the very first rule in the style sheet.
4. Save the changes, and verify that the styles are displayed as expected.

ACTIVITY 2-7

Importing Style Sheets

Activity Time:

5 minutes

Data Files:

- index.html

Before You Begin:

From the C:\085568Data\The Cascade\Activity 7\Starter\NewsParrot folder, open the index.html file in Internet Explorer and its source file in Notepad.

Scenario:

Your development team wants to decrease the font size of the paragraph text in each news page on the NewsParrot site (the pages that are accessed via the Main navigation section at the top of each page). The project team has also decided that all the news pages should share a common style sheet, to reduce code redundancies and make it easier to update their styles. The goal is to give all the news pages their own external style sheet. You need to apply the new style requirement in the news.css style sheet, and then import it from within each of the news pages: index.html, world.html, us.html, biz.html, tech.html, sports.html and pol.html.

What You Do	How You Do It
1. **Specify a smaller paragraph font size in the news.css style sheet.**	a. **Navigate to the My Computer\C:\085568Data\the cascade\Activity 7\Starter\NewsParrot folder and open news.css.**
	b. In the style sheet, **type `p { font-size: 14px; }`**
	c. **Choose File→Save and close the News.css - Notepad window.**

2. **Import the news.css style sheet from all the news pages in the site.**

   a. If necessary, **restore the Index.html - Notepad window.**

   b. In the Index.html - Notepad window, **click after `<!--` and press Enter.**

   c. **Type `@import "news.css";`**

   d. **Choose File→Save and close the Index.html - Notepad window.**

   e. In the Internet Explorer window, **click the Refresh button** to view the style change.

   f. **Similarly, import the news.css style sheet from the World News, U.S. News, Business, Technology, Sports, and Politics web pages, and save and close all the web pages.**

   g. **Close the Internet Explorer window.**

---

3. **Why does the imported style rule for paragraphs override the conflicting style in the linked style sheet?**

---

4. **If news.css were imported from the linked style sheet parrot.css, how would the paragraphs be displayed?**

TOPIC G

Create Inline Styles

You imported style sheets that cascaded according to their specificity and their origin. Sometimes you may have to include additional styles that are applicable to only one specific paragraph in a page. In this topic, you will create inline styles, which are the most local of all style sheet types.

After styling a site, you have been asked to style the text in one particular paragraph in red. In such cases you need not clog up the external, imported, or even embedded style sheets with a one-time style that is not used anywhere else on the page or throughout the site. You can create the single style you need without adding unnecessary code to an already existing style sheet.

Inline Styles

Inline styles are single instances of a style that are inserted directly into an element via the `style` attribute. All the style sheet types you have used thus far allow you to separate your style information from your HTML structure. Inline styles do not create any separation, but they are the most local style sheet type, which means they will take precedence over other conflicting styles.

Inline style adds flexibility, as you can always add an inline style to an element or one particular instance. This style is not meant to be shared or even repeated elsewhere on the page or throughout the site.

The most essential difference in terms of CSS syntax is that there is no selector, and no declaration. Instead, inline styles use the `style` attribute of HTML to insert CSS styles directly into HTML elements.

For example, in the following rule each of the elements have an inline style:

```
<div style="background-color: #ddd;">
<span style="font-variant: small-caps; font-size: 14px;">
```

Inline Style Usage

Though inline styles are the least powerful in terms of influence on a document or series of documents, there are many possible scenarios in which you can use inline styles. Some of the instances when you can use inline styles include:

- You might prefer to use inline styles when testing the effect on a particular element so you can modify your code from the location of that element.
- While prototyping or testing styles, you might find it easier to avoid external or even embedded style sheets.
- You may want to override an inherited style but would rather not create a new class or ID.
- Or, there are many DHTML-specific contexts wherein inline styles are the only solution.

Applying Inline Styles with the <span> Element

The `<span>` element is an inline, or text-level, element that's specifically designed to attach styles to text. On its own, it has no semantic meaning and has no effect on text, which often makes it the perfect host for inline styles.

How to Create Inline Styles

Procedure Reference: Create Inline Styles

To create inline styles:

1. If necessary, determine if your intended style is best applied inline.
2. Add the `style` attribute to the element you want to style.
3. Insert the required `property="value"` pairs as the value of the `style` attribute.
4. Verify the changes to the document.

ACTIVITY 2-8

Creating Inline Styles

Activity Time:

5 minutes

Data Files:

- staff.html

Before You Begin:

From the C:\085568Data\the cascade\Activity 8\Starter\Illuminati folder, open the staff.html file in Internet Explorer and its source file in Notepad.

Scenario:

Your project team has decided that the four names, on Illuminati's staff.html page, that represent the Board of Trustees should be distinguished in color from the other names in the full list of staff members. This style is only meant for this single instance—it will not be used by other sections of the page or site. You need to create a style that meets this requirement without adding any code to a style sheet.

What You Do	How You Do It
1. **True or False? Inline styles are single instances of a style that are inserted directly into an element via the style attribute.** __ True __ False	

2. **Create an inline style to apply a green shade to all the four members of the Board of Trustees.**

   a. In the Staff.html - Notepad window, **scroll down** to view the `<p>` tag below the `</div>` element.

   b. **Click after the `</b>` tag and type `<span style="color: #066;">`**

   c. **Click after Rachel Vincent, M.D., and type `</span>`**

   d. **Choose File→Save and close the Staff.html - Notepad window.**

   e. In the Internet Explorer window, **click the Refresh button.** The names are rendered in green, in accordance with the inline style rule.

   f. **Close the Internet Explorer Window.**

3. **What are the possible disadvantages of using inline styles?**

Lesson 2 Follow-up

In this lesson, you created and applied specific rules and placed them in appropriate style sheets, thus creating more efficient and logically organized style sheets that allow you to eliminate redundancies in your code.

1. **Why do you think implementing the cascade concept in your own development projects will help?**

2. **Which selector and style sheet types do you think you'll use most often, and why?**

Notes

LESSON 3
Designing Content Sections

Lesson Time
1 hour(s), 30 minutes

Lesson Objectives:

In this lesson, you will design content sections using box properties.

You will:

- Modify the margins and padding of elements.
- Create borders for an element.
- Control the height and width of elements.
- Create floating elements.
- Control content overflow.

Introduction

You created and placed specific rules in style sheets to make the latter efficient and logically organized. You also worked with elements that have default spacing and dimensions, but these default styles don't give the desired design outcome. In this lesson, you will learn how to design content sections by modifying element spacing, borders, and dimensions.

Creating a web page design using HTML coding is complex and time-consuming. To achieve the desired layout and design, you need to control spacing inside and between elements, modify the default size of elements, and arrange elements horizontally. Using CSS all aspects of web page design can be controlled without using code-heavy HTML tables, thereby reducing the amount of code in your HTML documents. CSS allows you to modify and update your designs quickly and easily.

TOPIC A

Control Margins and Padding

You created and applied specific rules and placed them in appropriate style sheets. At some point, you would likely apply margins to a word processed document or modify padding of tables in an HTML document. Margins and padding of elements provide the desired emphasis for the content sections of your document. In this topic, you will control the spacing inside and between elements.

Modifying the default spacing between page elements allows you to make vital adjustments to the placement and display of your content. This helps to establish the overall look and feel of your pages and makes it easier for users to read and navigate your content.

For example, the following figure shows a page with default spacing, resulting in somewhat *bunched up* content sections.

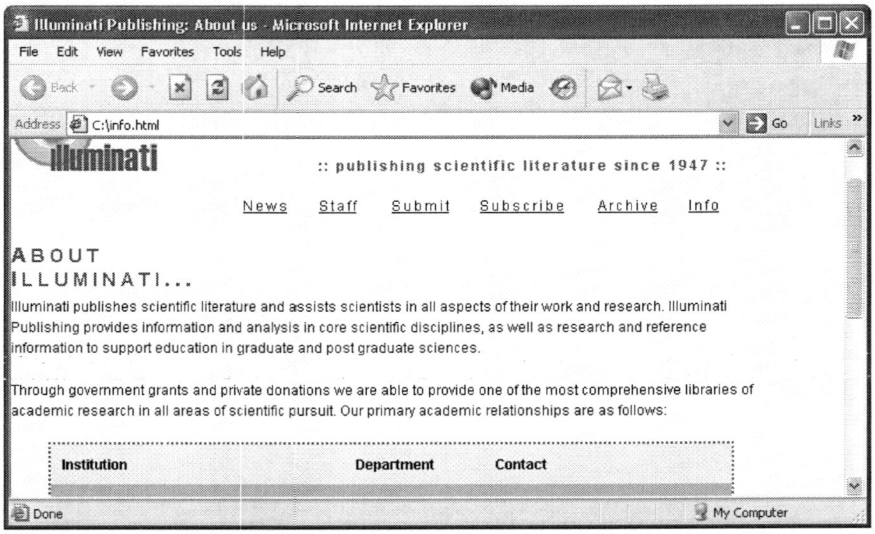

Web page with default spacing

The following figure shows the same page, but with added spacing to provide greater separation between content sections. This reduces the line length of the paragraph text, resulting in a cleaner, more readable design.

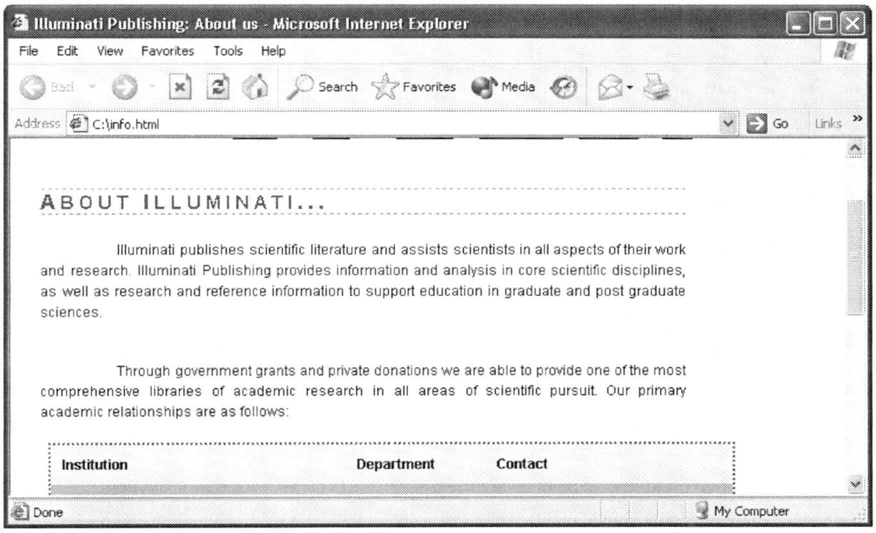

Web page with increased margin spacing

The Box Model

Box model is the formatting model of CSS, and it creates rectangular boxes for the elements in a document. There are three components of the Box model—the margin, border, and padding. Each component is controlled by its own properties, which are optional, as you don't have to specify an element's margin, padding, or border.

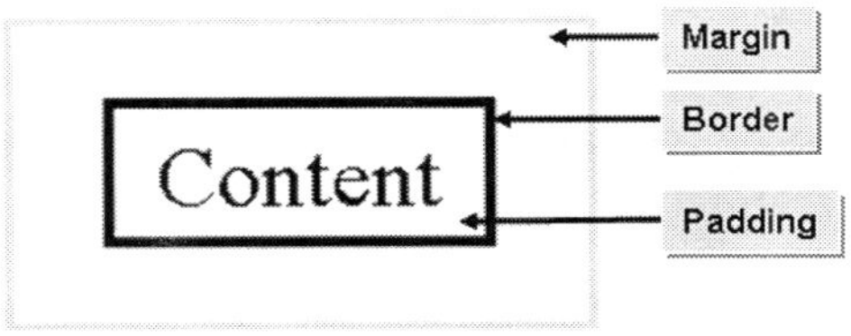

All the components of the Box model do not inherit from parent to child elements.

The 4.x browsers interpret the Box model differently; in particular, Navigator 4.x has incomplete or inaccurate support for the border properties.

Margin

Margin is the Box model component that defines the space between an element's box and its parent element, typically the *page canvas*, or <body> element. To set a margin, you can specify any unit of measurement that deals with length, such as pixels, percentages, inches, centimeters, or ems.

You can declare the margin as: `element { margin: 20px; }`

If you choose an absolute unit of measurement such as pixels or inches, the amount of margin will remain fixed, no matter what size the user's browser window is. If you use a relative unit of measurement such as percentages or ems, the amount of space that defines your margin will increase or decrease according to the size of the user's browser window. This is commonly referred to as a *fluid margin*.

Page Margins

The size of a page canvas is defined by the <body> element. To set a page margin, you simply apply margin styles using `body` as your selector.

When the <body> element has a margin set for it, all elements on the page are bound by its margins. The elements don't inherit the margins of the <body> element, but are simply confined by them. For example, a page with a 20-pixel margin applied to the <body> element, forces all page elements inside the margin.

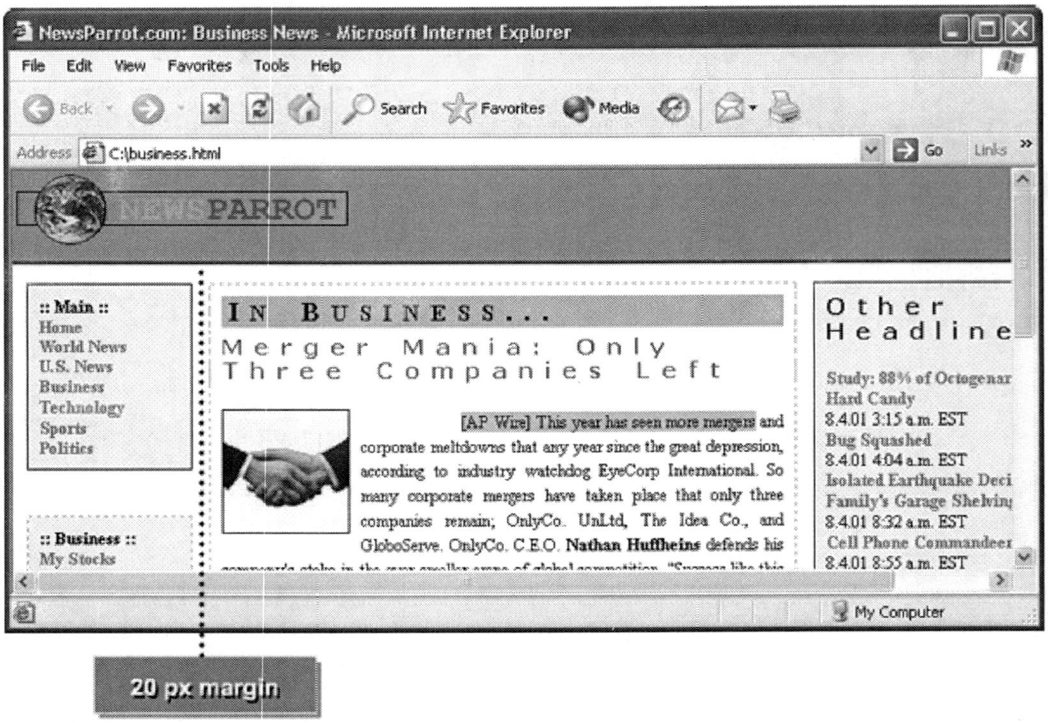

> HTML 4.0 recognizes the `<html>` element as an alternate definition of the page canvas. The 6.0 generation browsers allow you to manipulate the `<html>` element with CSS.

All browsers apply a default page margin, but there are subtle differences depending on the version and platform of the browsers. The following table lists the amount of margin that some of the more popular browsers apply to the page canvas.

Browser	Horizontal x Vertical Offset (In Pixels)
Internet Explorer	10 x 15
Netscape Navigator	8 x 8
Internet Explorer (Mac)	10 x 12

It is better if you set your own page margins due to the existing inconsistency. You can apply any margin value to override the default values that browsers apply, including a value of zero. Any explicit value will establish consistency across browsers.

Element Margins

Browsers apply default margins around page elements, just as page margins do. To establish consistency across browsers, you can override the default values by specifically declaring margin values for any element on a page.

For example, the following figure shows a `<div>` element that contains a paragraph. The parent of the `<div>` element is `<body>` or the page canvas. Therefore, its margin value is set between it and the left edge of the browser window. The paragraph also has a margin of 100 pixels, but it's offset farther than its parent because elements are confined by their parent's margins. In this case, the paragraph displays with a 100-pixel left margin, and is a total of 200 pixels from the left edge of the browser window. The same principle applies to all four sides of an element's box.

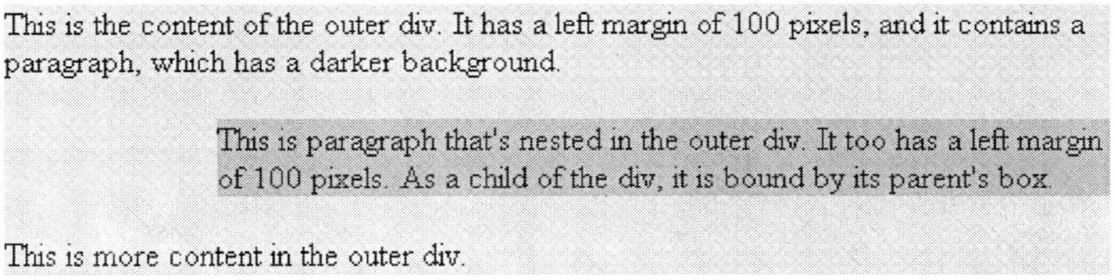

Margin Properties

There are five margin properties in CSS. The following table lists the various properties, their description, and an example for each.

Property	Description	Example
`margin-top`	Sets the top margin between the target element and the page, preceding element, or parent element.	`div { margin-top: 20px; }`
`margin-right`	Sets the right margin between the target element and the page, or any element to its right.	`div { margin-right: 12px; }`
`margin-bottom`	Sets the bottom margin between the target element and the page, or any element that follows it.	`div { margin-bottom: 20px; }`

Property	Description	Example
`margin-left`	Sets the left margin between the target element and the page, or any element to its left.	`div { margin-left: 12px; }`
`margin`	A shorthand property that allows you to set multiple sides of an element's margin at once.	`body { margin: 0px; }`

Setting the Margin Property

The `margin` property is a shorthand that can be used to set `margin-top`, `margin-right`, `margin-bottom`, and `margin-left` properties. To set the margin on all four sides of an element, you can simply write one value, as:

```
p { margin: 10px; }
```

If two values are specified, the top and bottom margins get the first value, and the left and right margins get the second value as in the following example:

```
p { margin: 5px 8px; } /* top,bottom:5px, left,right:8px */
```

If three values are specified, the top margin gets the first value, the left and right margins get the second value, and the bottom margin gets the third value as in the example:

```
div { margin: 2px 5px 10px; } /* top:2px, left,right:5px, bottom:10px
*/
```

For margin settings to be different on all four sides, you can specify four separate values, as shown in the example:

```
p { margin: 10px 20px 15px 5px; }
```

The order of these values declare the top, right, bottom, and left margins, respectively. Using the preceding code, paragraphs would have a top margin of 10 pixels, a right margin of 20 pixels, a bottom margin of 15 pixels, and a left margin of 5 pixels.

> There will be no commas between values in the shorthand. This is a syntax requirement for all CSS shorthand values.

Collapsing Margins

When CSS margins are adjoined vertically, they collapse—this means that the greater of the two margins is applied. For example, if an element has a bottom margin of 30 pixels, and an element directly below it has a top margin of 15 pixels, the total vertical margin between the two elements is 30 pixels, as shown in the following figure.

4 measurements Top Right Bottom Left

3 measurements T R/L Bottom

2 T/B R/L

1 TRBL all the Same

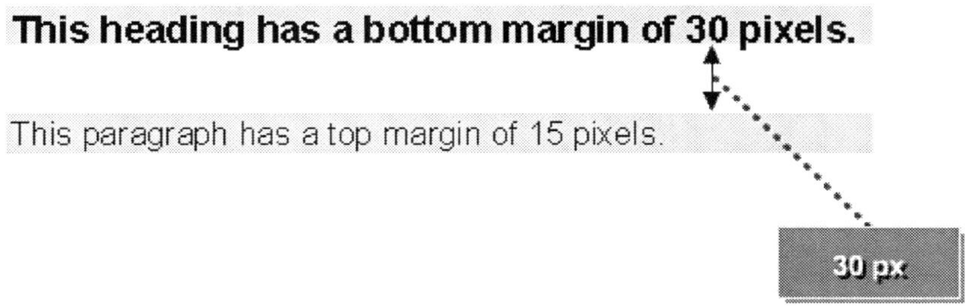

Margins only collapse vertically, and any horizontally adjoining margins are added for a total horizontal margin.

Padding

Padding is the Box model component that defines the space between an element's content and its box. Like margins, you can set all four sides of an element's padding.

For example, consider two paragraphs with a gray background; one with no padding and another with 12 pixels of padding around all four sides of its content. The background color of an element makes the padding visible.

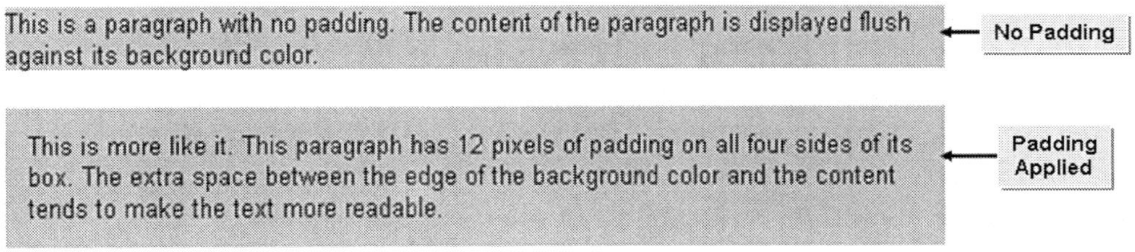

The Padding Properties

There are five padding properties in CSS. The following table lists the various padding properties, their description, and an example for each.

Property	Description	Example
`padding-top`	Sets the top padding between the element's content and its bounding box.	`div { padding-top: 8px; }`
`padding-right`	Sets the right padding between the element's content and its box.	`div { padding-right: 10px; }`
`padding-bottom`	Sets the bottom padding between the element's content and its box.	`div { padding-bottom: 8px; }`
`padding-left`	Sets the left padding between the element's content and its box.	`div { padding-left: 10px; }`

Property	Description	Example
`padding`	A shorthand property that allows you to set multiple sides of an element's padding at once.	`body { padding: 0px; }`

The padding Shorthand Property

As the margin shorthand, the `padding` shorthand property sets the `padding-top`, `padding-right`, `padding-bottom`, and `padding-left` properties at once. The order of values with respect to each side of an element's box is the same as the `margin` shorthand: top, right, bottom, and left.

Padding Table Cells

Padding inside table cells is usually controlled by the HTML `cellpadding` attribute. However, the `cellpadding` attribute only allows you to apply the same amount of padding to all sides of the cells in a table. Using CSS, padding can be set on any of the four sides of each table cell, or padding can be given to only specific table cells.

To set table cell padding with CSS, you have to set it directly on the `<td>` element or elements specifically, instead of the `<table>` element. For example, the effect of the code `td { padding: 2px 8px; }` can be seen in the following table.

Course Listing: Fall Semester

Course	Dept.	Instructor	Meets
Surviving Natural Selection	BIO	Dr. Fittest	M-W-F
DNA Made Easy	BIO	Dr. Wigginbotham	M-W-F
The Conundrum of True or False	PHI	Dr. Kant	M-W-F
Geometry I: Really Cool Shapes	MAT	Mr. Euclid, Jr.	M-W-F
Geometry II: Even Cooler Shapes	MAT	Mr. Euclid, Jr.	T-TH
Trigonometry: Off on Tangents	MAT	Bill Williams	Mon
Kafka: A Bug's Life	ENG	Dr. Samsa	M-W
English Comp: Avoiding Cliches	ENG	Dr. Partridge	Friday
Plato: Right About Atlantis	PHI	Dr. Hume	T-TH

The top and bottom of the table cells have 2 pixels of padding, and the left and right sides of each table cell have 8 pixels of padding.

Negative Margins

If you want to force an element outside of its container's margin, you can set a negative margin on that element. For example, the following code would produce a negative margin.

```
body { margin: 20px; }
h1 { margin-left: -20px; }
```

If the element's parent has no margin set for it, the negative margin would force 20 pixels of the element outside the viewable area of the browser window.

How to Control Margins and Padding

Procedure Reference: Control Margins and Padding

To set margins and padding on an element:

1. Estimate the amount of margin you need to set for the element.

   More often than not, when you set the margins and padding on an element, you will need to change your values one or more times before you find the display you're looking for, because it's often hard to correctly estimate the exact value you need.

2. Use one of the five margin properties to specify the margin you need for the element.
3. Apply the estimated margin value.
4. Save the changes and view the results.
5. Make changes to the margin value(s) as needed.
6. Perform the above steps to set the padding on the element.

ACTIVITY 3-1

Setting Margins

Activity Time:

20 minutes

Data Files:

- styles.css
- info.html

Before You Begin:

From the C:\085568Data\box model\Activity 1\Starter\Illuminati folder, open the info.html file in both Netscape Navigator and Internet Explorer. Also open the info.html's source file in Notepad.

Scenario:

You're now ready to modify the layout of the Illuminati's web pages. As you get started, you observe that the current default page margin is slightly different when viewed in a different browser. You and the project team have decided to remove all page margins to establish a consistent display across all browsers. You need to make changes in the styles.css style sheet by carrying out the following design requirements:

- Offset all text elements from the left and right edges of the page canvas.
- Add extra space between the paragraphs and the right edge of the page canvas, to make the line length of the text small for easier reading.
- Offset the copyright statement from the bottom of the browser window.
- Make sure that all margin lengths remain constant for all browser window sizes.

What You Do	How You Do It
1. **Remove the default page margins for all pages using the `margin` shorthand property.**	a. If necessary, **restore the Styles.css - Notepad window.** b. In the Styles.css - Notepad window, in the `body` rule, **click after `font-size: 12px;` and type `margin: 0px;`** c. **Choose File→Save.** d. **Minimize the Styles.css - Notepad window.** e. **Reload the page in both the Internet Explorer and Netscape Navigator.** The page will have no margins, so all the content starts at the immediate top-left side of the page canvas.

The inner table isn't flush against the left side of the browser window because it's centered on the page.

---

2. **How does setting the page margins to zero help you create precise element margins throughout your pages?**

What You Do	How You Do It
3. **Offset the left margin with an absolute unit of measurement for all paragraphs.**	a. **Restore the Styles.css - Notepad window.** b. In the `p` rule, **click after `line-height: 1.5em;` and type `margin-left: 25px;`** c. **Choose File→Save.** d. **Minimize the Styles.css - Notepad window.** e. **Reload the page in both Internet Explorer and Netscape Navigator.** The paragraphs will be offset 25 pixels from the left edge of the browser window. Notice that the headings and the copyright statement will still be flushed against the zero-margin canvas.

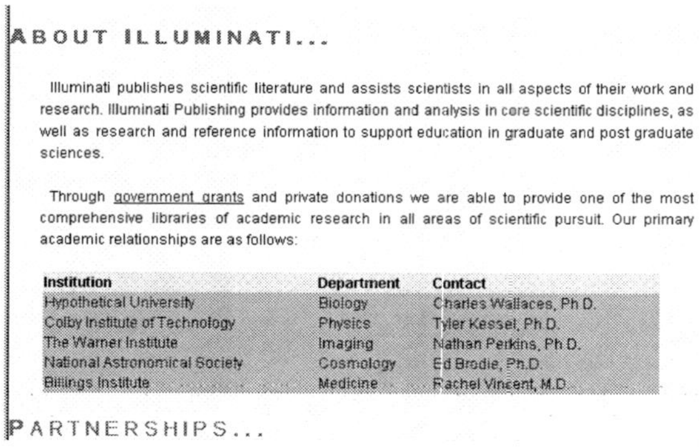

4. **Apply the same left margin to the `h1`, `h2`, and `address` elements.**

a. **Restore the Styles.css - Notepad window.**

b. In the `h1, h2` rule, **click after `font-variant: small-caps;` and type `margin-left: 25px;`**

c. In the `address` rule, **click after `font-style: normal;` and type `margin-left: 25px;`**

d. **Choose File→Save.**

e. **Minimize the Styles.css - Notepad window.**

f. **Reload the page in both the Internet Explorer and Netscape Navigator.** The headings, paragraphs, and the copyright statement will be aligned along the same margin.

---

5. **Verify that the margin length does not change at different browser window sizes.**

a. **Maximize the Internet Explorer or manually change its size**

b. **Observe the margin lengths** to verify that they remain fixed.

---

6. **Increase the paragraphs' right margin to a value greater than its left margin.**

a. **Restore the Styles.css - Notepad window.**

b. In the `p` rule, **click after `margin-left: 25px;` and type `margin-right: 75px;`**

c. **Choose File→Save.**

d. **Minimize the Styles.css - Notepad window.**

e. **Reload the page in both the Internet Explorer and Netscape Navigator.** The paragraphs are offset from the right side of their respective browser windows.

---

7. **Set the bottom margin to insert space after the copyright Statement.**

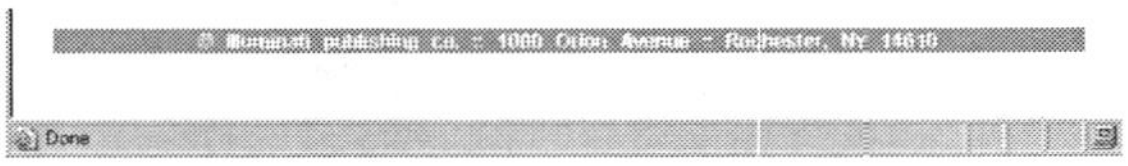

a. **Scroll down** to view the copyright statement.

b. Notice that there is no space between the copyright statement and the bottom of the canvas. **Restore the Styles.css - Notepad window.**

Depending on the current size of your browser window, you might need to reduce its height to observe that there's no space between the copyright statement and the bottom of the canvas (before applying the bottom margin).

c. In the `body` rule, **click after `margin: 0px;` and type `margin-bottom: 40px;`**

d. **Choose File→Save.**

e. **Close the Styles.css - Notepad window.**

f. **Reload the page in both Internet Explorer and Netscape Navigator. Scroll down** to view the change. The copyright footer on each page now has a 40-pixel offset from the bottom of the respective browser's canvas.

g. **Close both the Internet Explorer and Netscape Navigator windows.**

---

8. **What has happened to the implicit `0px` value of the bottom margin that is declared for the `<body>` element with the `margin` shorthand property?**

---

9. **What would the result be if the two properties were reversed in order (if the `margin: 0px` value was specified *after* the more specific `margin-left` value)?**

OPTIONAL ACTIVITY 3-2

Creating Negative Margins

Data Files:

- info.html

Before You Begin:

From the C:\085568Data\box model\Activity 2\Starter\Illuminati folder, open the info.html file in both Netscape Navigator and Internet Explorer. Also open the styles.css file.

Scenario:

In the styles.css style sheet, the margins are already set for the page canvas and the content paragraphs. The project team would like to see less space below each heading.

What You Do	How You Do It
1. **Decrease the amount of vertical white space below the headings.**	a. In the Styles.css - Notepad, in the `h1, h2` rule, **click after `margin-left: 25px;` and type `margin-bottom: -15px;`**
	b. **Choose File→Save.**
	c. **Close the Styles.css - Notepad window.**
	d. In the Internet Explorer window, **click the Refresh button.** The negative bottom margin values will be applied to all headings, reducing the white space below them.

The result is most clearly visible on the info.html page.

2. **What is the need for setting negative margins?**

    a) To force an element outside of its container's margin.

    b) To have the same margin settings on all four sides of an element.

    c) To force an element inside of its container's margin.

    d) To override the default value and establish consistency across browsers.

ACTIVITY 3-3

Modifying Element Padding

Activity Time:

5 minutes

Data Files:

- info.html
- styles.css

Before You Begin:

From the C:\085568Data\box model\Activity 3\Starter\Illuminati folder, open the info.html file in Internet Explorer. Also, open the styles.css file.

Scenario:

The Illuminati project team would like all paragraphs that have background colors to have a little extra space between their content and their boxes. This will allow the text in these elements to breathe, making them more readable, enhancing the overall design of these content sections. Use the styles.css style sheet to carry out the project team's request.

What You Do	How You Do It

The news.html and info.html pages have paragraphs with a light gray background.

1. **Give all "note" paragraphs sufficient padding on all sides to improve the readability of the text against its background color.**

PARTNERSHIPS...

In addition, Illuminati provides opportunities to associated companies and societies through publishing partnerships, advertising and sponsorship, reprints and content licensing. For more information on parterning organizations, you can *download this PDF file*.

a. In the Styles.css - Notepad window, **type `.note { background-color: #eee; padding: 10px; }` and press Enter.**

b. **Choose File→Save.**

c. **Minimize the Styles.css - Notepad window.**

d. In the Internet Explorer window, **click the Refresh button.** The "note" paragraph will have extra space on all four sides.

---

2. **Create a rule to add enough padding to both the `<th>` and `<td>` elements in the information table, providing adequate separation between the text and the table cells.**

Institution	Department	Contact
Hypothetical University	Biology	Charles Wallaces, Ph.D.
Colby Institute of Technology	Physics	Tyler Kessel, Ph.D.
The Warner Institute	Imaging	Nathan Perkins, Ph.D.
National Astronomical Society	Cosmology	Ed Brodie, Ph.D.
Billings Institute	Medicine	Rachel Vincent, M.D.

To achieve this with one new rule, you'll need to combine two contextual selectors.

a. **Restore the Styles.css - Notepad window.**

b. **Type `div th, div td { padding: 5px; }` and press Enter.**

c. **Choose File→Save.**

d. **Close the Styles.css - Notepad window.**

e. In the Internet Explorer window, **click the Refresh button.** The table headings and cells will have extra padding on all four sides.

f. **Close the Internet Explorer window.**

TOPIC B

Create Borders

You controlled element spacing to distinguish content sections and create white space. Borders provide emphasis and draw readers' attention to the elements. In this topic, you will distinguish content sections by creating borders, the third component of the Box model.

In a web page with lots of information, demarcating specific sections of content with borders adds aesthetic and functional value to the page. You can create borders around any element and control its style, width, and color. For example, the figure below shows a page with borders around certain elements. Borders clearly distinguish each content section, add unique character to the overall design, and help to draw the user's eye to the content sections you wish to emphasize.

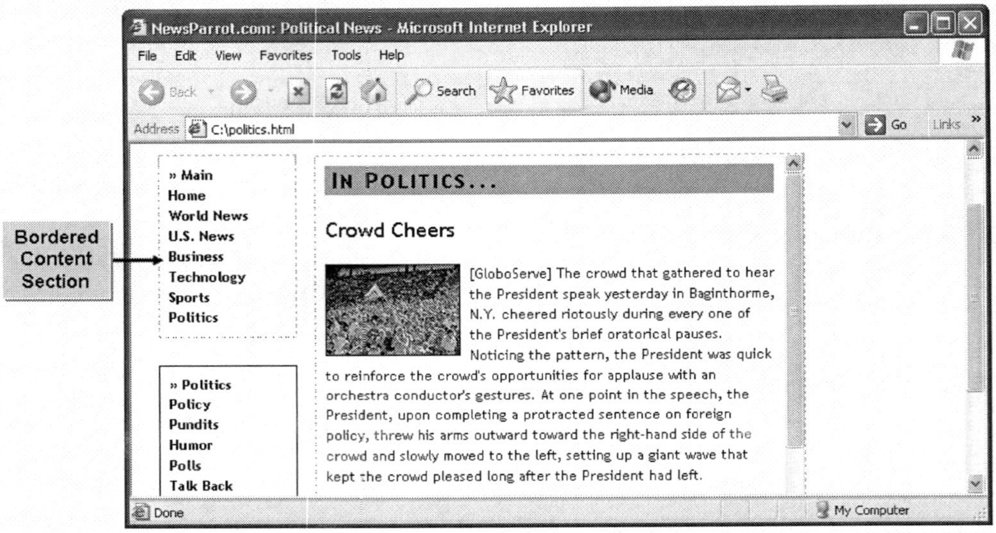

Borders

CSS *borders* are lines of various styles, colors, and widths that display on one or more outside edges of an element's bounding box. Borders provide a powerful way to distinguish content sections and contribute to a design's overall look and feel.

The Border Properties

There are several border properties for each side of an element's box: the top, right, bottom, and left sides. The following table lists these properties and their functionality.

Property	Description
`border-top-width`	Sets the width of a border on the top of an element.

Property	Description
`border-right-width`	Sets the width of a border on the right side of an element.
`border-bottom-width`	Sets the width of a border on the bottom of an element.
`border-left-width`	Sets the width of a border on the left side of an element.
`border-width`	Sets the width of a border on all sides of an element.
`border-top-style`	Sets the style of a border on the top side of an element.
`border-right-style`	Sets the style of a border on the right side of an element.
`border-bottom-style`	Sets the style of a border on the bottom side of an element.
`border-left-style`	Sets the style of a border on the left side of an element.
`border-style`	Sets the style of a border on all sides of an element.
`border-top-color`	Sets the color of a border on the top side of an element.
`border-right-color`	Sets the color of a border on the right side of an element.
`border-bottom-color`	Sets the color of a border on the bottom side of an element.
`border-left-color`	Sets the color of a border on the left side of an element.
`border-color`	Sets the color of a border on all sides of an element.

Netscape 4.x has only partial support for borders.

The following example illustrates how the `border` property can be used to create the desired border.

```
p.first { border-width: 2px;
border-style: dashed;
border-color: black;
background-color: #eee;
padding: 8px;

p.second { border-top-width: 4px;
border-top-style: double;
border-top-color: black;
background-color: #eee;
padding: 8px; }
```

The first rule creates a black, four-sided, two-pixel, dashed border around a paragraph, while the second rule creates a black, four-pixel, double border on the top side only, as shown in the following figure.

Amazingly, there has been nothing that could be reasonably deemed a "top story" for several weeks. This should not be seen as indicative of any failure on our part to cover the news, locate newsworthy stories, or assign reporters promptly. Literally *nothing* worthy of "top story" status has happened, in our opinion. Unlike other popular news sources, we never resort to "fluff" just to fill the space. We believe that no news is good news, and we hope you find this non-story refreshing.

Until something does happen that warrants such a headline, feel free to browse through our topical news sections, like sports, technology, and politics. Here at NewsParrot, we display the news as it happens, but only when and if it happens.

When borders are applied, they are drawn at the edge of the background color. The space between the content and the border is the elements' padding. When you apply borders around elements containing text, it's often a good idea to add some padding so that the text does not run up against the border, which can make the text difficult to read.

Border Shorthand Properties

All `border` properties have shorthand equivalents. As they involve less code, it is easier and more efficient to use shorthand properties. There is a partial shorthand, as well as the `border` shorthand property, which implicitly includes all partial shorthand. The following table lists the border shorthand types and the properties they implicitly include.

Property	Implicitly includes

`border-top`	`border-top-width`
	`border-top-style`
	`border-top-color`

`border-right`	`border-right-width`
	`border-right-style`
	`border-right-color`

`border-bottom`	`border-bottom-width`
	`border-bottom-style`
	`border-bottom-color`

`border-left`	`border-left-width`
	`border-left-style`
	`border-left-color`

`border`	`border-top`
	`border-right`
	`border-bottom`
	`border-left`

For example, the effect achieved using the `border` shorthand with the following rule: `div { border: 2px ridge #eee; }` achieves the same effect as with:

```
div { border-top: 2px ridge #eee;
border-right: 2px ridge #eee;
border-bottom: 2px ridge #eee;
border-left: 2px ridge #eee; }
```

Border Styles

The following table lists the various border styles with their description and example.

Border Style Keyword	Description	Example
`solid`	Creates a solid border.	p { border: 1px solid black; } p { border: 3px solid #eee; }
`ridge`	Creates a *mounded* border that darkens the specified color to create the required shading.	p { border: 2px ridge #eee; } p { border: 4px ridge #eee; }
`double`	Creates a solid double border.	p { border: 3px double black; } p { border: 5px double gray; }
`inset`	Creates the appearance that the element is inset into the document. The top and left sides of your color are darkened, and the right and bottom sides are lightened to create the inset effect.	p { border: 2px inset #eee; } p { border: 4px inset #eee; }
`outset`	Creates the appearance that the element is outset from the document. The top and left sides of your color are lightened, and the bottom and right sides are darkened to create the outset effect.	p { border: 2px outset #eee; } p { border: 4px outset #eee; }
`dotted`	Creates a dotted style.	p { border: 2px dotted black; } p { border: 4px dotted #ddd; }
`dashed`	Creates a dashed style.	p { border: 1px dashed black; } p { border: 3px dashed black; }
`groove`	Creates the effect of a light source coming at the border from the lower right side. The border color is lightened and darkened to create the required shading.	p { border: 3px groove #eee; } p { border: 5px groove #eee; }

All border styles are well supported in 6.0 and later generations of Internet Explorer and Netscape.

Border Widths

Any valid length value can be used to specify a border width. Pixel is the most logical and well supported unit of measurement for borders. There are three built-in keywords for specifying border width: `thin`, `medium` and `thick`.

- The `thin` value is equivalent to `2px`.
- The `medium` value is equivalent to `4px`.
- The `thick` value is equivalent to `6px`.

Netscape 6 and above has the best support for border styles at any width. Though Internet Explorer does a good job of rendering borders, there are some subtle differences. For example, a 1-pixel dotted border is displayed as a 1-pixel dashed border in Internet Explorer. You may find border styles and width measurements that suit best for any given design.

Borders and Inline Elements

You can create borders for block-level elements and inline elements. The border around an inline element will extend the length of the element text in the same way that the element's background color would be displayed. For example, the following code sets a border on a `<span>` element that's nested inside a paragraph:

`span { border: 2px dotted gray; }`The above code would produce the effect shown in the following figure:

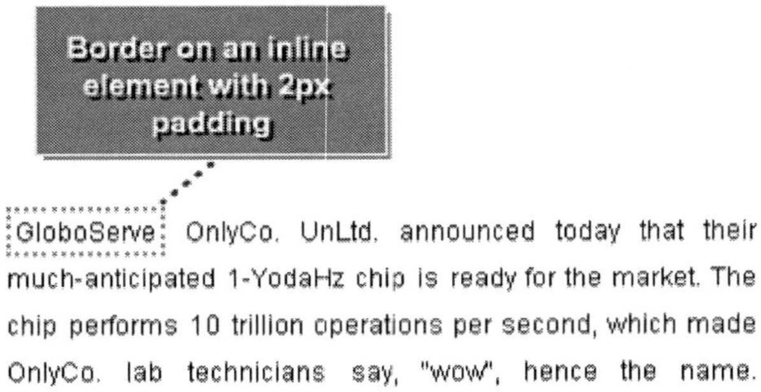

How to Create Element Borders

Procedure Reference: Create Element Borders

To apply borders for an element:

1. Determine which border style, width, and color that best suits your design goal.
2. Apply the border properties that will achieve the intended design, using border shorthands (whenever applicable) to reduce the amount of code in the style sheet.
3. Verify the results.
4. Modify the border styles as needed.

ACTIVITY 3-4

Creating Borders

Activity Time:

5 minutes

Data Files:

- info.html
- styles.css

Before You Begin:

From the C:\085568Data\box model\Activity 4\Starter\Illuminati folder, open the info.html file in Internet Explorer. Also, open the styles.css file.

Scenario:

You and the project team have decided that borders will enhance the presentation of the Illuminati site and lead the user to important content sections. Using the styles.css style sheet, you need to create borders that effectively distinguish the level-one headings, the inner content tables, and the "note" class paragraphs.

You may want to explore a variety of border styles, widths, and colors to determine which border style most effectively distinguishes each content section. Also, remember to keep your border code as lean as possible.

What You Do	How You Do It
1. **Create a border on the top and bottom sides of the level-one heading.**	a. In the Styles.css - Notepad window, **type** **`h1 { border-top: 1px dashed #699;border-bottom: 1px dashed #699; }`** **and press Enter.**
	b. **Choose File→Save.**
	c. **Minimize the Styles.css - Notepad window.**
	d. In the Internet Explorer window, **click the Refresh button.** The level-one heading will have a dashed border on the top and bottom sides.

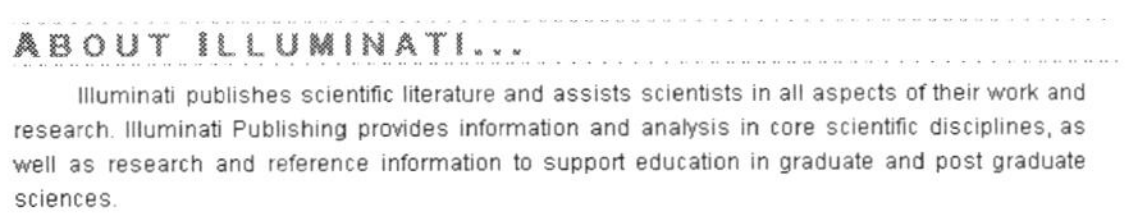

2. **Create a border around the information table.**

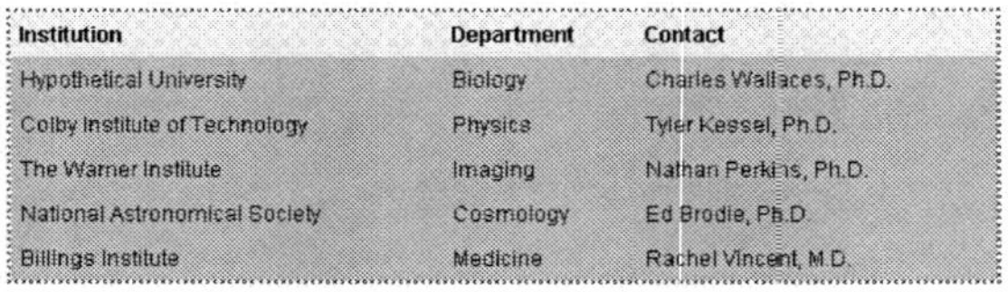

Institution	Department	Contact
Hypothetical University	Biology	Charles Wallaces, Ph.D.
Colby Institute of Technology	Physics	Tyler Kessel, Ph.D.
The Warner Institute	Imaging	Nathan Perkins, Ph.D.
National Astronomical Society	Cosmology	Ed Brodie, Ph.D.
Billings Institute	Medicine	Rachel Vincent, M.D.

a. **Restore the Styles.css - Notepad window.**

b. In the `div table` rule, **click after `background-color: #99ccb3;` and type `border: 2px dotted #366;`**

c. **Choose File→Save.**

d. **Minimize the Styles.css - Notepad window.**

e. In the Internet Explorer window, **click the Refresh button.** The table will have a dotted border on all four sides.

---

3. **Create a border around the "note" class paragraph.**

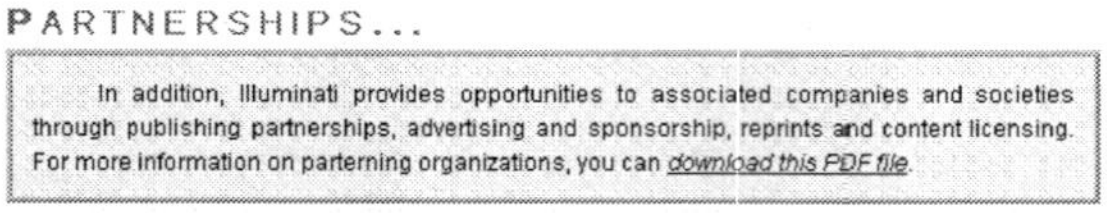

a. **Restore the Styles.css - Notepad window.**

b. In the first `.note` rule, **click after `padding: 10px;` and type `border: 3px ridge white;`**

c. **Choose File→Save.**

d. **Close the Styles.css - Notepad window.**

e. In the Internet Explorer window, **scroll down and click the Refresh button.** The "note" paragraph will have a ridged border on all four sides.

f. **Close the Internet Explorer window.**

TOPIC C

Control Element Dimensions

You distinguished content sections by creating borders. All the elements you styled have default dimensions. The height and width have been defined by the size of the browser window, the parent element, or the amount of content. In this topic, you will control element dimensions precisely.

Default element dimensions may not suit specific design. You will need a way to control the size of your page elements to achieve a desired layout. With CSS, you can control an element's height and width precisely, which is critical to designing content sections because it allows you to save page space, arrange elements within the confines of the page canvas, and maintain consistent width among common elements that are used across multiple pages. By just maintaining default dimensions, content sections will extend to the entire width of the browser window. However, by customizing the height and width of specific elements to create space for other content sections, and by reducing the line length of text, you can:

- Ensure that content sections remain fixed when the browser window is resized.
- Allow content sections to change size according to the size of the user's browser window.

For example, the following figure shows paragraphs with default dimensions that extend to the entire width of the browser window.

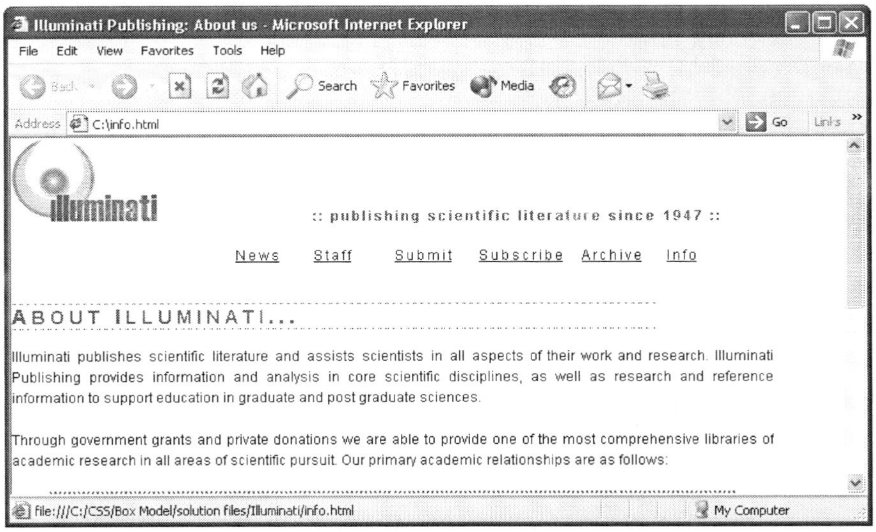

Paragraphs with default dimensions

The following figure shows the same page with customized height and width applied to the paragraph text.

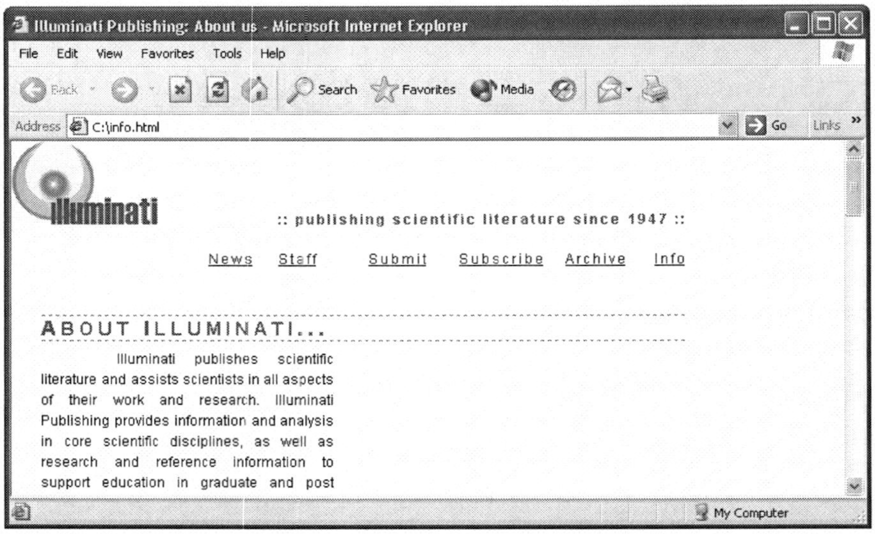

Paragraph with customized height and width

Element Dimensions

Height and width are an element's dimensions. For an effective and a precise layout, you need to customize the dimensions of your content sections. By default, block-level elements such as divisions and paragraphs extend across the entire width of the browser window minus the space created by margins or padding. And, these default dimensions won't always match the intended look and feel desired for the layout.

The height and width Properties

The `height` and `width` properties can be used to control the horizontal and vertical length of an element. If an absolute unit of measurement is used, the element's dimensions will be fixed, and it will not be influenced by the size of a user's browser window. If relative units of measurement are used, the element's dimensions will adjust to the size of a user's browser.

In instances where only the element's width is specified, the element's height is determined by the size of content in that element. For example, the code `div { border: 2px double gray; width: 250px; }` creates the result as shown in the following figure.

If the height of an element is increased beyond the height required by its content, the height value is honored. For example, the code `div { border: 2px double gray; width: 250px; height: 350px; }` creates the result as shown in the following figure.

Calculating an Element's Dimensions

When the width is declared for an element, it defines the width of the element's content, excluding any padding and borders. Padding and border widths are additional to the specified height and width settings. For example, in the following figure, the element occupies 200-pixel width, but the entire box is 224 pixels due to the padding and the border widths.

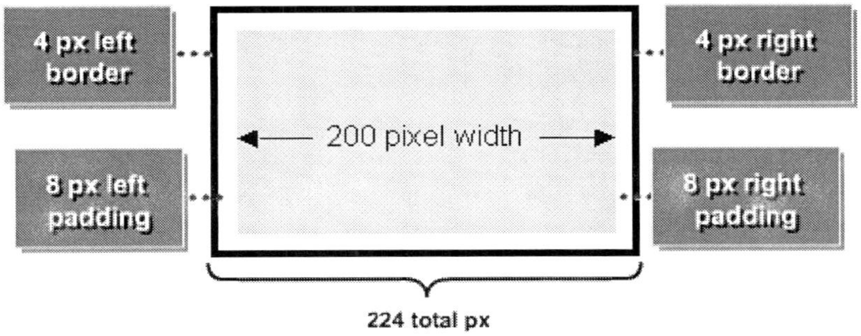

Netscape 7.1, Opera 5, and Internet Explorer 6 all support control over an element's dimensions equally. However, Internet Explorer prior to version 6 incorporates an element's padding and border widths into its overall specified width, which means there is less width for the content to display.

How to Control Element Dimensions

Procedure Reference: Control Element Dimensions

To customize an element's horizontal and vertical dimensions:

1. Estimate the dimensions you think you'll need for the element.
2. Determine which unit of measurement you want to use.

   You will likely find that pixels are the easiest unit of measurement with which to estimate and create pixel-precise dimensions.

3. Apply the `width` property with the estimated value.

4. Apply the `height` property to the element with the estimated value—if a height setting is needed.
5. Save and view the changes.
6. Modify the height and width value(s) until you achieve the desired dimension. This might entail several trial and error modifications until you get it exactly right.

ACTIVITY 3-5

Controlling an Element's Width

Activity Time:

5 minutes

Data Files:

- info.html
- styles.css

Before You Begin:

From the C:\085568Data\box model\Activity 5\Starter\Illuminati folder, open the info.html file in Internet Explorer. Also, open the styles.css file.

Scenario:

The Illuminati site project is coming along nicely. You still need to make a few minor changes to the dimensions of a few elements using the styles.css style sheet. In particular, you need to line up the right edge of the headings with the right edge of the paragraphs. You also need to apply this same width to the copyright footer and increase the copyright statement's height.

What You Do	How You Do It
1. **Use a width value to align the borders of the level-one headings to the right margin of the paragraphs.**	a. If necessary, **restore the Internet Explorer window.**
	b. **Notice that the border of the level-one headings extends beyond the paragraphs.**
	c. **Restore the Styles.css - Notepad window.**
	d. In the Styles.css - Notepad window, **click after `h1 { border-top: 1px dashed #699;border-bottom: 1px dashed #699;` and type `width: 550px;`**
	e. **Choose File→Save.**
	f. **Minimize the Styles.css - Notepad window.**
	g. In the Internet Explorer window, **click the Refresh button.** The headings will line up along the right margin of the paragraphs.
2. **Assign the same width value to the copyright footer.**	a. **Scroll down** to view the copyright footer.
	b. **Notice that the copyright footer's width is different from that of the other elements.**
	c. **Restore the Styles.css - Notepad window.**
	d. In the address rule, **click after `margin-left: 25px;` and type `width: 550px;`**
	e. **Choose File→Save.**
	f. **Minimize the Styles.css - Notepad window.**
	g. In the Internet Explorer window, **click the Refresh button**. The copyright footer will have the same width as the heading.

ABOUT ILLUMINATI...

Illuminati publishes scientific literature and assists scientists in all aspects of their work and research. Illuminati Publishing provides information and analysis in core scientific disciplines, as well as research and reference information to support education in graduate and post graduate sciences.

Through government grants and private donations we are able to provide one of the most comprehensive libraries of academic research in all areas of scientific pursuit. Our primary academic relationships are as follows:

3. **Increase the height of the copyright footer.**

a. **Restore the Styles.css - Notepad window.**

b. In the `address` rule, **type `height: 40px;`**

c. **Choose File→Save.**

d. **Minimize the Styles.css - Notepad window.**

e. In the Internet Explorer window, **click the Refresh button.**

---

4. **Pad the copyright text toward the middle of the box.**

Note that the extra padding increases the element's height further.

a. **Restore the Styles.css - Notepad window.**

b. In the `address` rule, **type `padding-top: 20px;`**

c. **Choose File→Save.**

d. **Close the Styles.css - Notepad window.**

e. In the Internet Explorer window, **click the Refresh button.**

f. **Close the Internet Explorer window.**

Topic D

Create Floating Elements

You controlled an element's dimensions, such as its height and width, to arrange content more precisely on a web page. There is no specific order in which a design must be constructed with CSS, but it makes sense to establish the dimensions of your content sections before you begin to arrange them on a page. Otherwise, your elements will have default widths, which may be excessively large, leaving little room for content to flow around them. In this topic, you will arrange adjacent elements horizontally and vertically to arrange content logically.

By floating elements side-by-side, you can arrange content both horizontally and vertically without having to use HTML tables. This results in much less code, as well as code that's easier to modify.

Floating Elements

To *float* an element means to align the element to either side of an adjacent element using the `float` property. With the `float` property, the `left` value forces the floated element to the left of adjacent elements, and the `right` value forces the floated element to the right of adjacent elements.

A float is to CSS what the align attribute is to the <img> tag in HTML. Both are used to move an element from its normal placement in the document and align it with another element.

The float Property

A `<div>` element when followed directly by another `<div>` element will by default display one above the other. To override this default display, you can float one element to the left or right of the other.

```
div1 { width: 250px;
border: 5px solid black;
padding: 5px;
float: left; }
```

The preceding code will produce the result shown in the following figure.

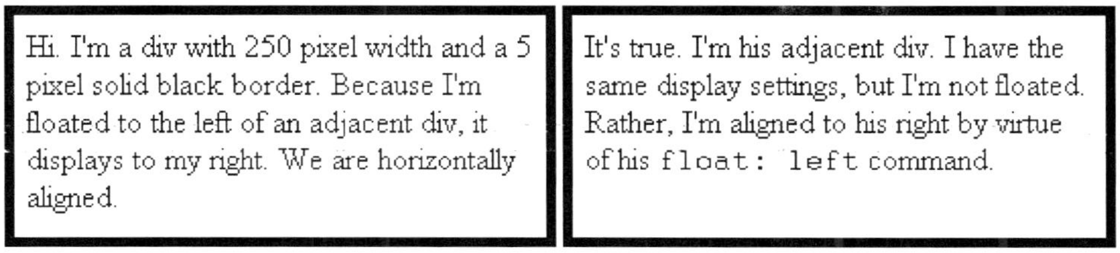

Floating Child Elements

When you float a nested or *child* element to one side of its parent element, the result is different from dealing with two adjacent element boxes. A child element that's floated to one side of its parent element is still contained in the parent's box, as shown in the following figure.

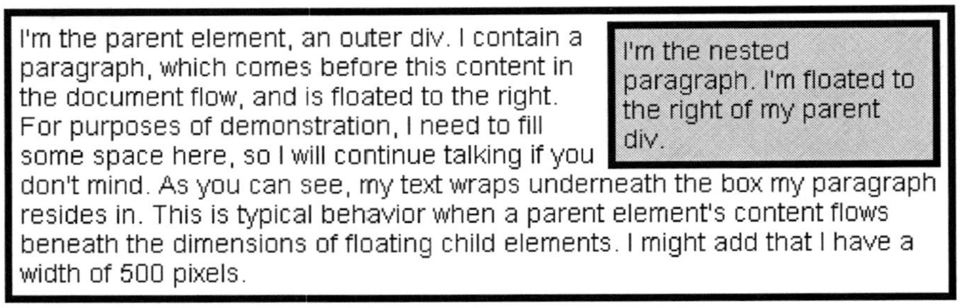

The clear Property

The `clear` property controls if an element allows floating elements to either its right or left side. This enables you to create vertically arranged content sections. The `clear` property is only valid on floated, block-level elements. When you use the `clear` property on an element, the `left` value declares that no element can display to its left side, and the `right` value declares that no element can display to its right side. The value `both` declares that no element can display on either side.

For example, a `<div>` element contains two paragraphs with the class names *first* and *second*, both of which are floated to the right. The second floated paragraph has `clear: right` set on it, which means that no content can display to its right. As a result, it is still displayed to the right of its parent in accordance with the `float: right` command, but is displayed below the first floated paragraph. If there was no `clear: right` set on the second paragraph, it would display in the middle to the left of the parent content, and to the left of the first floated paragraph.

For example:

```
div p.first, div p.second { float: right; }
div p.second { clear: right; }
```

The above code will produce the following result.

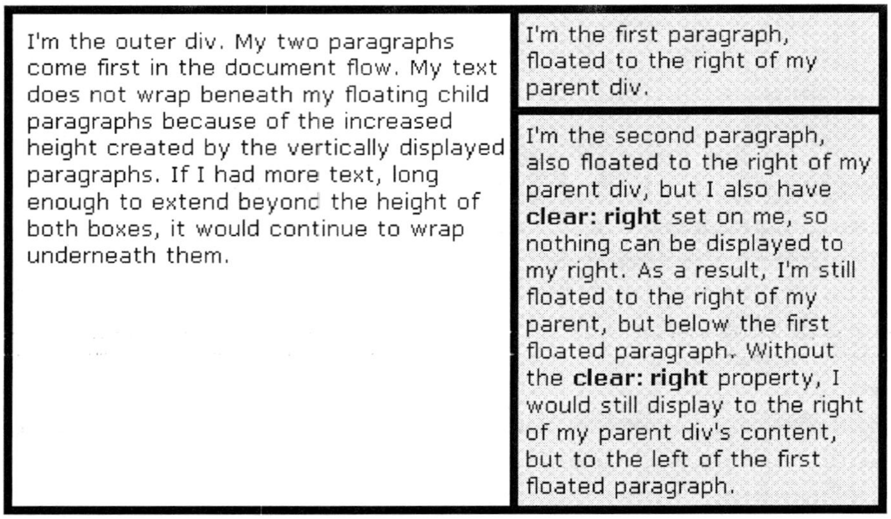

How to Create Floating Elements

Procedure Reference: Create Floating Elements

To achieve a desired layout by floating elements:

1. Start with elements having set dimensions.

   You don't always have to set your element's dimensions first, but you will likely find that it's much easier and more effective if you do so.

2. Determine how you want to arrange the elements.
3. Apply the `float` property and the required value.

   Use the `clear` property if you need to prevent elements from displaying to either side of your floated element.

4. Save and view the changes.
5. Modify the arrangement if necessary.

ACTIVITY 3-6

Arranging Elements with the Float Property

Activity Time:

5 minutes

Data Files:

- index.html
- parrot.css

Before You Begin:

From the C:\085568Data\box model\Activity 6\Starter\NewsParrot folder, open the index.html file in Internet Explorer. Also, open the parrot.css file.

Scenario:

You and the project team for the NewsParrot site have gone back to the drawing board. You are starting with a new design, wherein all content sections are controlled by box properties instead of code-heavy outer layout tables.

You have stripped out the old code from the index.html page and all the pages linked to it, and have redesigned each content section in separate boxes, complete with margin, padding, and border styles. Using the parrot.css style sheet, you need to arrange the content boxes according to the new design specification. The project team wants the Top Story content section to display to the right of both navigation boxes, and the images in each Top Story section should be arranged so that the text that follows it wraps around its right side.

What You Do	How You Do It

1. **Arrange both the navigation boxes so that they are vertically adjacent and to the left of the main Top Story section.**

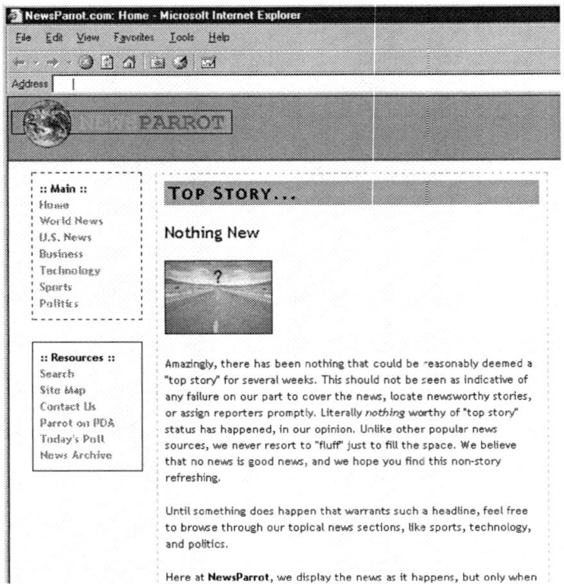

If you view the page in Netscape 6, it may not look like the image shown here. If this is the case, keep checking your work in Internet Explorer. The Netscape-based problem will be fixed in the following activity.

a. In the Parrot.css - Notepad, **scroll down to view the `#nav` rule. click after `height: 140px;` and type `float: left;`**

b. In the #nav2 rule, **click after `border: 1px solid black;` and type `float: left;`**

c. **Choose File→Save.**

d. **Minimize the Parrot.css - Notepad window.**

e. In the Internet Explorer window, **click the Refresh button.**

f. **Notice that the first navigation box is the first floated element, so it's arranged on the leftmost side. Depending on the width of your browser window, the second navigation box is either arranged to the left of the main Top Story section, or above it.**

You need to prevent any content from displaying to the left of the second navigation box in order to align the two navigation boxes vertically.

g. **Restore the Parrot.css - Notepad window.**

h. **Type `clear: left;`**

i. **Choose File→Save.**

j. **Minimize the Parrot.css - Notepad window.**

k. In the Internet Explorer window, **click the Refresh button.** The second navigation box will be displayed vertically adjacent to the first navigation box.

2. **Make the text that follows the image in the main Top Story section wrap around the right side of the image.**

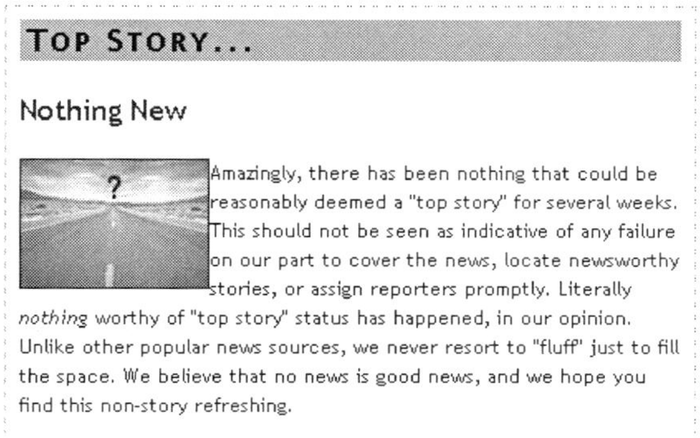

a. **Restore the Parrot.css - Notepad window.**

b. **Click after the `#nav2` rule and press Enter.**

c. **Type `#main img { float: left; }`**

d. **Choose File→Save.**

e. **Minimize the Parrot.css - Notepad window.**

f. In the Internet Explorer window, **click the Refresh button** to view the text flushed with the image. This is not yet a desirable effect in terms of readability and design.

---

3. **Add padding to the right of the image so that there's sufficient space between the image and its wrapping text.**

a. **Restore the Parrot.css - Notepad window.**

b. In the `#main img rule`, **click after `float: left;` and type `padding-right: 8px;`**

c. **Choose File→Save.**

d. **Close the Parrot.css - Notepad window.**

e. In the Internet Explorer window, **click the Refresh button.** There will be ample space between the image and the text that wraps around it.

f. **Close the Internet Explorer window.**

TOPIC E

Control Content Overflow

You arranged content sections by floating them to either side of their adjacent elements to achieve precise layouts. An element's content can define it's height if extra space is needed to accommodate the content. There may be times when you need an element to remain at a fixed height no matter how much content it contains. In this topic, you will modify height settings, and control how any overflowing content is displayed.

If you want to force an element to honor specified dimensions, no matter how much content it contains, you can control how any overflowing content is displayed. With this technique, you can save space on your pages without losing any content and ensure size conformity for a particular element that's used across multiple pages.

Content Overflow

Overflow occurs when an element's specified height is not large enough to contain its content. For example, take a <div> element that contains a heading and several links with a height of 100 pixels and width of 200 pixels. The element box may not be large enough to contain the element's content, so the content is forced through the bottom of the element box, which is delineated by its border.

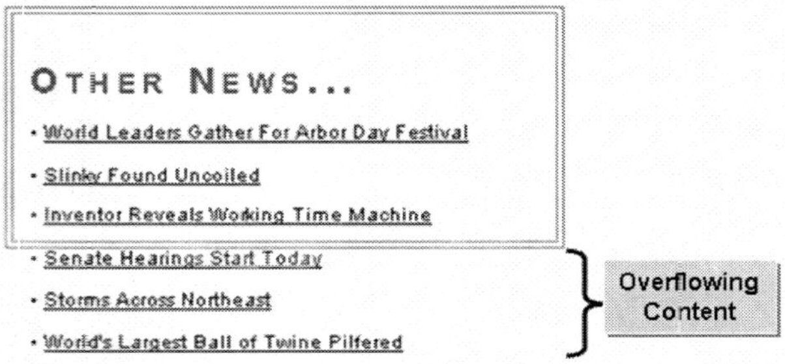

Both Netscape 7.1 and Internet Explorer 6 accept the content and increase the height of the element to accommodate any extra height needed to display the content. Netscape's interpretation is correct to the CSS specification, and the future versions of Internet Explorer will honor the specified height as well. When you use the overflow property on an element with overflowing content, the level of support between the two browsers is the same.

The overflow Property

The `overflow` property controls how the overflowing content is displayed. The following table lists the values of the `overflow` property and describes the relative behaviors of each.

Value	Description
`scroll`	Tells the browser to make all the content accessible by scrolling. Scroll bars are displayed even if the content doesn't overflow the container.
`hidden`	Tells the browser to *clip* any content that doesn't fit into the constrained region. Users would have no way to access the clipped content.
`visible`	Tells the browser to show all the content normally, even if it means extending the region's height and width dimensions.
`auto`	Allows the browser to determine the best way to display all the content. If the content extends beyond the size of the region, scroll bars are displayed. If the content is small enough to fit within the region, it's displayed normally.
`inherit`	Tells the browser to use the overflow value of the element's parent element, assuming the parent element is assigned a value.

Scrollable Content Sections

A scrollable content section is one that displays a scroll bar to access overflowing content. It's a powerful design technique, but it doesn't work on all elements. The <div> element produces the most reliable results across browsers. If the element that you want to make scrollable is not a <div> element, you can either change it to a <div> element or simply nest your element in a new <div> element.

The following figure shows an example of a scrollable table.

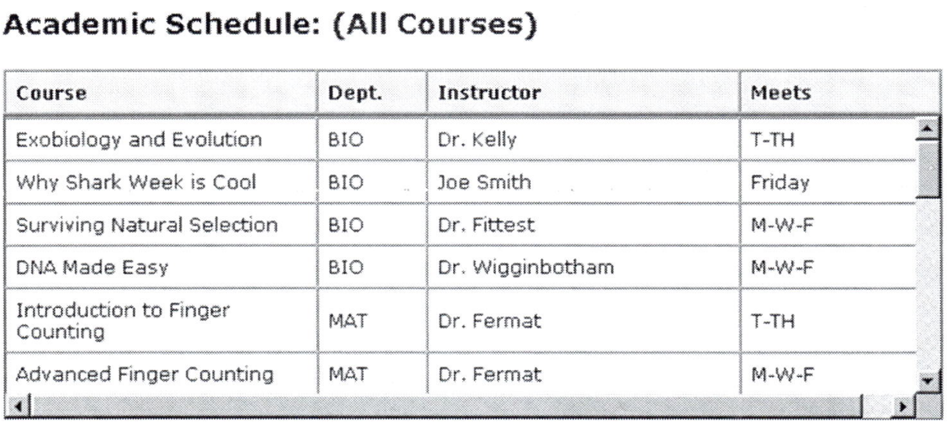

Academic Schedule: (All Courses)

Course	Dept.	Instructor	Meets
Exobiology and Evolution	BIO	Dr. Kelly	T-TH
Why Shark Week is Cool	BIO	Joe Smith	Friday
Surviving Natural Selection	BIO	Dr. Fittest	M-W-F
DNA Made Easy	BIO	Dr. Wigginbotham	M-W-F
Introduction to Finger Counting	MAT	Dr. Fermat	T-TH
Advanced Finger Counting	MAT	Dr. Fermat	M-W-F

When you create a scrollable content section, you can also customize the scroll bar colors.

Applying the overflow: auto Property

If, for example, you have a table on your page that holds data, to ensure that this table doesn't occupy more space than you want, simply wrap the table in a <div> element and apply whatever height and width values you need to that <div> element. You can then apply the `overflow: auto` property to allow users to access the data without having to compromise your intended layout.

How to Control Content Overflow

Procedure Reference: Control Content Overflow

To control content overflow:

1. Determine the dimensions you need for your <div> element.

   > The <div> element produces the most reliable results across different browsers. If the element you're working with is not <div>, change it to a <div> if possible, or simply nest the element in a new <div> container.

2. Set its dimensions with the `height` and `width` properties.
3. Save and view the changes to make sure the element's dimensions are right.
4. If necessary, modify the height and width.
5. Use the `overflow` property and the value that best displays the overflowing content.

   > The `auto` value is the most commonly used value for the `overflow` property because it allows users to access overflowing content with a scroll bar.

6. Save and view the changes to make sure your content section displays as expected.

ACTIVITY 3-7

Creating a Scrollable Content

Activity Time:

5 minutes

Data Files:

- index.html
- parrot.css

Before You Begin:

From the C:\085568Data\box model\Activity 7\Starter\NewsParrot folder, open the index.html file in both Netscape Navigator and Internet Explorer. Also, open the parrot.css file.

Scenario:

The design edict has been handed down. All Top Story sections must fit into a specific height and width, no matter how long the content might be. In the parrot.css style sheet, you need to constrain the Top Story section to a specific height and allow users to access any overflowing content with a scroll bar.

What You Do	How You Do It
1. **Resize the height of the main content section so that it lines up horizontally with the top of the first navigation box and the bottom of the second navigation box.**	a. In Parrot.css - Notepad window, in the `#main` rule, **click after `margin-top: 13px;` and type `height: 311px;`**
	b. **Choose File→Save.**
	c. **Minimize the** Parrot.css - Notepad **window.**
	d. In the Internet Explorer window, **click the Refresh button.**

2. **Allow the size of the content to dictate if a scroll bar is required.**

   You may see subtle differences in the way the boxes line up when viewed in the Internet Explorer and Netscape Navigator. This is due to minor support discrepancies with floating elements.

   a. **Restore the Parrot.css - Notepad window and type `overflow: auto;`**

   b. **Choose File→Save.**

   c. **Close the Parrot.css - Notepad window.**

   d. In the Internet Explorer window, **click the Refresh button.** The Internet Explorer displays a scroll bar because the content occupies a larger space than the specified dimensions.

   e. **Close the Internet Explorer window.**

   f. In the Netscape Navigator window, **click the Reload button.** The results are consistent.

   g. **Close the Netscape Navigator window.**

Lesson 3 Follow-up

In this lesson, you designed content sections using box properties. With CSS, designing and creating the desired visual effect for your web page becomes easy.

1. **Analyze a website of your choice that does not have appropriately designed content sections. What properties would you apply and why?**

2. **Explain how margins and padding will improve the design?**

LESSON 4

Controlling Layout with Positioning

Lesson Time
1 hour(s), 30 minutes

Lesson Objectives:

In this lesson, you will control your page layouts with CSS positioning.

You will:

- Arrange elements with absolute positioning.
- Create a fixed multi-column layout.
- Create a fluid multi-column layout.
- Arrange the elements relative to their normal position in the document flow.
- Control the display of layered elements.
- Apply fixed positioning to an element.

Introduction

You used box properties to design and arrange content sections. Box properties can be used effectively for simple arrangements of content, but they are not appropriate for elaborate layout designs. In this lesson, you will use positioning to create complex, precise layouts, and control the display of overlapping elements.

CSS positioning allows you to achieve any layout design without heavy coding. You don't have to use code-heavy HTML tables to establish multiple column layouts or other complex arrangements. With positioning, you can create layout templates that control the design of multiple pages, which greatly simplifies your code, makes your pages load faster, and makes the task of updating your layouts much easier.

TOPIC A

Control Layout with Absolute Positioning

You customized spacing inside and between elements and created a variety of border styles to achieve visual separation and emphasis. Sometimes, the default arrangement of elements as they appear in the HTML code can make the process of establishing a layout more difficult. In this topic, you will position elements on a page without being limited by their location in the HTML code.

Positioning provides you the flexibility to arrange elements in a desired location on a page because positioning is not limited by the document structure. Positioning is a powerful and flexible layout tool, because elements will always display in the specified location, no matter what the context of the page may be.

Positioning

Definition:

Positioning refers to a family of CSS properties that specifically addresses the position of elements on a page. There are three types of positioning, namely, `absolute`, `relative`, and `fixed`. All of them require the `position` property, which accepts three values that determine the method of positioning in use.

To set an element's position on a page, you need to specify the coordinates using the `top` and `left` properties. These properties are only valid on positioned elements.

The `position` property also accepts a fourth value, `static`, which is the default. It creates no effect, as if the `position` property is not specified.

Example: Absolute Positioning

Absolute positioning uses the `absolute` value:

```
element { position: absolute;
top: 20px; left: 40px; }
```

This code would position the selected element 20 pixels from the top of its parent element and 40 pixels to the left.

Example: Relative Positioning

Relative positioning uses the `relative` value:

```
element { position: relative;
top: 10px; left: 8px; }
```

This code would position the selected element 10 pixels from the top of its normal location in the document and 8 pixels to the left.

Example: Fixed Positioning

Fixed positioning uses the `fixed` value:

```
element { position: fixed;
top: 0px; left: 0px; }
```

This code would permanently affix the selected element to the upper-left edge of the browser window.

Absolute Positioning

Absolute positioning is a method of layout wherein the elements you arrange on a page are removed from their normal place in the flow of HTML elements. With absolute positioning, the top leftmost edge of an element's parent is the reference point on which the coordinates are based. By default, each coordinate is set to `top: 0px` and `left: 0px`. When `<body>` is the parent element, the reference point is at the upper-left edge of the page canvas.

In the following example:

```
div { position: absolute;
left: 330px;
top: 165px; }
```

The code will set a <div> element as absolutely positioned, 330 pixels from the left edge of the page canvas and 165 pixels from the top, as shown in the following figure.

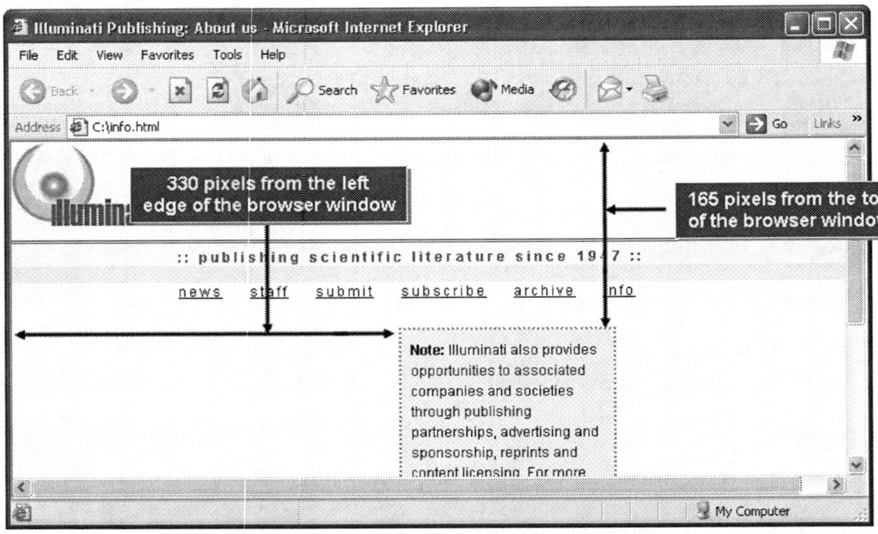

When an absolutely positioned element has a parent element other than <body>, its coordinates are set in relation to the upper-left edge of that parent element, no matter where that element is on the page.

For example, the following figure shows a <div> element that's nested inside an outer <div> element. The child <div> element will be absolutely positioned at 230 pixels to the left of its parent and three pixels from the top. Here, as the parent <div> element has a three-pixel border, positioning the child element three pixels from the top brings it directly below the parent's border.

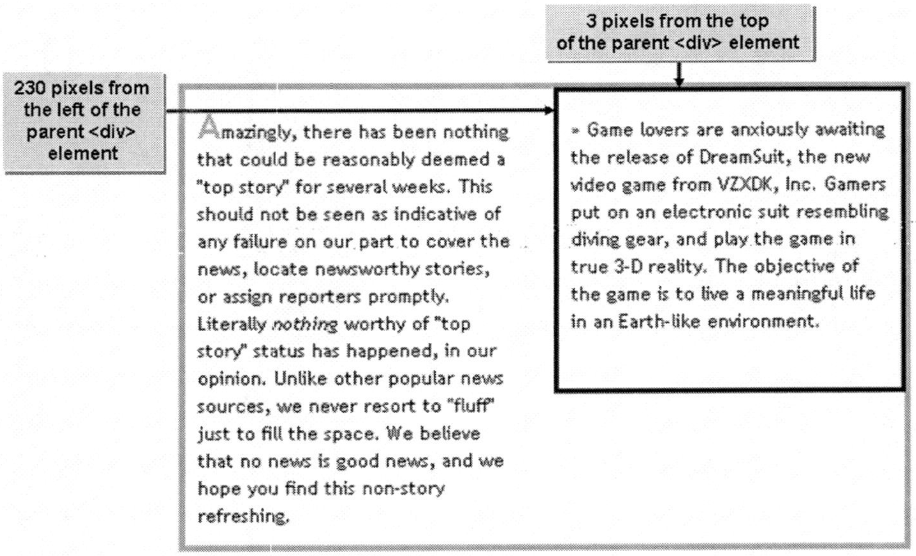

How to Control Layout with Absolute Positioning

Procedure Reference: Control Layout with Absolute Positioning

To absolutely position an element:

1. Determine where you want the element to display on the page.
2. Estimate the amount of offset you will need to position the element in the desired location.
3. Use the `position: absolute` property to remove the element from the document flow.

   Most developers use pixels to define the coordinates of positioned elements because pixels are the most logical choice when you're attempting to achieve pixel-precise layouts of content sections. Pixel dimensions are also fairly easy to estimate.

4. Use the `top` and `left` properties to apply the estimated offset.
5. Save and view the changes to check the position of the element.
6. Modify the values of the `top` and `left` properties until the element is positioned precisely where you want it.

   Unless you have a lot of experience in positioning elements, you will have to, by trial and error, find the exact coordinates for the elements.

ACTIVITY 4-1

Positioning Content Sections

Activity Time:

5 minutes

Data Files:

- info.html
- styles.css

Before You Begin:

From the C:\085568Data\positioning\Activity 1\Starter\Project folder, open the info.html file in both Netscape Navigator and Internet Explorer and its source file in Notepad.

Scenario:

You are asked to make some layout revisions to the info.html page of the Illuminati site. You need to position the "note" element to the right of the paragraphs, and then position the "promo" element directly under it.

What You Do	How You Do It
1. **Position the "note" element to the right of the paragraphs.**	a. In Info.html - Notepad window, in the `#note` rule, **click after `background-color: #eee;` and type `position:absolute;top:225px;` ⇒ `left:550px;`**
	b. **Choose File→Save.**
	c. **Minimize the Info.html - Notepad window.**
	d. **Reload the page in both Internet Explorer and Netscape Navigator.** The page footer moves up closer to the table holding the staff data. This is because the "note" element is absolutely positioned, which means it is removed from the document flow. The footer section moves ***up*** the document flow as if the "note" element is not there.

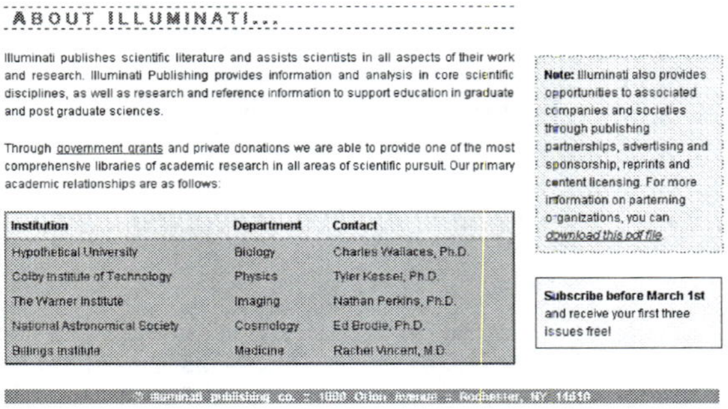

What You Do	How You Do It
2. **Position the "promo" element under the "note" element, using the same left offset.**	a. **Restore the Info.html - Notepad window.**
	b. In the `#promo` rule, **click after `background-color: #FFC;` and type `position:absolute;top:450px;` ⇒ `left:550px;`**
	c. **Choose File→Save.**
	d. **Close the Info.html - Notepad window.**
	e. **Reload the page in both Internet Explorer and Netscape Navigator.**
	f. **Close both the browsers.**

not correct screen shot

The file will have a slightly different appearance depending on which browser you're using.

TOPIC B

Create a Fixed Multi-Column Layout

You used absolute positioning to create simple arrangements of elements on a single page. There may be instances in your own development projects where you need to create templates to establish a consistent layout for multiple pages. In this topic, you will create a more complex layout that controls the design of multiple pages.

Complex, multi-column layouts are one of the most popular designs on the web. Creating complex layouts for multiple pages typically requires code-heavy HTML tables. Using positioning, you can create a template that applies a complex layout to multiple pages in a site without much code. By combining positioning with width settings, you can display a layout consistently, no matter what size a user's browser may be.

Fixed Layouts

A *fixed layout* is a layout wherein content sections remain fixed in relation to each other and the page canvas, even when the browser window is resized.

To apply a fixed layout, you need to set a fixed width for content sections. A fixed width is simply a width expressed using an absolute unit of measurement such as pixels. Even if the size of the browser window is changed by a user, the page layout will not be affected if the elements have a fixed width.

For example, the following figure shows an example of a fixed layout. The elements are absolutely positioned, and all the elements have fixed dimensions with their height and width values set in pixels. Here, the browser window is just large enough to view the page content.

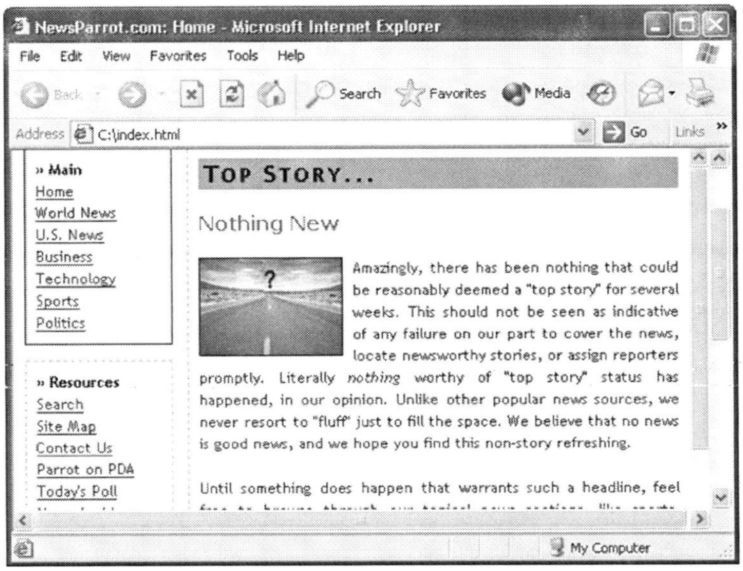

Web page with fixed layout in a small browser window

The following figure shows the same page with the browser window maximized. Even here the elements do not expand to fill in the extra space provided by the larger browser window.

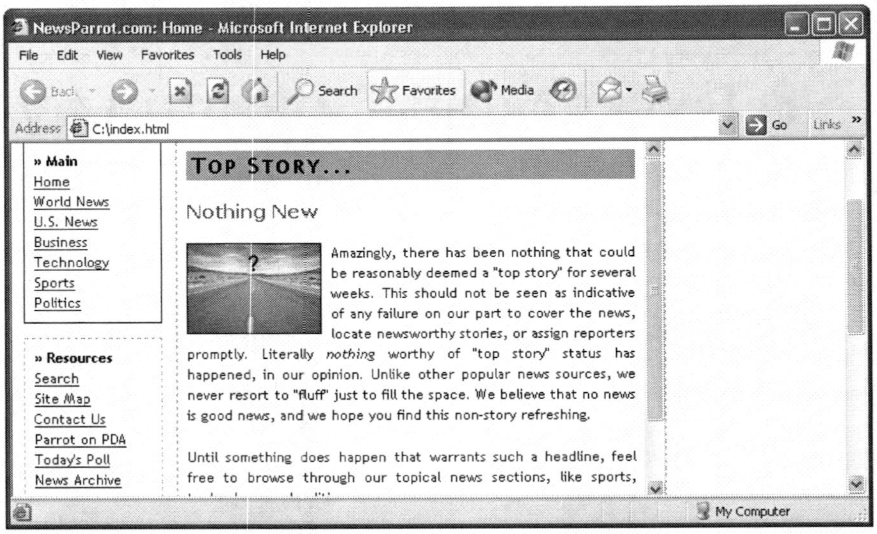

Web page with fixed layout in a large browser window

Fixed layout is the most commonly used layout design on the web. You can visit any website of your choice and adjust the size of your browser window. If the content sections don't change in dimension or position relative to the top and left side of the browser window, you're looking at a fixed layout.

How to Create a Fixed Multi-Column Layout

Procedure Reference: Create a Fixed Multi-Column Layout

To create a fixed multi-column layout:

1. Set fixed widths to your content sections by using an absolute unit of measurement.
2. Determine where you want the content sections to display on the page.
3. Estimate the amount of offset you will need to position each content section in the desired location.
4. Set the elements as absolutely positioned, and use the `top` and `left` properties to apply the estimated offsets to each content section.
5. Save and view the changes to check the position of each content section.
6. Modify the values of the `top` and `left` properties until the content sections are positioned where you want them.
7. Resize the browser window to make sure that the content sections remain fixed in place.

ACTIVITY 4-2

Creating a Fixed Multi-Column Layout

Activity Time:

10 minutes

Data Files:

- tech.html
- parrot.css

Before You Begin:

From the C:\085568Data\positioning\Activity 2\Starter\Project folder, open the tech.html file in both Netscape Navigator and Internet Explorer. Also, open the parrot.css file.

Scenario:

Your project team wants the NewsParrot design to consist of three content columns that remain fixed at any browser window sizes. You have been provided with a mockup of the desired layout and a style sheet, parrot.css. You need to re-create the layout from the given material.

The six pages that are accessible from the Main navigation box share the same structure. The home page, however, is slightly different. You decide to focus on those six pages and create a layout template they can share.

What You Do	How You Do It
1. **Position the main Top Story section to the center of the page.** View your changes on any of the site's pages other than index.html.	a. In the Parrot.css - Notepad window, in the `#main` rule, **click after `border: 1px dashed orange;` and type `position:absolute;top:85px;` ⇒ `left:140px;`**
	b. **Choose File→Save.**
	c. **Minimize the Parrot.css - Notepad window.**
	d. **Reload the web page in both Internet Explorer and Netscape Navigator.**

2. **Position the Other Headlines section to the right of the main section.**

   Note that the elements that are not positioned continue to shift upwards as each element is removed from the document flow.

   a. **Restore the Parrot.css - Notepad window.**

   b. In the `#headlines` rule, **click after `background-color: #eee;` and type `position:absolute;top:85px;` ⇒ `left:570px;`**

   c. **Choose File→Save.**

   d. **Minimize the Parrot.css - Notepad window.**

   e. **Reload the web page in both Internet Explorer and Netscape Navigator.**

---

3. **Position the first navigation box in the upper left-hand corner of the page.**

   a. **Restore the Parrot.css - Notepad window.**

   b. In the `#nav` rule, **click after `border: 1px solid black;` and type `position:absolute;top:85px;` ⇒ `left:10px;`**

   c. **Choose File→Save.**

   d. **Minimize the Parrot.css - Notepad window.**

   e. **Reload the web page in both Internet Explorer and Netscape Navigator.** You may notice some problems with overlapping elements; however, these can be easily remedied.

---

4. **Position the second navigation box so that it lines up vertically below the first one.**

   a. **Restore the Parrot.css - Notepad window.**

   b. **In the `#nav2` rule, click after `border: 1px dashed orange;` and type `position:absolute;top:260px;` ⇒ `left:10px;`**

   c. **Choose File→Save.**

   d. **Minimize the Parrot.css - Notepad window.**

   e. **Reload the web page in both Internet Explorer and Netscape Navigator.**

5.	Position the third navigation box so that it lines up vertically below the second one.	a. Restore the Parrot.css - Notepad window. b. In the `#nav3` rule, click after `border: 1px solid black;` and type `position:absolute;top:420px;` ⇒ `left:10px;` c. Choose File→Save. d. Minimize the Parrot.css - Notepad window. e. Reload the web page in both Internet Explorer and Netscape Navigator.
6.	Position the page footer below the other elements so that it lines up between the left edge of the browser window and the bottom of the Other Headlines section.	a. Restore the Parrot.css - Notepad window and press the Page Down key. b. In the `#footer` rule, click after `text-align: center;` and type `position:absolute;top:580px;` ⇒ `left:10px;` c. Choose File→Save. d. Close Parrot.css - Notepad window. e. Reload the web page in both Internet Explorer and Netscape Navigator.
7.	Verify your changes in all the pages. The home page, index.html, will require additional styles—you will work on that page later.	a. Click all the links—except the Home link—in the Main navigation box of both the browsers. b. Compare the corresponding pages on both the browsers.
8.	Verify that the positioned layout is fixed.	a. Change the size of the browser window when viewing any of the pages other than index.html. b. Verify that the content sections do not change size or position when the browser window is resized. c. Close both the browsers.

ACTIVITY 4-3

Modifying the Layout of the Home Page

Activity Time:

5 minutes

Data Files:

- index.html

Before You Begin:

From the C:\085568Data\positioning\Activity 3\Starter\Project folder, open the index.html file in both Netscape Navigator and Internet Explorer and its source file in Notepad.

Scenario:

You now have a series of pages all absolutely positioned in a fixed multi-column layout. You need to finish the changes to the NewsParrot site by modifying the home page, index.html, which is slightly different from the other pages—it only has two navigation boxes plus an additional What's Hot section. From the style sheet embedded in index.html, you need to position What's Hot section between the Top Story section and the page footer.

What You Do	How You Do It
1. **Position the What's Hot section between the Top Story section and the page footer.**	a. In the Index.html - Notepad window, in the `#hot` rule, **click after `padding: 8px;` and type `position:absolute;top:415px;` ⇒ `left:10px;`**
	b. **Choose File→Save.**
	c. **Close the Index.html - Notepad window.**
	d. **Reload the web page in both Internet Explorer and Netscape Navigator.**
	e. **Close both the browsers.**

2. **A fixed layout is a layout wherein content sections remain fixed in relation to each other and the page canvas, even when the browser window is resized.**

   __ True

   __ False

TOPIC C

Create a Fluid Multi-Column Layout

You applied a fixed layout that allows you to guarantee the size of your content sections in any browser window. But there may be instances where you have to create flexible layouts to suit your design requirements. In this topic, you will modify the fixed layout design so that the content sections will expand or contract to accommodate the varying browser window sizes.

With fixed layouts, users with smaller browser windows or small monitors may have to scroll horizontally to view the content. With a fluid layout design, you can ensure that your content is displayed on screen irrespective of the browser window size, precluding the need to scroll horizontally.

Fluid Layouts

A *fluid layout* is one that accommodates to the size of a user's browser. When a browser window is resized, the fluid layout will *reflow* so that its dimension will increase or decrease to fill the available space. It is also referred to as a *flexible layout.*

For example, the following figures show an example of a fluid layout. The first figure displays a web page in a small browser window, while the second image shows the same page in a larger browser window. In both the images, the Top Story and footer sections reflow to occupy the extra space provided by the larger browser window.

A normal HTML document that has no CSS styles or layout tables is said to be fluid.

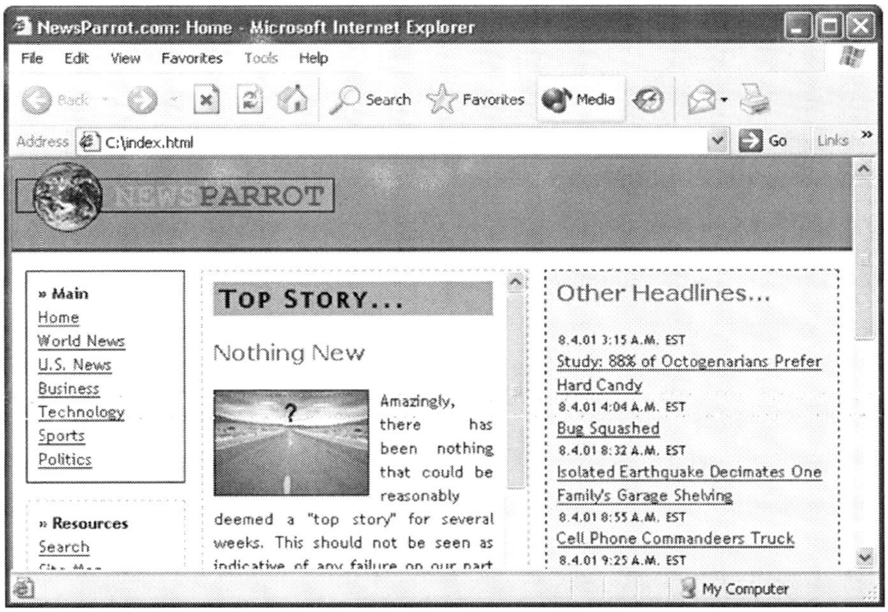

Web page with fluid layout in a small browser window

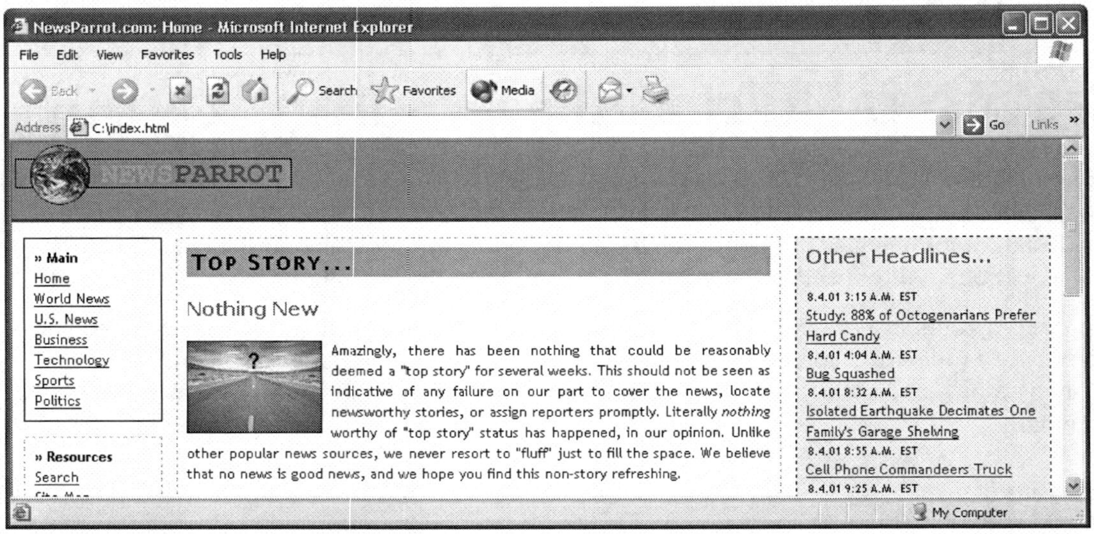

Web page with fluid layout in a large browser window

In a fluid design, all content sections need not be fluid. Fixed and fluid content sections can be integrated to achieve the desired result. For example, in the preceding figures, it wouldn't be appropriate to have the navigation boxes fluid. First, because they're not wide enough to warrant being fluid and, second, because it's a good idea to give content sections like navigation boxes a fixed width, to ensure that your link text is displayed as intended.

To make an element fluid, you can use three different methods:

- Set the element width using a relative unit of measurement.
- Use the left and right margins to control the displayed width of the element.
- Position the element, and use the `right` property instead of the `left` property to establish its relationship to the browser window.

A fluid design involves more imagination than code. You will need to think the design, contemplate what you want the design to do, and which styles will achieve it.

The right and bottom Properties

Positioning elements using the `right` and `bottom` properties is a great way to establish a fluid layout, as you can ensure that an element will remain in place with reference to the right side of the browser window. These properties are additional coordinate options you have with any positioned element. They work the same as the `top` and `left` properties.

The `right` property declares the offset amount between an element's upper right edge and the right edge of its parent element, typically the page canvas. The `bottom` property declares the offset amount between an element's lower right edge and the lower right edge of its parent element. For example, in the following figure, the `<div>` element is positioned using the `right` and `bottom` properties, as follows:

```
div#note { position: absolute;
right: 10px;
bottom: 10px; }
```

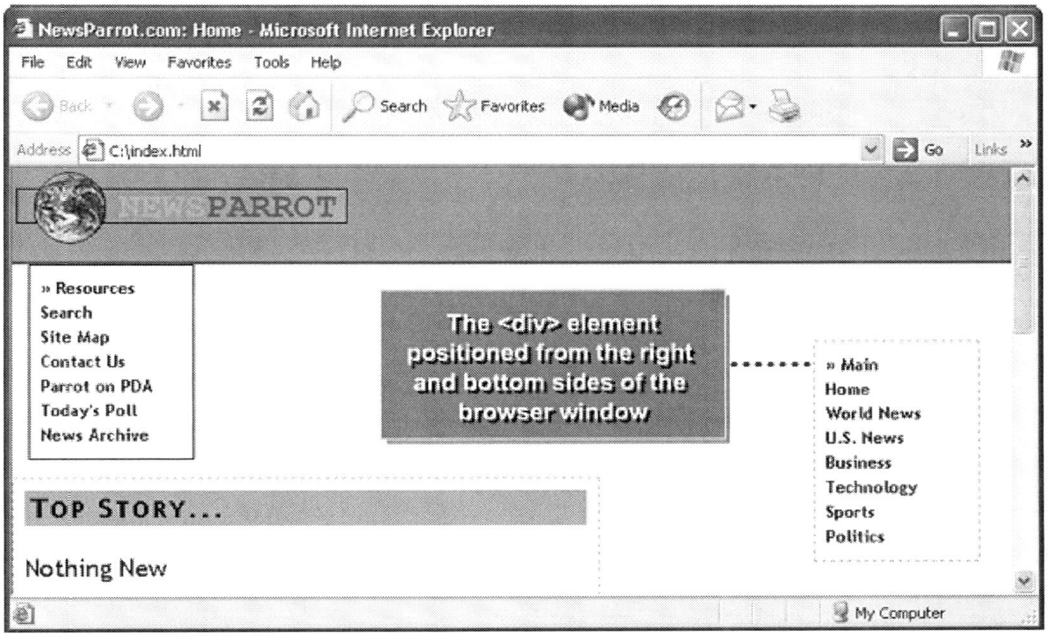

The following figure shows the same element in a larger browser window. Note that the element remains in its position relative to the bottom-right edge of the page canvas.

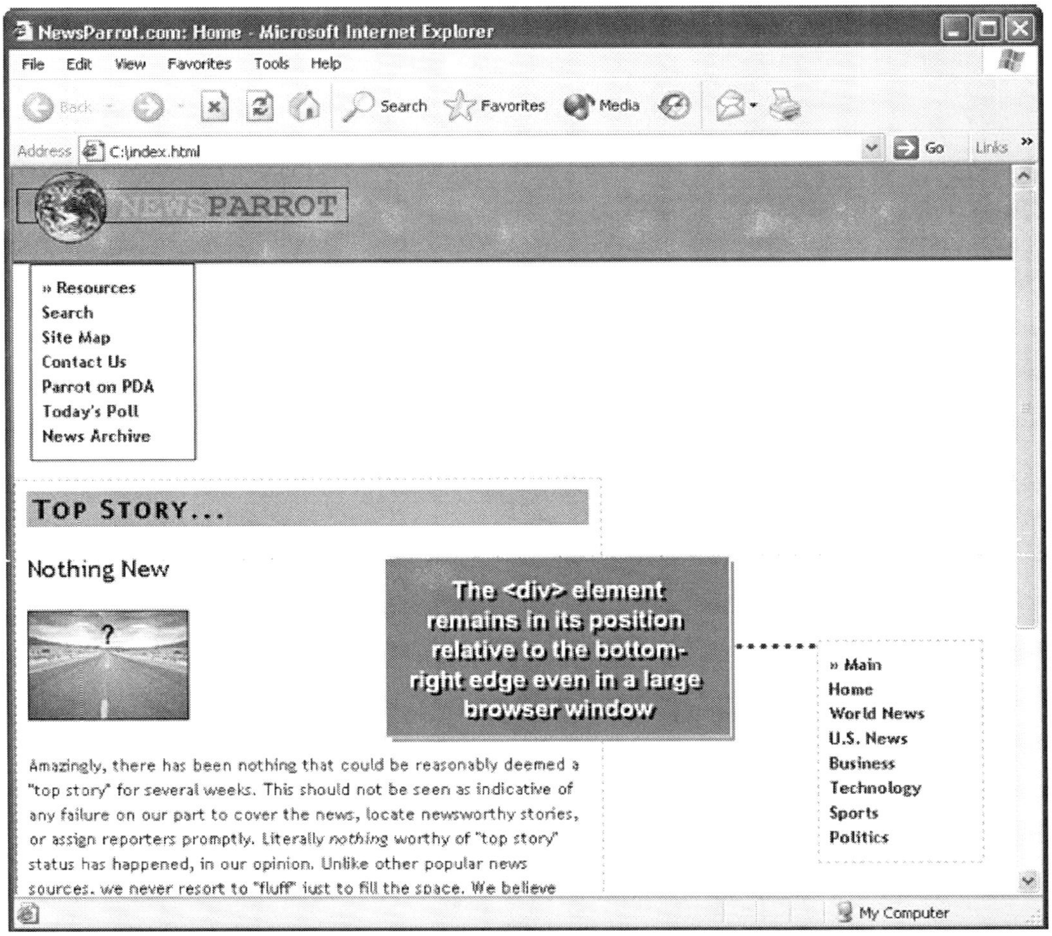

The `right` and `bottom` properties are only supported in the 6.0 and later generation of browsers. In instances where you're not certain about the browsers used, you should use alternative methods or use a script to refer users with older browsers to a safer version of the page.

How to Create a Fluid Multi-Column Layout

Procedure Reference: Create a Fluid Multi-Column Layout

To create a fluid multi-column layout:

1. Determine which content section(s) should have a fluid width.
2. If necessary, remove any fixed width value for the element(s) you want to have a fluid width.
3. Use margins to establish the fluid element(s)' placement on the page.
4. Position the rightmost content section in relation to the right edge of the browser window.

   Generally, the exact procedure you will need to follow will depend on the specifics of your project.

5. Save and verify the position of the elements.
6. If necessary, modify the positioning coordinates until the content sections are positioned where you want them.
7. Resize the browser window to make sure the elements reflow as expected.

ACTIVITY 4-4

Creating a Fluid Layout

Activity Time:

10 minutes

Data Files:

- index.html
- parrot.css

Before You Begin:

From the C:\085568Data\positioning\Activity 4\Starter\Fluid folder, open the index.html file in both Netscape Navigator and Internet Explorer. Also, open the parrot.css file.

Scenario:

Your project team decides that the NewsParrot design should accommodate a variety of browser window sizes. From the parrot.css style sheet, you need to change the existing design from a fixed layout to a fluid layout.

What You Do	How You Do It

Focus on the site's pages *other* than the home page, index.html. You will modify the home page in the next activity.

1. **Which content sections should have fluid width, and why?**

2. **Which content sections are best left with fixed width, and why?**

3. **Make the width of the Top Story section adjust to the size of the browser window.**

   a. In the Parrot.css - Notepad window, in `#main` rule, **select `width: 400px;`**

   b. **Choose Edit→Delete.**

   If you want to be able to see your edits at a later date, you can *hide* the removed styles in a CSS comment rather than delete them.

   c. **Select `position: absolute;top: 85px;left: 140px;`**

   d. **Choose Edit→Delete.**

   e. **Choose File→Save.**

   f. **Minimize the Parrot.css - Notepad window.**

   g. **Reload the web page in both Internet Explorer and Netscape Navigator.** Without fixed width, the element's width is determined by the size of the browser window. It's partially ***hidden*** behind the other elements because they're still positioned—removed from the document flow.

4. **Why is it necessary to remove the main content section's width?**

5. **Why is it also necessary to remove the positioning properties from the *main* element?**

---

6. **Re-create the previous layout of the Top Story section by using the margins.**

   a. **Restore Parrot.css - Notepad window.**

   b. **Type**
   ```
   margin-left:140px;margin-top:14px;
   margin-right:240px; ⇒
   margin-bottom:12px;
   ```

   c. **Choose File→Save.**

   d. **Minimize the Parrot.css - Notepad window.**

   e. **Reload the web page in both Internet Explorer and Netscape Navigator.**

   f. **Resize the browser windows to verify the change.** The margins of the Top Story section change when the browser is resized.

---

7. **The Top Story section may be displayed in the right spot, but why does the Other Headlines section overlap with the main content section at larger browser window sizes?**

---

8. **How can you make the Other Headlines section react to the resizing of the browser window along with the main content section?**

---

9. **Position the Other Headlines section to the right edge of the browser window and give it the same offset from the right edge as the navigation boxes are from the left.**

a. **Restore the Parrot.css - Notepad window.**

b. In the `#headlines` rule, **select `left: 570px;`**

c. **Choose Edit→Delete.**

d. **Click after `border: 1px` and select `dashed black`.**

e. **Choose Edit→Delete.**

f. **Press Spacebar and type `solid black`**

g. **Click after `background-color: #eee;` and type `right:10px;`**

h. **Choose File→Save.**

i. **Minimize the Parrot.css - Notepad window.**

j. **Reload the web page in both Internet Explorer and Netscape Navigator.**

k. **Resize both the browser windows** to verify the change.

At this point, the fluid layout of the Top Story section and the headlines section should be successful, but the page footer remains a problem.

---

10. **How can you give the page footer a flexible width while keeping a fixed distance between the left edge of the browser window and the left edge of the Headlines section?**

---

11. **Make the page footer respond to the size of the browser window, and set a fixed distance between the elements.**

    a. **Restore the Parrot.css - Notepad window and scroll down** to view `#footer` rule.

    b. In the `#footer` rule, **select `width: 530px;` and choose Edit→Delete.**

    c. **Select `position: absolute;` ⇒ `top: 580px;left: 10px;` and choose Edit→Delete.**

    d. **Type `margin-left:10px;` ⇒ `margin-right:240px;`**

    e. **Choose File→Save.**

    f. **Close the Parrot.css - Notepad window.**

    g. **Reload the web page in both Internet Explorer and Netscape Navigator.**

    h. **Resize both the browser windows** to verify the change.

    i. **Close both the browsers.**

    The home page requires additional modifications—you will work on that page in the next activity.

OPTIONAL ACTIVITY 4-5

Creating a Fluid Layout for the Home Page

Activity Time:

5 minutes

Data Files:

- index.html

Before You Begin:

From the C:\085568Data\positioning\Activity 5\Starter\Fluid folder, open the index.html file in Internet Explorer and its source file in Notepad.

Scenario:

You're almost finished and ready to present your new fluid layout to the project team. You still need to set the fluid design for the home page, index.html, which contains the What's Hot section. You need to modify the styles of this content section so that it flows with the other fluid elements.

What You Do	How You Do It
1. **Make the What's Hot section fluid and set its left and right margins by using values of the navigation box and the Top Story section, respectively.**	a. In the Index.html - Notepad window, in the `#hot` rule, **select `width: 525px;` and choose Edit→Delete.**
	b. **Select `position: absolute;top: 415px;left: 10px;` and choose Edit→ Delete.**
	c. **Type `margin-left:10px;` ⇒ `margin-right:240px;`**
	d. **Choose File→Save.**
	e. **Minimize the Index.html - Notepad window.**
	f. In the Internet Explorer window, **click the Refresh button.**

2. **Create an equal amount of white space between the top and bottom of the What's Hot section.**

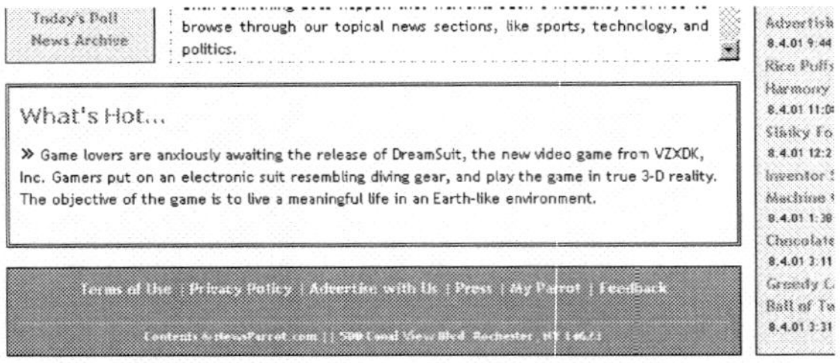

a. **Restore the Index.html - Notepad window.**

b. **Type `margin-bottom:10px;`**

c. **Choose File→Save.**

d. **Close the Index.html - Notepad window.**

e. In the Internet Explorer window, **scroll down and click the Refresh button.**

f. **Close the Internet Explorer window.**

TOPIC D

Control Layout with Relative Positioning

You modified layouts using absolute positioning, a method of positioning that removes elements from the document flow. But you may encounter a situation where you don't want to lose the natural flow of elements in your layout. In this topic, you will position elements and preserve the document flow.

Relative positioning can be used to position elements without affecting the placement of content following it. In the following example of a simple layout, if you use absolute positioning to arrange Content Section 2 to the right of Content Section 1, the latter will be moved from the normal flow of elements, and the page footer will move upward to occupy the space it formerly occupied. With relative positioning, you can position Content Section 2 in the same location while retaining the normal document flow, and the page footer also remains in its default location.

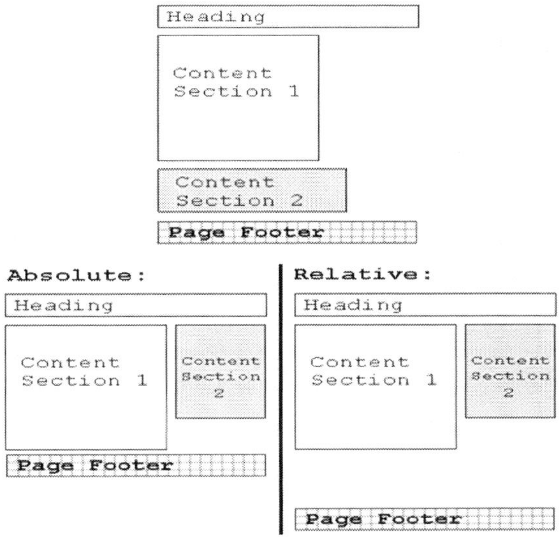

Relative positioning preserves the normal document flow

Relative Positioning

Relative positioning is a method of positioning elements where the elements remain in the document flow. Coordinates of a relatively positioned element are relative to their default position in the document, the position on the page that it would normally occupy.

For example, if a nested element is relatively positioned, its coordinates are calculated from the point that the element would normally begin, as shown in the following figure.

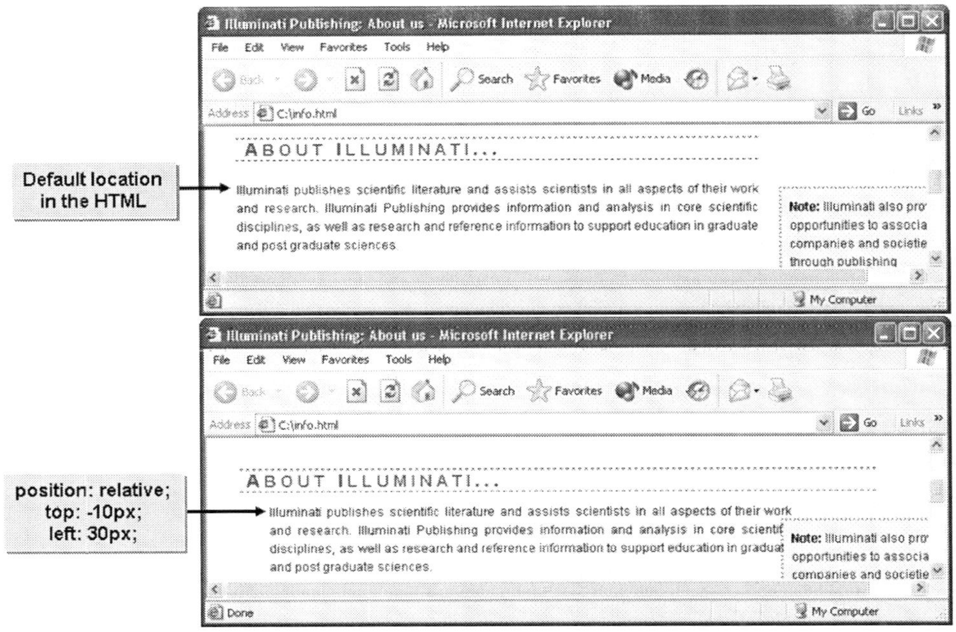

When you relatively position an element, the element that follows it in the document flow is not affected. For example, if you relatively position a `<div>` element so that it is displayed 20 pixels higher in the document than in its normal position, the elements that follow it will not shift up to fill the available space. The normal document flow is not altered.

Negative Coordinate Values

When designing a page with relative positioning, you need to use negative values for the coordinates. If you specify `top: 0px` for a relatively positioned element, it will remain in its normal vertical position. Negative values are the only way you can move a relatively positioned element up in the document. For example, the following code positions a `<div>` element 40 pixels up from its normal position in the document flow:

```
div { position: relative;
top: -40px; }
```

How to Control Layout with Relative Positioning

Procedure Reference: Control Layout with Relative Positioning

To relatively position an element:

1. Determine where you want your element to display on the page.
2. Estimate the amount of offset you will need to position the element in the desired location.
3. Use the `position: relative` property to set the element without removing it from the document flow.
4. Use the `left` or `right`, `top` or `bottom` properties to apply the required offset.
5. Save the changes and verify the position of the element.
6. Modify the coordinate values until the element is positioned where you want it.

ACTIVITY 4-6

Arranging Elements with Relative Positioning

Activity Time:

5 minutes

Data Files:

- staff.html

Before You Begin:

From the C:\085568Data\positioning\Activity 6\Starter\Relative folder, open the staff.html file in both Netscape Navigator and Internet Explorer and its source file in Notepad.

Scenario:

The Illuminati project team has asked you to make a few modifications to the staff.html page. The team wants to make the element containing the text "The 2001 Editorial Board of Trustees" display to the left of the staff picture table. The team also wants the copyright statement to remain in its current place on the page.

The existing layout consists of margin settings, which establish the position of elements on each page. You need to carry out the design requirements while retaining the normal document flow.

What You Do	How You Do It
1. **Position the Board element to the left of the staff picture table without affecting the position of the copyright statement.**	a. In the Staff.html - Notepad window, in the `#board` rule, **click after `text-indent: 0px;` and type `position:relative;top:-200px;`**
	b. **Choose File→Save.**
	c. **Minimize the Staff.html - Notepad window.**
	d. **Reload the web page in both Internet Explorer and Netscape Navigator.** The copyright statement does not shift up to fill in the space left by the positioned element.

2. **Move the staff picture table to the right to create space for the Board element.**

a. **Restore the Staff.html - Notepad window.**

b. In the table rule, **click after** **`margin-left: 25px;`** **and type** **`position:relative;left:100px;`**

c. **Choose File→Save.**

d. **Close the Staff.html - Notepad window.**

e. **Reload the page in both Internet Explorer and Netscape Navigator.**

f. **Close both the browsers.**

TOPIC E

Control the Display of Layered Elements

You have controlled layouts and arranged elements using relative positioning. Sometimes, for design purposes, you may want to place multiple elements in the same location. You can fit a lot of content into a small space by positioning multiple elements in the same location on a page. In this topic, you will control which element is displayed on top in a series of overlapping elements.

By positioning multiple elements in the same location on a page, and controlling which element is displayed on top, you can present more content in a small space with a simple script. This provides users the flexibility to select the content they want to access.

For example, you can visit a website of your choice where there is tabbed content sections. When a user clicks a tab, a script is activated to display only the desired content. Thus, the total amount of available content occupies a lesser page space than it would otherwise require.

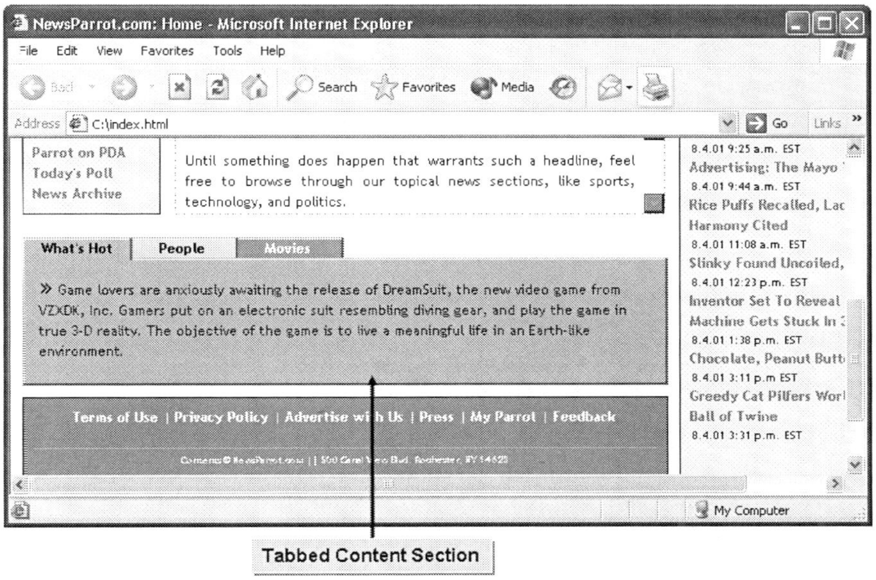

Layered Elements

When you position multiple elements in the same location on a page, you create a series of *layers*. The order in which overlapping elements are displayed is called the stacking order. By default, the last element in the document flow is positioned on top of the others.

For example, the following figure shows three <div> elements that are positioned such that they partially overlap each other.

The term *layers* in this context is not the same as the <layer> tag, which is an unofficial HTML element supported only by older versions of Netscape Navigator.

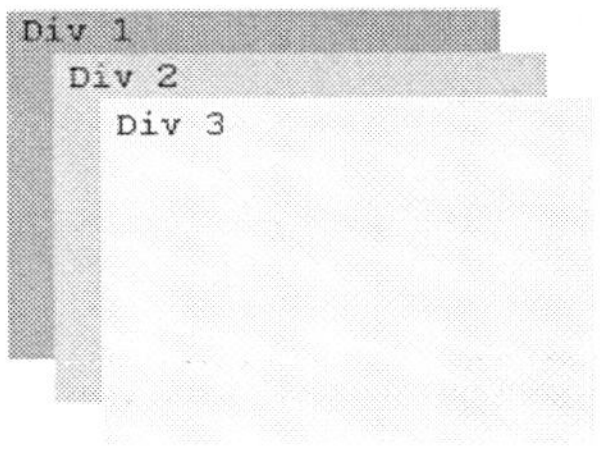

Overlapping <div> elements

The z-index Property

You can control the stacking order of overlapping, positioned elements with the `z-index` property. An element's `z-index` is specified in integers; the higher the number, the higher the element appears in the stacking order. If two or more elements have the same `z-index` value, or if no `z-index` is specified for either element, the order in which the elements appear in the document source determines their stacking order. The element defined last in the document source displays on top.

For example, in the following code the three <div> elements will be positioned such that they partially overlap each other:

```
#div1 { position: absolute;
        top: 10px; left: 10px;
        z-index: 1; }
#div2 { position: absolute;
        top: 20px; left: 20px;
        z-index: 2; }
#div3 { position: absolute;
        top: 30px; left: 30px;
        z-index: 3; }
```

Values of the z-index property need not be sequential.

The stacking order of layered elements is best implemented with a script to make the layers dynamic. Dynamic layers give users control over what content is displayed.

The z-index.html file located in the Instructor Demo folder demonstrates how the `z-index` of layered elements, when combined with a simple script, allows users to access the desired content.

How to Control the Display of Layered Elements

Procedure Reference: Control the Display of Layered Elements

To control the stacking order of elements:

1. Set uniform dimensions for two or more elements by using the `height` and `width` properties.
2. Position each element in the same location on the page.
3. Assign the highest `z-index` value to the layer you want displayed on top.
4. Use a script to allow users to control which layer is displayed on top.

The scripting aspect of this technique is beyond the scope of this course, but there are several sites on the web that offer such scripts for free.

ACTIVITY 4-7

Controlling the Stacking Order of Elements

Activity Time:

5 minutes

Data Files:

- index.html

Before You Begin:

From the C:\085568Data\positioning\Activity 7\Starter\Layers folder, open the index.html file in both Netscape Navigator and Internet Explorer and its source file in Notepad.

Scenario:

Based on a request from the NewsParrot design team, you created a tabbed content section on the home page, index.html, to display the site's special features. This content section consists of three `<div>` elements that serve as content panels; each panel has another `<div>` element positioned above it to serve as its selectable tab. A developer has already implemented a script that allows users to select the content they want by clicking on a tab. You need to change the default stacking order of the elements so that the panels display in the same order they appear in the HTML, with the What's Hot panel displayed on top.

The panels are positioned in the exact location on the page, and each tab is positioned so that they're always visible for users to select. Each element in this content section has outset borders to create the appearance of tabs.

What You Do	How You Do It
1. **Observe the default stacking order of the overlapping layers.** **Why is the Movies layer displayed on top?**	

2. **Set the stacking order to display the layers as they appear in the HTML.**

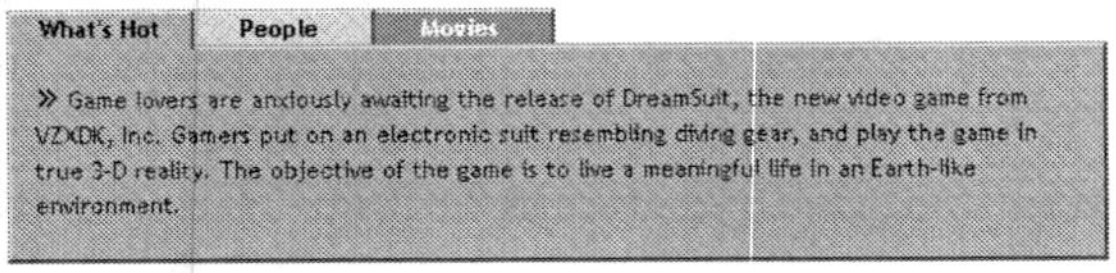

a. In the Index.html - Notepad window, **scroll down** to view the div element under <!-- What's Hot -->. **Click after <div class="panel" id="panel0" style="background-color: #ea6; and type z-index:3;**

b. In the div element under <!-- People -->, **click after <div class="panel" id="panel1" style="background-color: #ddd; and type z-index:2;**

c. In the div element under <!- Movies -->, **click after <div class="panel" id="panel2" style="color: white; background-color: #7e92ba; and type z-index:1;**

d. **Choose File→Save.**

e. **Close the Index.html - Notepad window.**

f. **Reload the web page in both Internet Explorer and Netscape Navigator.** The What's Hot layer is now displayed because it's at the top of the stacking order, with the highest z-index value.

---

3. **Verify that each tab still activates its associated panel.**

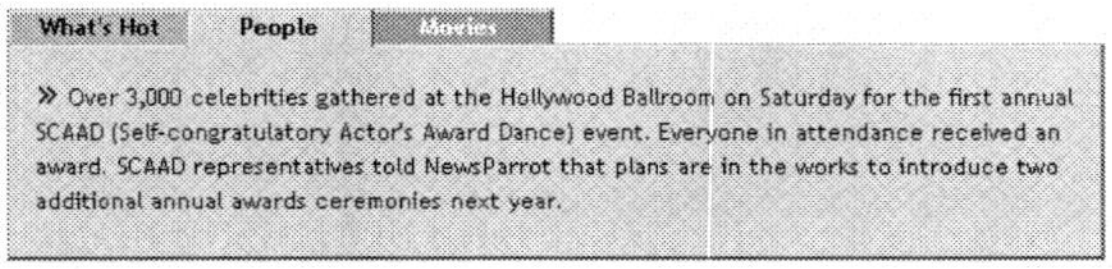

a. **Click on a tab** to activate its content panel.

b. **Go through each tab** to make sure the script works correctly.

c. **Close the Internet Explorer window.**

TOPIC F

Apply Fixed Positioning

You have determined the display of layered elements by controlling their stacking order. You have used both absolute and relative positioning to arrange page elements which keep scrolling with the page content. There may be occasions when you want an element to remain in its specified position at all times. In this topic, you will use fixed positioning to position an element so that it remains in its specified location even when the document is scrolled.

Fixed positioning allows you to keep important content sections visible at all times. For example, if you have a `<div>` element—at the top of your page—containing navigation links that should be visible even if a user scrolls down to the bottom of the page, you can use fixed positioning to permanently affix the `<div>` to the specified location on the page canvas.

This effect is traditionally handled with HTML frames, which involve multiple documents and more coding. With fixed positioning, you can create frame-like effects with only a single style rule.

Fixed Positioning

Fixed positioning is a positioning method wherein an element is affixed to the browser window, or *viewport*, in a specified location. It does not scroll with other page content. Fixed positioning is similar to absolute positioning in that an element is removed from the document flow. However, with fixed positioning, the `top`, `left`, `right`, and `bottom` coordinates are always relative to the viewport. The viewport is different from the page canvas in that it is not defined by an HTML element and cannot be manipulated.

An element with a fixed position acts like an HTML frame. If you have an HTML frame at the top of your document, it will not scroll with the active document.

For example, the following figure shows a page with a top navigation bar that has a fixed position. It does not scroll along with the page content.

Because fixed elements do not scroll with page content, you will need to make sure that your fixed content is always displayed on top in the stacking order, so that other content scrolls beneath it. By default, content will scroll underneath an element with a fixed position.

However, if the scrolling content is also positioned, either absolutely or relatively, it will scroll on top of the fixed element, in accordance with the default stacking order of positioned elements. You can force content to scroll underneath an element with a fixed position by giving the fixed positioned element a higher `z-index` value.

Fixed positioning is supported by Netscape Navigator 6 and later, and Opera 5 and later. Internet Explorer, as of version 6, ignores this type of positioning.

How to Apply Fixed Positioning

Procedure Reference: Apply Fixed Positioning

To apply fixed positioning:

1. Determine where on the page canvas you want the fixed element to display.
2. Estimate the amount of offset you will need to position the element in the desired location on the page.
3. Use the `position: fixed` property and value to prevent the element from scrolling.
4. Use the `top` or `bottom`, `left` or `right` properties to establish the offset you need.
5. Determine if you want the page content to scroll underneath or on top of the fixed element, if applicable.
6. Give the fixed element a `z-index` value to set the desired stacking order.
7. Save and verify the changes.
8. Modify the offset of the positioned element, if necessary, until it displays in the desired location on the page.

ACTIVITY 4-8

Applying a Fixed Position

Activity Time:

5 minutes

Data Files:

- index.html

Before You Begin:

From the C:\085568Data\positioning\Activity 8\Starter\Layers folder, open the index.html file in Netscape Navigator and its source file in Notepad.

Scenario:

The client, NewsParrot, wants to reserve the top of its home page for banner advertisements. NewsParrot informs you that it can increase ad revenues if the banner is always visible, no matter where the user scrolls on the page. NewsParrot has provided you with an animated advertisement, and you have already positioned it in the desired location on the page.

In the index.html file, you need to make the top section of the page visible at all times, so that it does not scroll with the page content.

What You Do	How You Do It
1. **Prevent the top section from scrolling along with the document content.**	a. In the Index.html - Notepad window, in the embedded style sheet, **scroll down, click after <!-- and press Enter.**
	b. **Type `#top{position:fixed;}`**
	c. **Choose File→Save.**
	d. **Minimize the Index.html - Notepad window.**
	e. **Scroll through the document.** The page content overlaps the fixed content section because no `z-index` values are set and because the page content is defined later in the source rather than in the top section.
	You may need to decrease the size of your browser window to activate the page's scroll bar.

2. **Make the page content scroll underneath the top section.**

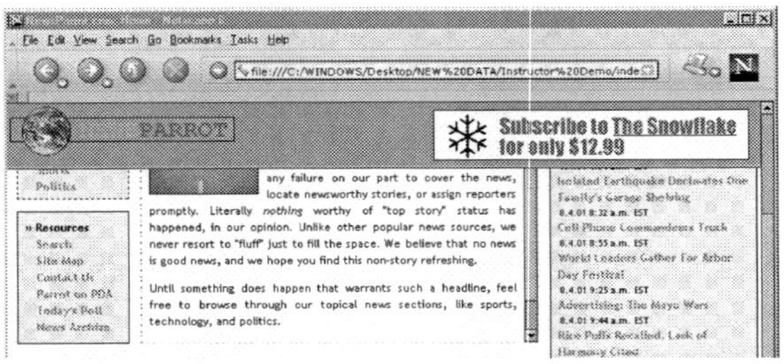

a. **Restore the Index.html - Notepad window. Click after `#top{position:fixed;` and type `z-index:20;`**

b. **Choose File→Save.**

c. **Close the Index.html - Notepad window.**

d. In the Netscape Navigator window, **click the Reload button and scroll up.**

e. **Notice that the content scrolls underneath the top section.**

f. **Scroll through the document** to verify that the content scrolls underneath the top section.

g. **Close the Netscape Navigator window.**

If you view the changes in Internet Explorer, you'll see that it safely ignores the `position: fixed` rule, so no harm is done to the layout. The top section remains absolutely positioned, in accordance with the rule on the site's linked style sheet.

Lesson 4 Follow-up

In this lesson, you controlled layouts with CSS positioning. Positioning precludes the need for HTML tables to achieve complex layouts because it greatly reduces and simplifies coding and also makes it easy to update and load your pages.

1. **Do you think you'll use positioning in your own development projects, or rely on box properties to arrange your content sections? Why?**

2. **In your own projects, do you think you will create fixed or fluid layouts? Why?**

LESSON 5

Enhancing an Existing Design

Lesson Time
1 hour(s), 30 minutes

Lesson Objectives:

In this lesson, you will enhance an existing design.

You will:

- Customize cursors to meet established guidelines.
- Customize link styles in their various states.
- Apply styles to form elements.
- Declare a background image for a page and modify its display characteristics.
- Modify the display characteristics of an HTML list.
- Define content from a style sheet.

Lesson 5

Introduction

You controlled complex layouts with positioning, making it easy to update and load your pages. But these layout designs alone may not be enough to keep your users engaged with your web content. In this lesson, you will enhance your existing designs to provide an environment that is visually engaging and that which helps users to effectively access the information provided.

There's more to web content than just text elements and arrangement of content sections. To make your designs look complete and appealing, you need to incorporate the other types of web content into your design scheme. By customizing the design of non-text elements such as forms and background images, or by providing visual cues for your interactive content, you can greatly enhance user experience and make your website more engaging and accessible.

Topic A

Customize Cursors

You controlled complex layouts by using positioning. The way a component in a user interface is displayed can be customized to suit design requirements and objectives. In this topic, you will customize the display of the cursor.

By customizing the cursor, you can provide users with visual cues regarding the functionality of your elements. For example, you can display the cursor as a question mark when it is over a particular link or other element on a page. This provides the cue that "help is available," so users can more effectively use the information provided on the web pages.

The following figure shows a link containing a `title` attribute with the information to the user that the link will launch the email client. The Help cursor is activated when a user's mouse is positioned over the link.

Cursor Styles

Cursor styles are CSS keywords that specify the cursor to display when a user places the mouse pointer over an element. You're familiar with the default cursors that browsers display when the mouse pointer is placed over plain text or links. When the mouse pointer is moved over a hyperlink, the cursor changes to a hand icon, providing a visual cue that the item is clickable. Cursors vary across different platforms, but most browsers display the same cursor for each element type.

The cursor can be customized with the `cursor` property and several different keyword values, as:

```
element { cursor: keyword; }
```

When indicating a link or clickable region, specify both the *pointer* and *hand* values, as:

```
element { cursor: pointer; cursor: hand; }
```

Internet Explorer, prior to version 6, supports the `hand` value but not `pointer`. Specifying both ensures that your cursor will work in all versions of Internet Explorer.

The following table lists the available cursor style keywords, their appearance, and also describes how each one is meant to be used.

Property/Keyword Value	Display	Description
`cursor: default`	Default cursor for an element.	Displays the default cursor for an element. Most browsers use the same default cursor styles.
`cursor: auto`	Determined by the browser in use.	Provides the browser control over what cursor is displayed. This value creates the same effect as the default value.
`cursor: text`		The standard icon for text elements.
`cursor: crosshair`		Provides an aiming tool. This cursor can be useful in DHTML applications.
`cursor: move`		Indicates that an element can be moved. This cursor can be useful in DHTML applications in which page elements can be moved via drag-and-drop.
`cursor: pointer`	Internet Explorer (PC):  Netscape 6 and above: 	This is the default cursor used for links. This is also useful for clickable regions that have no automatic cursor. For IE 4 through 5.5, use `cursor: hand`.
`cursor: wait`		Indicates that a page is loading or some other task is in process. Avoid using this cursor except to communicate that the user is currently waiting for some process to be completed.
`cursor: help`		Indicates that an element offers some sort of assistance or information.
`cursor: x-resize`	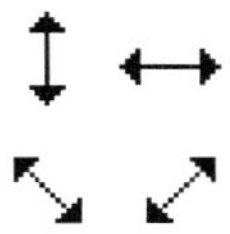	Specifies a direction, where `x` equals one of eight directional abbreviations: `n` (north), `e` (east), `s` (south), `w` (west), and the compass points such as `ne` for northeast, `sw` for southwest, etc.

Custom Cursors

You can create and specify your own custom cursor. To do this, you need to specify the location of an existing cursor file with a .cur extension. Like other CSS properties that declare an image, you can use the `url` and parentheses to specify the file name or location of your cursor file, as follows:

```
a.help { cursor: url("mycursor.cur"); }
```

For browsers that don't support custom cursors, you can declare a secondary option, the same way that you specify multiple font face options when you use the `font-family` property. If the user's browser does not support custom cursors, it will use your second choice. For example:

```
a.help { cursor: url("mycursor.cur"), help ; }
```

How to Customize Cursors

By customizing cursors you can help communicate or reinforce the intent of your page elements.

Guidelines

To customize the cursor effectively:

- Choose a cursor that matches the element's functionality or intent.
- Don't apply cursor styles arbitrarily.

Example:

You can declare the link cursor for a clickable element that is not a hyperlink, such as a form button or a dynamic element. The default cursor might not adequately indicate how the element is intended to be used.

It's important not to get carried away with cursor styles. Cursor icons like the hand and hourglass are well-established user interface conventions that give the user important feedback. Manipulating these conventions arbitrarily can be a disservice to your site visitors.

ACTIVITY 5-1

Customizing Cursors

Activity Time:

5 minutes

Data Files:

- index.html

Before You Begin:

From the C:\085568Data\enhancement\Activity 1\Starter\NewsParrot folder, open the index.html file in both Netscape Navigator and Internet Explorer. Also, open its source file in Notepad.

Scenario:

You need to improve the usability of the tabbed content section on the NewsParrot home page, index.html. The clickable tabs currently display with the default cursor for text elements: the I-beam. This cursor does not provide an effective visual cue that the region is clickable, which might confuse users and detract from the usability of this content section.

You also decide to change the cursor for the Feedback link in the footer so that users might be more inclined to read the tooltip associated with it. You have already inserted `class="help"` attributes in the link tags for each of the Feedback links. You simply need to apply the cursor style to these links.

The Feedback links also have a `title` attribute which defines the tooltip message.

What You Do	How You Do It
1. **Display the standard link cursor when the mouse pointer is hovered over the tabbed section.**	a. In the Index.html - Notepad window, **scroll down to view the `.tab` rule, click after `width: 90px;` and type `cursor:pointer;cursor:hand;`**
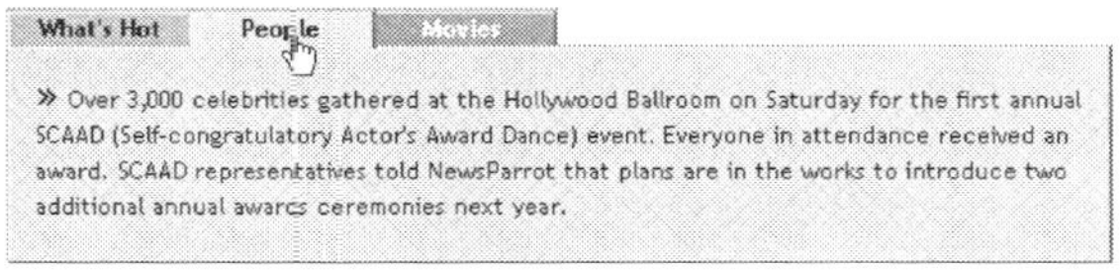	b. **Choose File→Save.**
	c. **Minimize the Index.html - Notepad window.**
	d. **Verify that both browsers display the change in cursor type when the mouse pointer is placed over each of the three tabs.**

2. **Display the Help cursor for the Feedback link.**

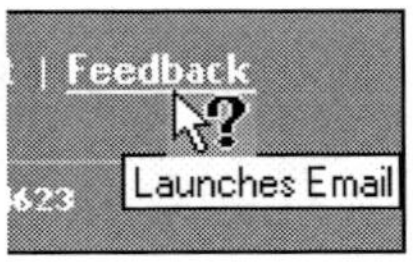

a. **Restore the Index.html - Notepad window.**

b. In the embedded style sheet, **click after `<!--` and press Enter.**

c. **Type `.help{cursor:help;}`**

d. **Choose File→Save.**

e. **Close the Index.html - Notepad window.**

f. **Notice that a question mark is displayed when the mouse pointer is placed over the Feedback link, indicating that information is available.**

g. **Close both the browsers.**

ACTIVITY 5-2

Applying Image Cursors

Activity Time:

5 minutes

Data Files:

- index.html
- chili.cur

Before You Begin:

From the C:\085568Data\enhancement\Activity 2\Starter\NewsParrot folder, open the index.html file in Internet Explorer and its source file in Notepad.

Scenario:

The NewsParrot design team has provided you with a customized cursor file, chili.cur, and has asked you to apply it to the What's Hot content panel on the home page, index.html.

This activity will not work in Internet Explorer versions earlier than version 6, or in any version of Netscape (up to and including Netscape 7).

What You Do	How You Do It
1. **Display the customized cursor for the What's Hot content panel.**	a. In the Index.html - Notepad window, in the embedded style sheet, **click after <!-- and press Enter.**

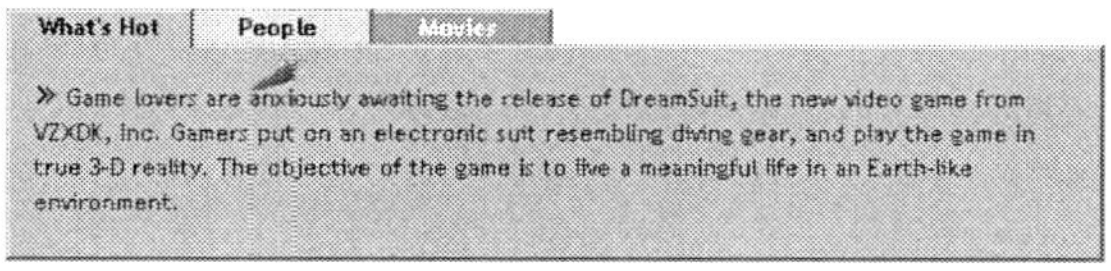

b. **Type**
```
#panel0{cursor:url("chili.cur");}
```

c. **Choose File→Save.**

d. **Close the Index.html - Notepad window.**

e. In the Internet Explorer window, **click the Refresh button.**

f. **Notice the changes by moving the mouse pointer over the What's Hot panel.**

g. **Close the Internet Explorer window.**

2. **The cursor: text keyword is used for what purpose?**
   a) To display the standard icon as the default cursor for an element.
   b) To display the standard icon as the default cursor for text elements.
   c) To display the standard icon as the default cursor for text links.
   d) To display the standard icon as the default cursor for links.

TOPIC B

Customize Link Styles

You customized the cursor to provide users visual cues regarding the functionality of your page elements. Dynamic styles can enhance the usability of your websites because they can provide important feedback to your users. In this topic, you will customize link styles to change dynamically as visitors navigate through them.

By customizing the link styles, you can provide visual feedback to users indicating which links they have visited, which links they have not yet visited, and which link is selected. By doing so, you can override the default styles that browsers apply to links, and incorporate the links into your site's color scheme.

If you don't set your own link styles, your links might display in different colors according to the browser in use. The default link colors that different browsers apply might not suit your established color scheme. Customizing your link styles allows you to avoid potential color clashes, establish style consistency across all browsers, and enhance your site's overall color scheme.

Link States

The status of a link is called the link's state. It is defined by user activity. There are four different *link states*:

- The default state:

  The state in which a link exists before it is clicked.
- The hover state:

  The state when a user positions the mouse pointer over a link.
- The active state:

  The moment between the pressing and releasing of the mouse button.
- The visited state:

  The state after a link has been clicked.

You can help users navigate through your site by providing visual feedback for the links in all their states.

Most browsers display links as blue underlined text, and visited links as purple underlined text. However, Netscape 6 displays links as navy underlined text and visited links as gray underlined text by default.

Pseudo-Classes

Pseudo-classes define the style for each link state. Pseudo-classes have a unique syntax and can be used to override default link colors and text styles. All pseudo-classes begin with a colon, followed by the pseudo-class. The following table lists the pseudo-classes attached to the `a` element.

Pseudo-class	Description
`a:link`	Sets the style for links that have not yet been visited.
`a:visited`	Sets the style for visited links.
`a:hover`	Sets the style for links when the mouse pointer is moved over it.
`a:active`	Sets the style for links when clicked.

Just like regular classes, each pseudo-class has a specificity of 10. Since they're usually attached to the link element, the total specificity of a typical selector such as `a:hover` is 11, 1 for the `a` element, and 10 for the pseudo-class.

When you apply styles using just the link element `a` as your selector, all links will pick up those styles in all of their states. This allows you to set styles that you want applied to all link states, and then use pseudo-class rules to apply the state-specific styles you need.

`:focus` is a pseudo-class which does not apply to links. It can be used to change the style of a form control when the cursor is placed in a particular form field.

Order of Pseudo-Classes

It is important to follow the order in which you list your link state rules. To successfully set styles in all link states, you need to list your rules in the order as:

```
a:link { your styles }
a:visited { your styles }
a:hover { your styles }
a:active { your styles }
```

For example, if the `a:visited` rule is specified last, the visited link styles won't change in the active or hover state because each pseudo-class rule has the same specificity. In the cascade, conflicting styles in a later rule override those in an earlier rule, unless the earlier rule is more specific. So, the `a:visited` rule will override conflicting styles in both the `a:hover` and the `a:active` rules.

Using Classes and Pseudo-Classes in the Same Selector

Classes and pseudo-classes can be combined in your selectors as they provide flexibility. For example, if you only specify your link styles once using the rules, all your links will pick up those styles. But if you want another section of a page to have different link styles, you need to target those links more specifically by using classes.

For any link that you want to give a different set of styles, you can insert a class attribute into your link tags with whatever class name you want. You can then set up rules for these links as:

```
a.ClassName:link { your styles }
a.ClassName:visited { your styles }
a.ClassName:hover { your styles }
a.ClassName:active { your styles }
```

Pseudo-classes should be listed last in a selector.

How to Choose the Appropriate Link Style

Link styles enhance the overall usability of a website by communicating the status of the user's navigation.

Guidelines

To create effective link styles:

- The colors you choose for all link states should provide enough contrast against the background color.
- Colors that complement your existing color scheme need to be used.
- Styles that force surrounding content to shift when in the hover state should be avoided.
- Styles such as increased font sizes or letter spacing for link text in the hover state will likely force the text around the link to move, which can reduce the usability of your links.

Example:

The bad_link_styles.html file located in the Instructor Demo folder contains a navigation bar with link colors that do not provide enough contrast against the page background color, making the links difficult to see. The font size also increases when a user hovers over a link, which forces the other links around it to reflow or change position. This can be distracting and frustrating for users.

The good_link_styles.html file contains the same series of links, but with more effective styles as shown below. In this example, it's easy to distinguish the link text color against the background color, and the links are bold to provide even more contrast. The hover style changes the link background color to white and the link text color to black, and this more clearly shows that the link is selected.

Effective link styles

How to Customize Link Styles

Procedure Reference: Customize Link Styles

To customize the link styles:

1. Determine which colors or styles you want to apply to each link state, to complement the existing color scheme and help users navigate through your site pages.
2. Set up the pseudo-class rules.
   a. Type `a:link { your styles }` and press Enter.
   b. Type `a:visited { your styles }` and press Enter.
   c. Type `a:hover { your styles }` and press Enter.
   d. Type `a:active { your styles }`
3. Save the changes.
4. Activate all link states to test the styles.

ACTIVITY 5-3

Customizing Styles for Link States

Activity Time:

5 day(s)

Data Files:

- index.html
- parrot.css

Before You Begin:

From the C:\085568Data\enhancement\Activity 3\Starter\NewsParrot folder, open the index.html file in Internet Explorer. Also, open the parrot.css file.

Scenario:

All the layout components for the NewsParrot site project are complete, and you're now ready to give some finishing touches to the design. In the parrot.css style sheet, you want to replace the color of links in all of their states with colors that complement the existing color scheme.

The links are already bold: an existing rule for the `a` element has set this style, which inherits to all four link states. Also, the links in the page footer already have their own color styles; they need to be different because the page footer has a different background color than the other links in the page.

What You Do	How You Do It
1. In the parrot.css style sheet, **observe the existing rule for the a element.** **What's the difference between using the a element as a selector and using the `a:link` selector?**	
2. **Verify that the existing link styles do not change dynamically.**	a. If necessary, **restore the Internet Explorer window.** b. In the Internet Explorer window, **hover over the links in the Main navigation box.** The link styles do not change. c. **Click the World News and Home links.** d. **Notice that the link styles do not change.**

3. **Make visited links black.**

   a. **Restore the Parrot.css - Notepad window and scroll down** to view the a rule.

   b. **Click to the right of the a rule, press Enter and type `a:visited{color: black;}`**

   c. **Choose File→Save.**

   d. **Minimize the Parrot.css - Notepad window.**

   e. In the Internet Explorer window, **click the Refresh button.**

   f. **Notice that the visited link text is now black.**

---

4. **Make all links turn dark orange on mouseover.**

   a. **Restore the Parrot.css - Notepad window and press Enter. Type `a:hover{color:#F90;}`**

   b. **Choose File→Save.**

   c. **Minimize the Parrot.css - Notepad window.**

   d. In the Internet Explorer window, **click the Refresh button.** Notice that the links turn dark orange whenever the mouse pointer is moved over them.

---

5. **Underline the links on mouseover.**

   a. **Restore the Parrot.css - Notepad window. Click to the right of the `a:hover{color:#F90;` rule and type `text-decoration:underline;}`**

   b. **Choose File→Save.**

   c. **Minimize the Parrot.css - Notepad window.**

   d. In the Internet Explorer window, **click the Refresh button.** Notice that the links are underlined whenever the mouse pointer is moved over them.

---

6. **Underline and turn the link text to red when activated.**

   a. **Restore the Parrot.css - Notepad window. Click to the right of the `a:hover` rule and press Enter.**

   b. **Type `a:active{color:red; ⇒ text-decoration:underline;}`**

   c. **Choose File→Save.**

   d. **Close the Parrot.css - Notepad window.**

   e. In the Internet Explorer window, **click the Refresh button.** Notice that the links turn red and underlined whenever the mouse pointer is held down over them.

   f. **Close the Internet Explorer window.**

---

7. **In your opinion, do these styles enhance the usability of the links and complement the existing design?**

TOPIC C

Customize Forms

You customized link styles in all user-defined states, thereby providing important feedback to the user about the status of your links. You might want to customize the appearance of your forms. In this topic, you will incorporate your site's color scheme into your form pages.

As you probably know, web forms always look the same by default—gray form controls and white background for input fields. With CSS, you can override these default styles, which allows you to integrate the design of your form pages to your site's established design and color scheme. Customizing your forms effectively can also enhance their usability.

How to Enhance Form Design

Forms, like links, are intended for user interaction, so their usability is critical to a successful design. If the forms are excessively or inappropriately styled, users won't be able to successfully interact with your forms.

Guidelines

To ensure that your styles enhance the usability of your forms:

- The colors you choose should provide enough contrast against your background color.

- Colors should complement your existing color scheme.
- Colors should provide effective cues for users interacting with your form controls.
- Styles that make it difficult for users to identify the form are to be avoided.
- Font sizes that do not make the form input fields excessively large are to be used.
- When you set a font size for an input field, the size of the form field changes to accommodate the size of the text that will be displayed in it.

Example:

The following figure shows a form with styles that enhance the design of the form without detracting from the form's overall usability. Here, both form sections have a one-pixel inset border attached to the `<fieldset>` element, and the input fields have a one-pixel solid black border and gray background. The text in the Personal Info fields are displayed in bold white, and the options in the Select list are displayed in bold black.

These styles do not detract from the usability of the form, and the customized design is arguably more appealing than the default form style.

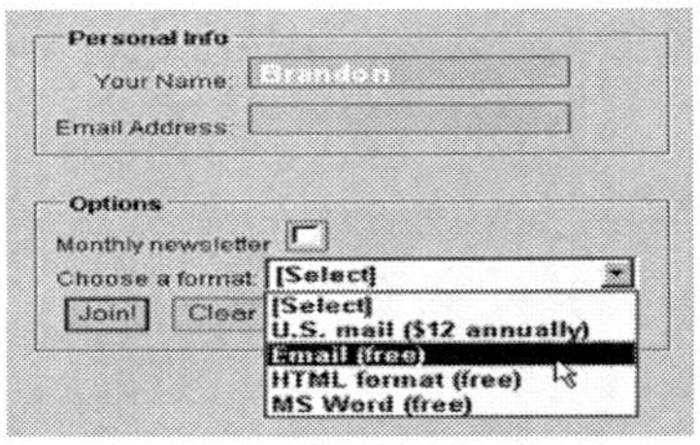

CSS styles applied to form elements

Form Elements

Forms do not have CSS properties of their own. But any CSS styles can be applied to form elements to override their default display and enhance their design. For example, you can:

- Apply background color to input fields.
- Create border around your form controls.
- Reinforce the form field that is receiving the user's focus.
- Apply text and font styles to form text.
- Customize the design of form buttons.

How to Customize Forms

Procedure Reference: Customize Forms

To customize the appearance of your forms:

1. Determine which styles you want to add, and to which form element(s).
2. Apply styles such as color, border, text, and font styles.
3. Save and view the changes.
4. Determine if the form's styles meet the established guidelines.

5. Make any necessary modifications.

ACTIVITY 5-4

Customizing Form Styles

Activity Time:

15 minutes

Data Files:

- custom.html

Before You Begin:

From the C:\085568Data\enhancement\Activity 4\Starter\NewsParrot folder, open the custom.html file in both Netscape Navigator and Internet Explorer. Also, open its source file in Notepad.

Scenario:

The NewsParrot design team wants the My Parrot form page, custom.html, to fit into the color scheme and general design of the other pages on the site. Because the form styles will only apply to this page, you decide to add your styles in the page's embedded style sheet.

The form in its current state is already distinguished from most web forms because you decided to use the `<fieldset>` and `<legend>` elements of HTML 4.0, which allow you to design and organize your form elements logically. The borders around each form section are automatically drawn by the `<fieldset>` element.

What You Do	How You Do It
1. **Give all fieldsets extra padding on all sides.**	a. In the Custom.html - Notepad window, in the embedded style sheet, **click to the right of `<!--` and press Enter. Type `fieldset{padding:10px;}`**
	b. **Choose File→Save.**
	c. **Minimize the Custom.html - Notepad window.**
	d. **Verify the changes in both browsers.** The fieldset elements have extra space inside them to separate the form controls they contain.

2. Modify the fieldset borders to more accurately fit in with the existing color scheme.

   a. Restore the Custom.html - Notepad window. Click to the right of `fieldset {padding:10px;` and type `border: 2px outset #7E92BA;`

   b. Choose File→Save.

   c. Minimize the Custom.html - Notepad window.

   d. Verify the changes in both browsers.

---

3. Modify the color and typography of the legend text to better fit the existing color scheme.

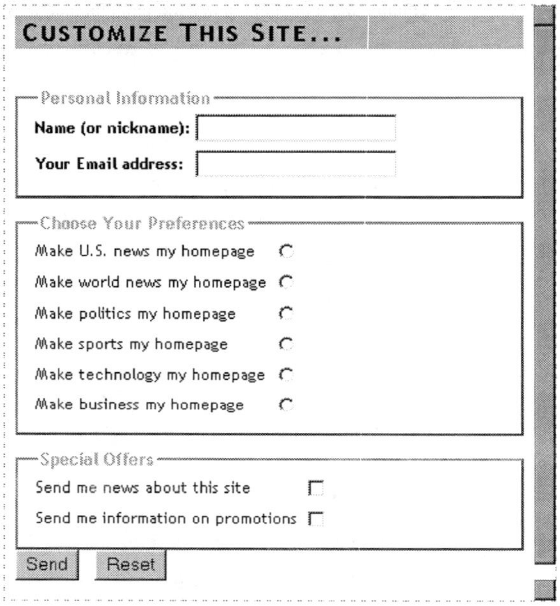

You need to use `legend` as your selector.

   a. Restore the Custom.html - Notepad window. Click to the right of the `fieldset` rule and press Enter.

   b. Type

```
legend{color:#F90;font-weight:⇒
bold;font-size:larger;}
```

   c. Choose File→Save.

   d. Minimize the Custom.html - Notepad window.

   e. Verify the changes in both browsers.

---

4. Change the background and text colors for all form input controls.

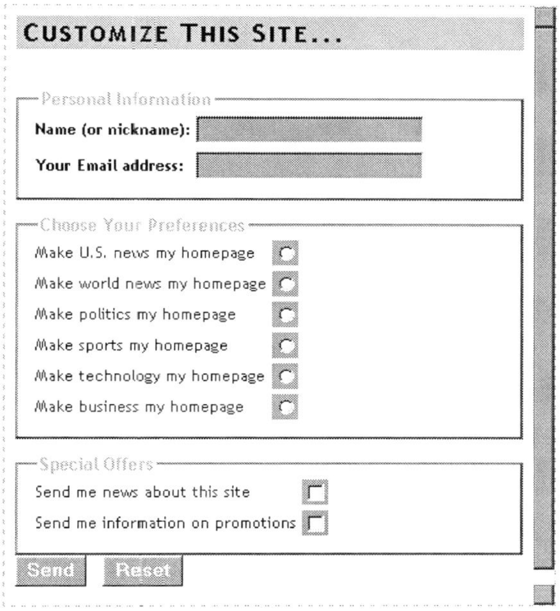

a. Restore the Custom.html - Notepad window and press Enter.

b. Type **`input{color:#fff; ⇒ background-color:#7E92BA; ⇒ font-weight:bold;}`**

c. Choose File→Save.

d. Minimize the Custom.html - Notepad window.

e. Verify the changes in both browsers.

---

5. Give all form controls a small margin and a border.

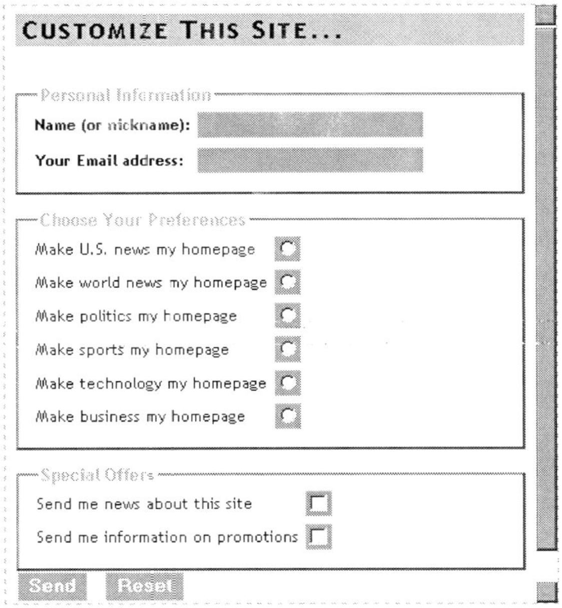

a. Restore the Custom.html - Notepad window. Click to the right of the `input{color:#fff; ⇒ background-color:#7E92BA; ⇒ font-weight:bold;` rule and type **`border:1px solid #F90;margin:1px;`**

b. Choose File→Save.

c. Minimize the Custom.html - Notepad window.

d. Verify the changes in both browsers.

If you explore border styles on form elements, you will likely find that 1-pixel values often work best. Larger border widths can make the forms look odd, and this might detract from the usability of the form.

---

6. **Add space between the buttons and the content above them.**

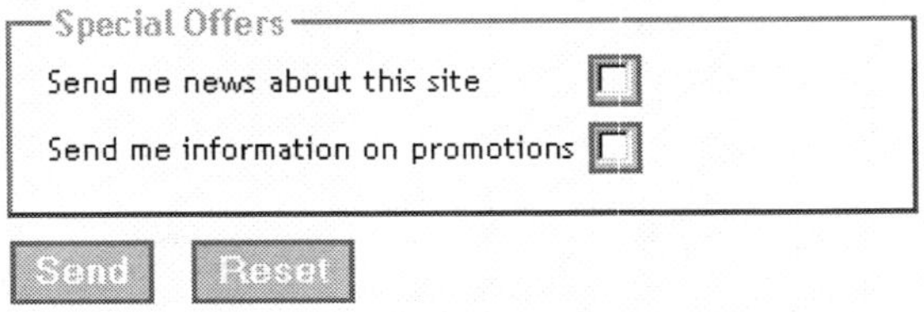

The button code is contained in a `<div id="buttons">` element. Use this ID as your selector.

a. **Restore the Custom.html - Notepad window. Click to the right of the `input` rule and press Enter.**

b. **Type `#buttons{margin-top:10px;}`**

c. **Choose File→Save.**

d. **Minimize the Custom.html - Notepad window.**

e. **Verify the changes in both browsers.**

---

7. **Center the buttons to the content.**

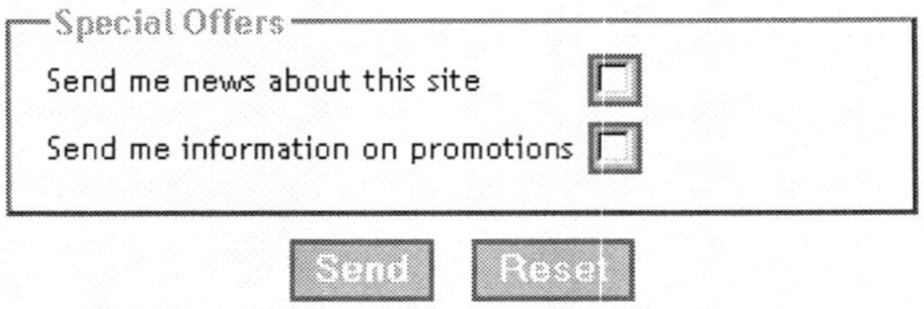

a. **Restore the Custom.html - Notepad window. Click to the right of `#buttons{margin-top:10px;` and type `text-align:center;`**

b. **Choose File→Save.**

c. **Close the Custom.html - Notepad window.**

d. **Verify the changes in both browsers.**

e. **Close both the browsers.**

TOPIC D

Work with Background Images

You customized form designs to match your existing design and color scheme. Background images also play an important role in your website's appearance. In this topic, you will display and manipulate background images to enhance your designs further.

In your experience with HTML, you may have used an image to create a page background. With CSS, you have far greater control over how background images are displayed, and you can also display images behind any page element. With full control over how your background images are displayed, your designs can be enhanced and made effective.

Background Image Styles

Background image styles are a family of properties specific to background images. They are used to control the position of a background image, the horizontal and vertical direction of the image's tiling, and its status against the page canvas, either fixed or scrolling.

The five CSS properties specific to background images are:

- `background-image`, which declares a background image for an element.
- `background-repeat`, which controls the direction of image tiling.
- `background-position`, which controls the precise position of a background image.
- `background-attachment`, which determines if a background image should scroll with page content.
- `background`, which is a shorthand property that declares the other four background image properties at once.

The background-image Property

With the `background-image` property, you can use any image as a background for the entire document or a specific element on a page. The property's value must start with `url`, followed immediately by a parenthesis containing the file name or path to the image, as:

```
body { background-image: url(background.gif); }
```

Background Images on Page Elements

When a background image is declared for any element other than the `<body>` element, the image you insert behind the element will fill the size of the element's set dimensions, no matter how large the image might be. If your image is larger than the element you set it to, any overflowing portions of the image are clipped. The element will not stretch to accommodate the background image.

To get around this, you can use the `height` and `width` properties to set the element to the same size as your image.

Background Images

Using images as the background is a common design technique. Background images are set on the `<body>` element to create an image-based page canvas. With straight HTML, the only background technique you can use is a tiling background, wherein a single image is repeated vertically and horizontally to create a complete background. CSS provides more control over a background image's behavior.

For example, the following figure shows the background image, the large "i" on the right, is positioned precisely on the page and that it does not tile in either direction.

By applying background images with CSS, you can declare images from within your style sheets rather than in your HTML code using `<img>` tags. This reduces the amount of code in the HTML documents and updates the background images in multiple pages by changing a few lines of code.

Background Image Tiling

The way background images repeat behind an element is called tiling. By default, background images tile vertically and horizontally, filling the entire page canvas or element, just as in HTML. With the `background-repeat` property, you can override this default behavior and specifically declare how you want a background image to tile on the page or behind an element.

The background-repeat Property

The `background-repeat` property accepts four values:

- `repeat`
- `no-repeat`
- `repeat-x`
- `repeat-y`

The `repeat` value is the default and the `no-repeat` value prevents the background image from tiling in either direction.

For example:

```
body { background-image: url(ideabg.gif);
background-repeat: no-repeat; }
```

The above code will produce the result shown in the following figure.

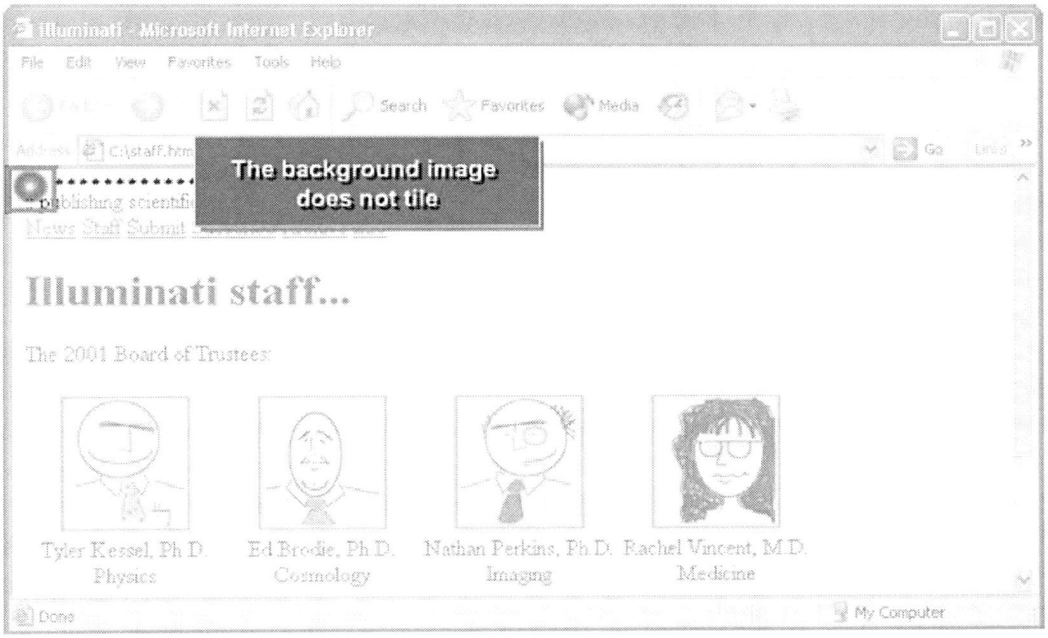

The `repeat-x` value makes a background image repeat horizontally.

For example:

```
body { background-image: url(background.gif);
background-repeat: repeat-x; }
```

The above code will produce the result shown in the following figure.

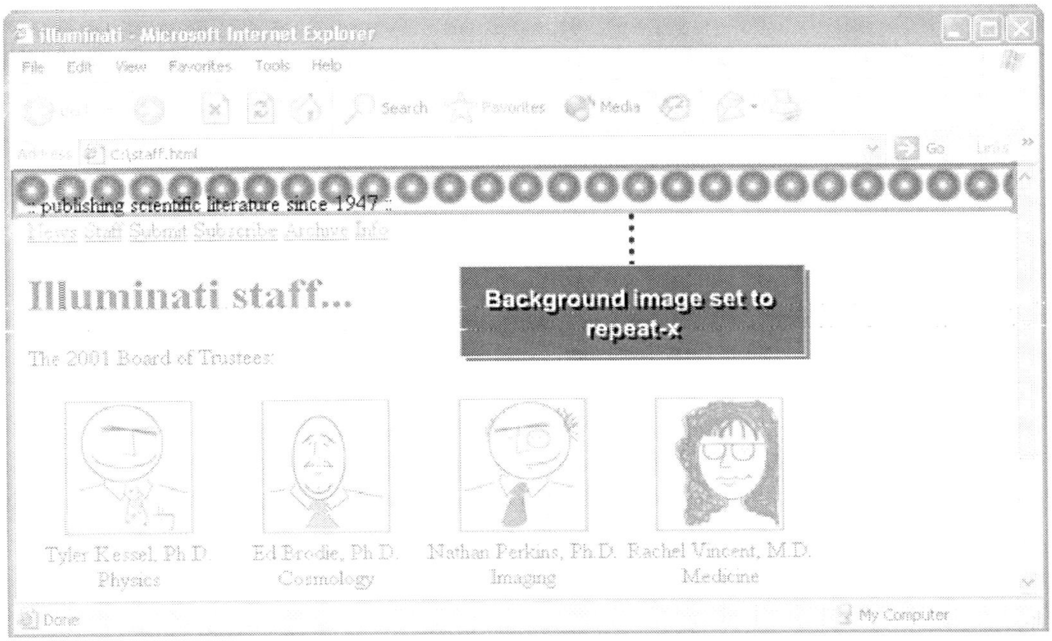

The `repeat-y` value can be used to make a background image repeat vertically.

For example:

```
body { background-image: url(ideabg.gif);
background-repeat: repeat-y; }
```

This code will produce the result shown in the following figure.

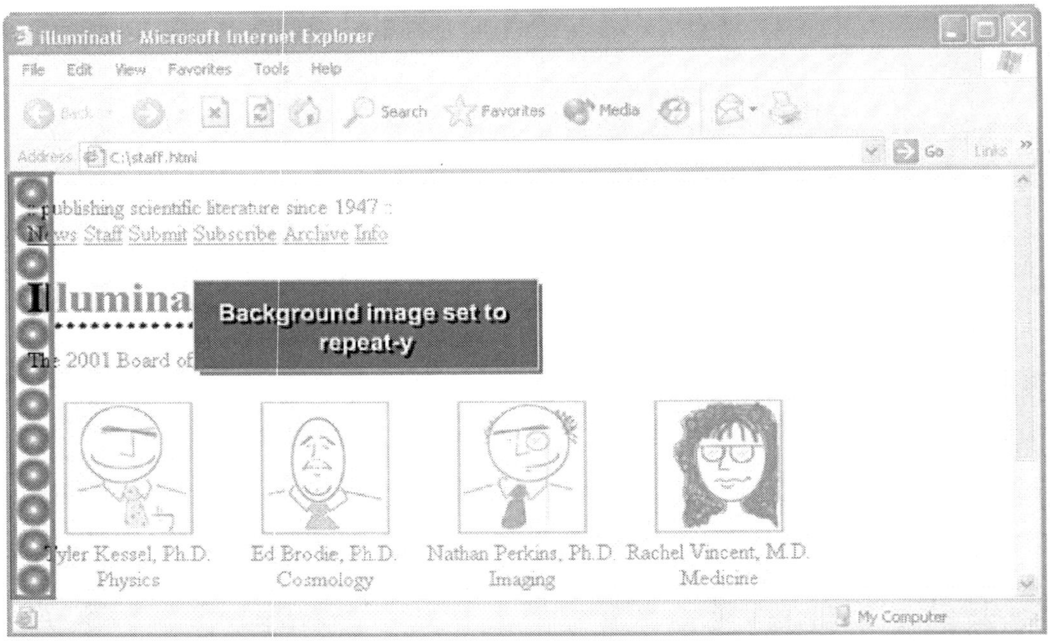

Positioning Background Images

When a background image is set to `no-repeat`, there is only one single image on the page or behind an element. The image can be positioned precisely with the `background-position` property, on the page canvas or behind a particular element on the page.

The position can be specified in either length values, percentages, or the keywords `top`, `right`, `bottom`, `left`, or `center`. These values are specified in pairs representing the horizontal and vertical positions. The first value represents the horizontal position, and the second specifies the vertical position. For example:

```
body { background-image: url(background.gif);
background-repeat: no-repeat;
background-position: 40% 20%; }
```

The preceding rule states that the image be positioned 20% from top and 40% to the left of the page, as shown in the following figure.

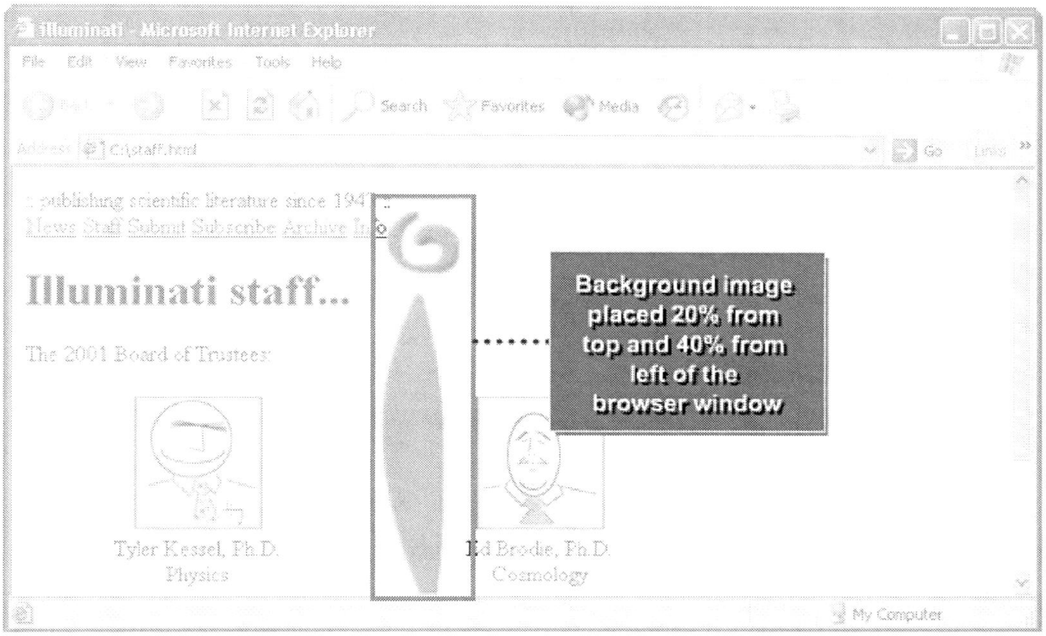

If the horizontal position is the same value as the vertical position, you can simply use one value, as:

```
body { background-image: url(background.gif);
background-repeat: no-repeat;
background-position: 30%; }
```

This rule positions the background image at the center of the page, 30% from the leftmost edge of the <body> element and 30% from the top. The single value 50% will produce the same effect as the keyword `center`. If you choose the keyword `bottom`, the bottom of the image is positioned at the bottom of the page. If you choose the keyword `top`, the top of the image is positioned at the top of the page.

Fixed Background Images

All background images scroll along with the page content. If you want to affix a background image to the page canvas or behind another scrolling element, you can use the `background-attachment` property.

The `background-attachment` property accepts two values: `scroll`, which is the default, and `fixed`, which secures the image to the page canvas or other scrolling element. The image will not move when a user scrolls through the page. As a user scrolls through a document, the elements on the page appear to float above the fixed image.

The background Shorthand Property

The `background` property is a shorthand property that is used to consolidate every property relating to background images. All five background properties are implicit in the shorthand. You can specify values for one property, or all five, in any order. For any value left out, that property's default value is assumed. For example, a rule can be specified as:

```
body { background: url(image.gif) no-repeat fixed 10% 20%; }
```

This is a more efficient way to set the `background-image`, `background-repeat`, `background-attachment`, and `background-position` properties all at once. Each value implies the property it's associated with.

How to Work with Background Images

Procedure Reference: Work with Background Images

To display and manipulate background images:

1. Declare an image for the element using

   ```
   YourElement { background-image: url(YourImage.gif); }
   ```

2. Determine if you want the image to tile and on which direction it should tile.
3. Use the `background-repeat` property to control how the image tiles.
4. Determine if you want to position the element and where on the page you want it to display.
5. Use the `background-position` property to control the image's position on the page or behind an element.
6. If necessary, use the `background-attachment: fixed` property and value if you want to affix the image to the page canvas.
7. Save and verify the changes.

ACTIVITY 5-5

Applying a Background Image

Activity Time:

5 minutes

Data Files:

- archive.html

Before You Begin:

From the C:\085568Data\enhancement\Activity 5\Starter\Illuminati folder, open the archive.html file in both Netscape Navigator and Internet Explorer. Also, open its source file in Notepad.

Scenario:

The Illuminati design team would like to see a background image along one side of the archive.html page. You are given a small background image but haven't been informed on which side of the page the image should tile. From the embedded style sheet in archive.html, you need to declare a background image, dot.gif, on the page canvas and modify its display characteristics.

What You Do	How You Do It
1. **Declare dot.gif as the background image for the page.**	a. In the Archive.html - Notepad window, in the embedded style sheet, **click to the right of `<!--` and press Enter. Type `body{background-image: ⇒ url(dot.gif);}`** b. **Choose File→Save.** c. **Minimize the Archive.html - Notepad window.** d. **Verify the changes in both browsers.** The default tiling looks inappropriate.
2. **Make the image tile vertically.** 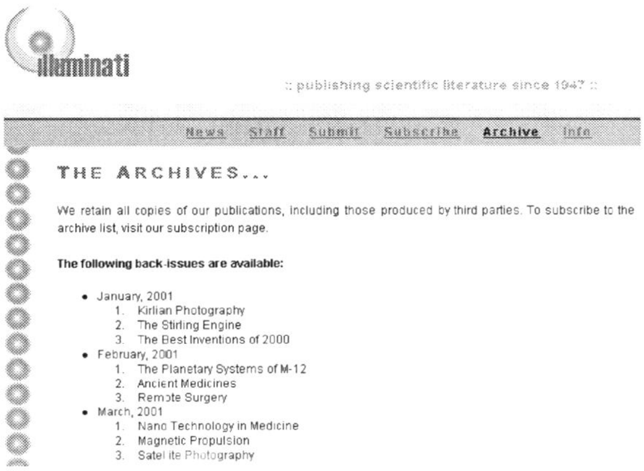	a. **Restore the Archive.html - Notepad window. Click after `body{background-image: ⇒ url(dot.gif);` and type `background-repeat:repeat-y;`** b. **Choose File→Save.** c. **Close the Archive.html - Notepad window.** d. **Verify the changes in both browsers.** e. **Close both the browsers.**

If you make the image tile horizontally, the background image will be partially obscured behind the illuminati logo.

3. **Why is the background image hidden behind the logo and link sections?**

To make a background image display behind the elements on a page, those elements must either have no background color or the transparent background color value.

ACTIVITY 5-6

Displaying a Positioned Background Image

Activity Time:

10 minutes

Data Files:

- archive.html

Before You Begin:

From the C:\085568Data\enhancement\Activity 6\Starter\Illuminati folder, open the archive.html file in both Netscape Navigator and Internet Explorer. Also, open its source file in Notepad.

Scenario:

The Illuminati project team has decided that the tiled background image idea doesn't adequately reinforce the Illuminati identity, and has sent you back to the drawing board. You decide to use a different image, watermark.gif, and position it at the right-center of the page, an area with available white space. You also decide that the watermark image should always be displayed, even if the document is scrolled.

What You Do	How You Do It
1. **Replace the current image with the watermark.gif image.**	a. In the Archive.html - Notepad window, in the `body` rule, **select `dot.gif` and choose Edit→Delete.**
	b. **Type `watermark.gif`**
	c. **Choose File→Save.**
	d. **Minimize the Archive.html - Notepad window.**
	e. **Verify the changes in both browsers.**

2. **Prevent the image from tiling.**

a. **Restore the Archive.html - Notepad window.** In the `body` rule, **select `repeat-y`.**

b. **Choose Edit→Delete and type `no-repeat`**

c. **Choose File→Save.**

d. **Minimize the Archive.html - Notepad window.**

e. **Verify the changes in both browsers.** Notice that the image is partially obscured.

---

3. **Position the image in the center of the page canvas.**

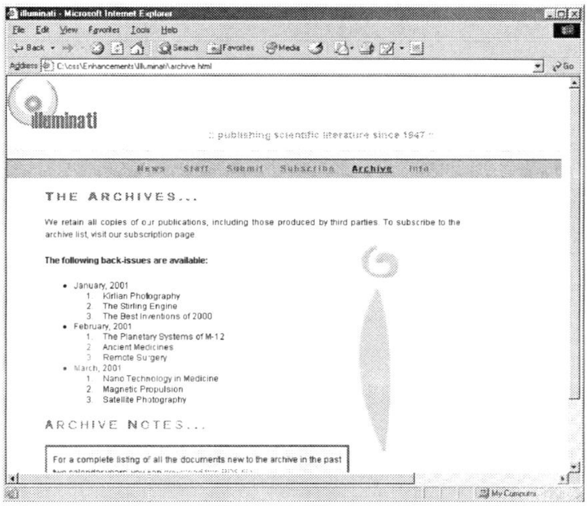

a. **Restore the Archive.html - Notepad window.** In the `body` rule, **click after `no-repeat;` and type `background-position: 5in 2.5in;`**

b. **Choose File→Save.**

c. **Minimize the Archive.html - Notepad window.**

d. **Verify the changes in both browsers.**

4. **Prevent the image from scrolling with the document.**

   a. **Restore the Archive.html - Notepad window. Press Enter and type** **`background-attachment:fixed;`**

   b. **Choose File→Save.**

   c. **Close the Archive.html - Notepad window.**

   d. **Verify the changes in both browsers.** Notice that the image does not scroll with the document because it's fixed on the canvas.

   e. **Close both the browsers.**

   You might need to decrease the size of your browser window to enable the page's scroll bar.

TOPIC E

Customize Lists

You controlled the display of background images and modified their display characteristics to create a more effective visual impact for your users. You might need to customize the lists your site contains. In this topic, you will customize the appearance of lists using properties meant specifically for them.

You can specify the list labels you want to display by using HTML attributes. However, using CSS allows you to control list styles in ways that HTML can't. Perhaps most importantly, controlling the display of your lists with CSS rather than HTML allows you to reduce the amount of code and update your list styles quickly and easily.

List Styles

List styles are CSS properties that are used to present ordered, hierarchical information like indices, definitions, and tables of content. There are three list style properties targeting the list item labels, such as the bullets or alphanumeric characters that define the list items in both ordered and unordered lists:

- The `list-style-type` property allows you to specify one of 10 label (bullet) types.
- The `list-style-position` property allows you to control where your list labels are displayed.
- The `list-style-image` property allows you to use images as list labels.

To customize the design of HTML lists, you can use the three list-specific properties, as well as any other CSS property that controls text-based elements, including the box properties, text and font properties, color properties, and positioning.

The list-style-type Property

With the `list-style-type` property, you can specify the type of label you want your ordered or unordered list to have. Following are the keywords that you can use.

Keyword	Label Description
`disc`	Displays standard, solid bullets.
`circle`	Displays circular labels.
`square`	Displays square labels.
`decimal`	Displays sequential, integer values.
`lower-alpha`	Displays sequential, lowercase letters.
`upper-alpha`	Displays sequential, uppercase letters.
`lower-roman`	Displays sequential, lowercase roman numerals.
`upper-roman`	Displays sequential, uppercase roman numerals.
`none`	No list item labels are displayed.

It makes sense to reserve the `disc`, `circle`, and `square` values for unordered lists and the other values for ordered lists, to retain the intended structure and visual meaning of the list.

The list-style-image Property

With the `list-style-image` property, you can apply images as list labels. The syntax for this property's values is the same as other image-embedding properties in CSS; first the property, then `url`, followed immediately by parentheses containing the location or file name of the image, as:

```
ul { list-style-image: url(image.gif); }
```

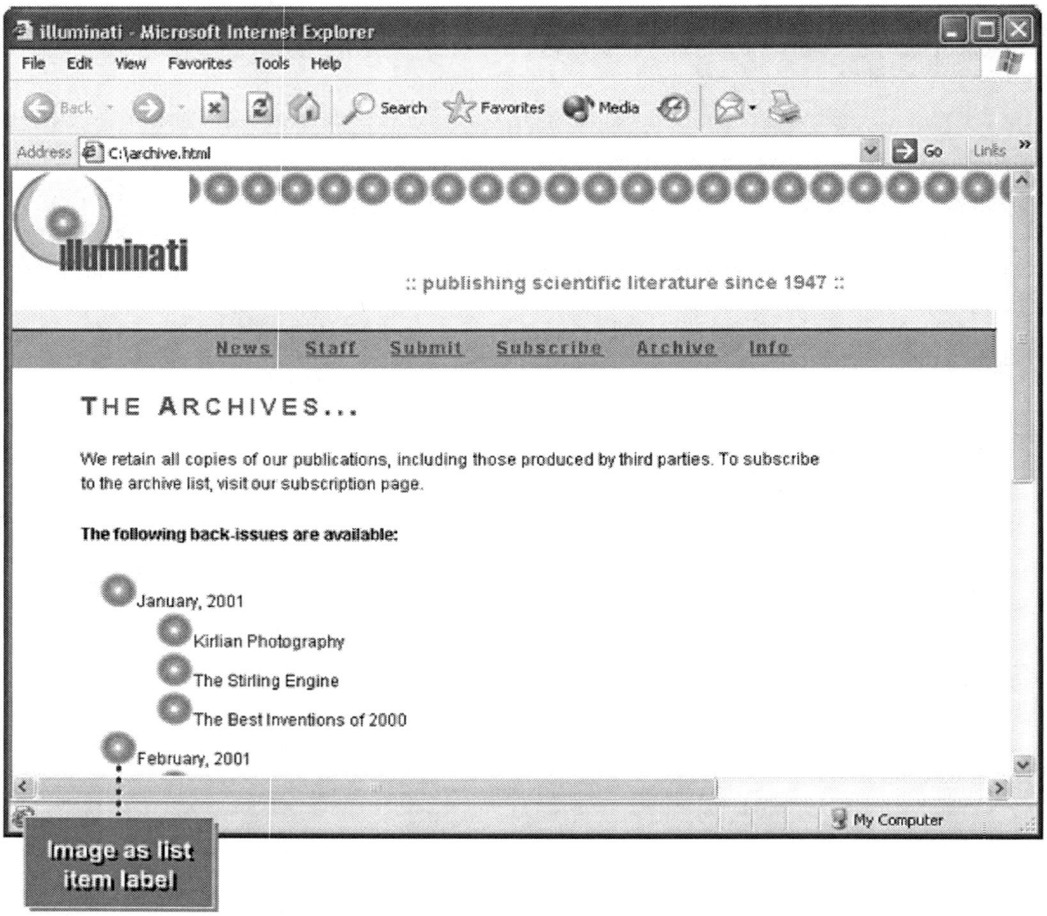

The list-style-position Property

The `list-style-position` property accepts two values: `inside` and `outside`. The `outside` value is the default. Every list item creates a box, just like other elements. Normally, a list item's label is displayed just outside of this box, to the left. To display the label inside the list item's box, you can use the `inside` value. The following figure shows an example of both positions. When a list item is positioned inside, any text that runs to a new line will start at the same point that the label starts.

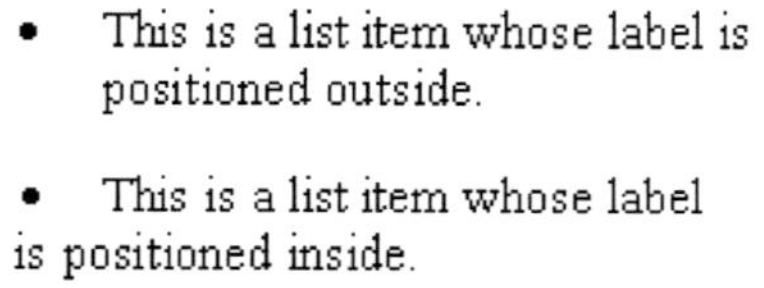

The list-style Shorthand Property

The `list-style` is another shorthand property that combines `list-style-type`, `list-style-position`, and `list-style-image` in one property. As with other shorthand properties, the values of the `list-style` shorthand property are separated by a space, as follows:

```
ol { list-style: url(image.gif) lower-roman outside; }
```

You may want to specify both an image label and a built-in label type. If a browser doesn't support the `list-style-image` property, it will display your second choice instead.

How to Customize Lists

Procedure Reference: Customize Lists

To customize the design of HTML lists:

1. Determine how you want to customize your list(s).
2. Use any of the three list-specific properties to customize the appearance of the bulleted lists.
3. Use any other CSS property that acts on text to customize the appearance of the list text.
4. Verify the results.

ACTIVITY 5-7

Styling Lists

Activity Time:

10 minutes

Data Files:

- archive.html
- folder.gif

Before You Begin:

From the C:\085568Data\enhancement\Activity 7\Starter\Illuminati folder, open the archive.html file in both Netscape Navigator and Internet Explorer. Also, open its source file in Notepad.

Scenario:

You're almost finished with the design proof for the Illuminati site project. You are, however, asked to make a few modifications to the site's styles. Because there's only one page—archive.html—on the Illuminati site that contains a list, you decide to use an embedded style sheet. You are asked to apply the following styles:

- Make the list item text bold.
- Use the folder.gif image for unordered list item labels.

What You Do	How You Do It
1. **Bold the `<ul>` element.** Note that the unordered list contains separate ordered lists. This will have an effect on your list styles.	a. In the Archive.html - Notepad window, in the embedded style sheet, **click to the right of `<!--` and press Enter.** b. **Type `ul{font-weight:bold;}`** c. **Choose File→Save.** d. **Minimize the Archive.html - Notepad window.** e. **Verify the changes in both the browsers.** All the lists display in bold text because the `<ul>` element contains the `<ol>` element and, since the style is attached to the parent element, it inherits through the other list elements `<ol>` and `<li>`.

2. **How can you make only the unordered list item text display in bold and the ordered list text in normal?**

What You Do	How You Do It
3. **Disable the bold style on the ordered list text.**	a. **Restore the Archive.html - Notepad window and press Enter.** b. **Type `ol{font-weight:normal;}`** c. **Choose File→Save.** d. **Minimize the Archive.html - Notepad window.** e. **Verify the changes in both browsers.** The ordered list is displayed with normal text.

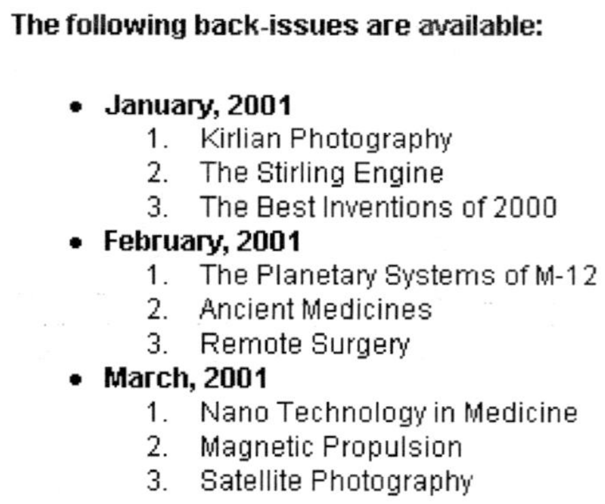

4. **Use the folder.gif image as the label for unordered list items.**

   a. **Restore the Archive.html - Notepad window.** In the `ul` rule, **click to the right of `font-weight:bold;` and type `list-style-image:url(folder.gif);`**

   b. **Choose File→Save.**

   c. **Minimize the Archive.html - Notepad window.**

   d. **Verify the changes in both browsers.** The image is displayed as the label for all the list items for the same reason that the bold style was applied to the entire list—inheritance.

---

5. **Turn off the image labels for ordered list items.**

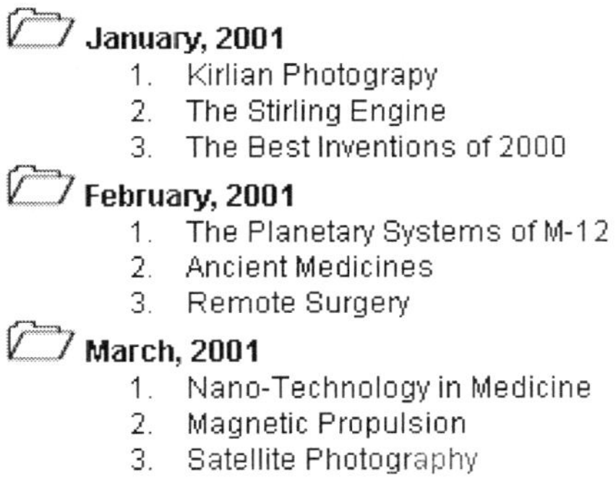

   a. **Restore the Archive.html - Notepad window. Click to the right of `ol{font-weight:normal;` and type `list-style-image:none;`**

   b. **Choose File→Save.**

   c. **Close the Archive.html - Notepad window.**

   d. **Verify the changes in both browsers.**

   e. **Close both browsers.**

TOPIC F

Create Generated Content

You customized HTML lists. Using CSS list attributes reduces the amount of code and updates your list styles quickly and easily. There may be occasions when you need to add ancillary content to your site pages but you don't have the time or resources to add new content to all the HTML documents in your site. In this topic, you will generate content from a style sheet.

By specifying content from a style sheet rather than individual HTML documents, the task of updating a website can be completed in a fraction of the time it would otherwise require. You will also have much less code in your HTML documents, so your pages will load faster. For example, you can display images without having to clog up your documents with `<img>` tags. You can also include text content to provide cues or other information to users without having to edit any HTML.

Generated Content

A generated content is text or images that is specified directly from a style sheet. The content itself is not defined in an HTML document. The generated content allows you to:

- Display text content before and/or after an element.
- Display an image before and/or after an element.
- Display quotation marks before and after an element.

Generated content is supported in Netscape 6 and Opera 5. It is not supported in Internet Explorer 6.

For example, the following figure, which is not specified in the HTML using the `<img>` tag, shows an image at the end of the text. The image is declared in the document's style sheet as generated content.

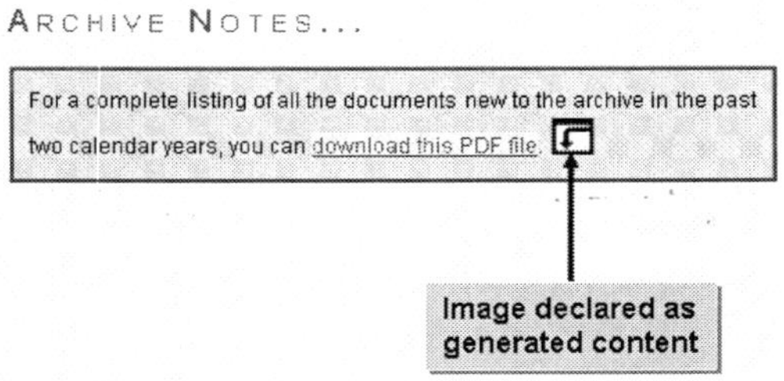

Creating Generated Content

The `content` property specifies the content you want to display before and/or after an element. To specify that the content should come before or after the target element, you use the `:before` or `:after` pseudo-element. Specifications for elements that are recognized only by CSS are called pseudo-elements. The syntax is the same as for pseudo-classes:

```
selector:pseudo-element { property: value; }
```

You can also combine classes with pseudo-elements, as:

```
selector.class:pseudo-element { property: value; }
```

The `:before` and `:after` pseudo-elements only apply to generated content, and are valid in conjunction with the `content` property.

The CSS-2 specification includes many other generated content properties that are not currently supported in any browser such as the 6.0 generation of Internet Explorer and Netscape.

To display an image before an element, your rule would be:

```
element:before { content: url(image.gif);
```

If you need to control the quotation marks for certain elements, there are four predefined keywords that you can use:

- `open-quote`
- `close-quote`
- `no-open-quote`
- `no-close-quote`

To make paragraphs display in quotation marks, your rules would follow this syntax:

```
p:before { content: open-quote; }
p:after { content: close-quote; }
```

Keyword values cannot be enclosed in quotes. The effect of the preceding rules is shown in the following figure.

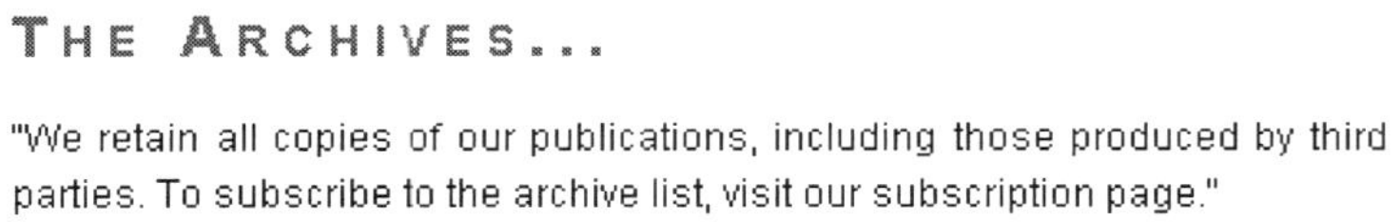

To display a string of text, the value of the `content` property must be enclosed in quotes, as:

```
p.note:before { content: "NOTE:"; }
```

This rule declares that all paragraphs of the class "note" should display with the word "NOTE:" before the paragraph element's text. If you then want to add style to this generated content, you can add any text or font property after the `content` property as:

```
p.note:before { content: "NOTE:";
 color: navy;
font-weight: bold; }
```

Generated content inherits the styles of the element it's associated with.

How to Create Generated Content

Procedure Reference: Create Generated Content

To create generated content:

1. Determine what content you want to display before or after a page element.
2. Determine if you want the content to appear before or after the element, or both.
3. In the style sheet, use the `:before` and `:after` pseudo-elements to declare where the content should be displayed.

4. Use the `content` property to define the content you want to display.
5. Apply any additional style rules to the generated content.
6. Save and view the changes.

ACTIVITY 5-8

Creating Generated Content

Activity Time:

5 minutes

Data Files:

- index.html
- parrot.css

Before You Begin:

From the C:\085568Data\enhancement\Activity 8\Starter\NewsParrot folder, open the index.html file in Netscape Navigator. Also, open the parrot.css file.

Scenario:

The NewsParrot design team has a few more design instructions for you. From the parrot.css style sheet, you need to specify a small image, icon.gif, before all links in the Other Headlines section. This will help distinguish individual links from among link text that often spans multiple lines. You also need to enhance the *current* link style for Netscape users by specifying an asterisk (*) before all links that represent the currently loaded page. To save time, you decide to achieve these design enhancements using generated content.

What You Do	How You Do It
1. **Display the icon.gif image before all links in the Other Headlines section.**	a. In the Parrot.css - Notepad window, **click to the right of `/* Global Styles */` and press Enter two times.**
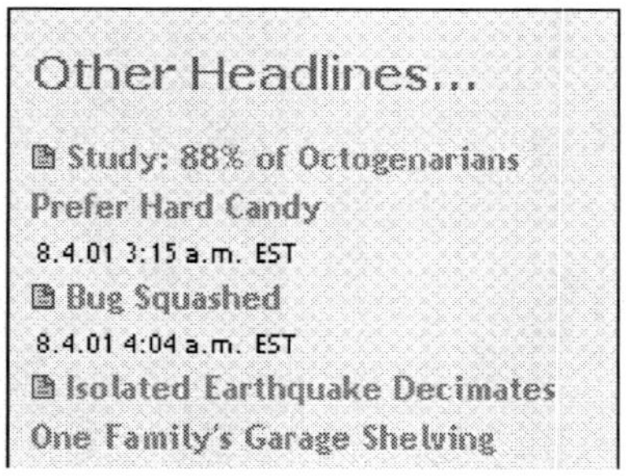	b. **Type `.other:before{content:url ⇒ (icon.gif);}`**
	c. **Choose File→Save.**
	d. **Minimize the Parrot.css - Notepad window.**
	e. In the Netscape Navigator window, **click the Reload button.**
The classes that style these links have already been entered in index.html.	f. **Notice that the icon.gif image is displayed before each news story.**

2. **Display an asterisk before all current links in the Main navigation box.**

   Note that the asterisk inherits the existing color style for the current link.

   a. **Restore the Parrot.css - Notepad window and press Enter. Type** `a.current:before{content: "* ";}`

   b. **Choose File→Save.**

   c. **Close the Parrot.css - Notepad window.**

   d. In the Netscape Navigator window, **click the Reload button.**

   e. **Notice that the current link is displayed with a generated asterisk.**

   f. **Close the Netscape Navigator window.**

Lesson 5 Follow-up

In this lesson, you enhanced an existing design by incorporating all web content into your design scheme, and by providing visual cues to help users access and understand the content. With these techniques, you can greatly enhance user experience and make your website more engaging and accessible.

1. **For a project you are currently involved in or one that you have in mind, what styles will you apply to make the content in the site more accessible?**

2. **Find a website that does not effectively incorporate all of its content into its existing design, and describe how you will improve it?**

Notes

LESSON 6

Creating Alternate Style Sheets

Lesson Time
1 hour(s), 10 minutes

Lesson Objectives:

In this lesson, you will create alternate style sheets, and link your pages to them to enhance the accessibility and functionality of your websites.

You will:

- Create and enable an alternate style sheet to enhance accessibility.
- Create an alternate style sheet that applies a user's system font and color settings.
- Create a print style sheet.

Introduction

You enhanced an existing web design by incorporating content and by providing visual cues to help the users access and understand the provided content. You can also include a style sheet that can be enabled or disabled by users. In this lesson, you will create alternate style sheets that users can select for more personalized viewing.

By creating alternate style sheets, you take your designs beyond the author-control level, and into the hands of your users. You can significantly improve the usability and accessibility of your websites by allowing users to choose alternate style sheets with features such as larger text, or user-defined system fonts and colors.

TOPIC A

Create Accessible Style Sheets

You enhanced an existing design and provided visual cues to help users access the content. Many users prefer to modify certain aspects of design to suit personal needs. In this topic, you will link pages to alternate style sheets that users can choose to activate.

By providing alternatives to primary style sheets, you can accommodate users for whom accessibility is critical. For example, you can ensure that users with vision problems can easily increase the font size of your text, or provide color options for users who are color-blind. Anything you do to make your website more accessible can help build loyalty among your users, which is critical to the success of any website.

Link Relationships

The relationship between a document and a linked style sheet is called a *link relationship*. A link relationship is defined with the `rel` attribute of the `<link>` tag. Three different relationships, namely, persistent, preferred, and alternate can be defined in a linked style sheet.

Persistent Style Sheets

A style sheet that's always enabled is called the *persistent style sheet*. All style sheets you have created in this course are persistent. A persistent style sheet will apply to a page whenever it's requested. Generally, this relationship is used for style sheets that contain layout rules and any other design aspects that you want applied at all times.

Preferred Style Sheets

The default style sheet that is disabled when a user selects an alternate style sheet is called a *preferred style sheet*. As the designer, it's your preferred style sheet. This relationship is used to establish your preferred styles, which will apply to a page whenever it is requested, and can only be disabled if a user selects an alternate style sheet.

Alternate Style Sheets

An *alternate style sheet* is an optional alternative to your site's preferred style sheet that the user can select. When a user selects an alternate style sheet, the preferred style sheet is disabled but the persistent style sheet remains linked to the document. For example, all layout-specific rules can be in a persistent style sheet, and all font and color rules in a preferred style sheet, which users can disable in favor of an alternate style sheet that changes the font and color styles.

Creating Link Relationships

- To create a relationship between a document and a persistent style sheet, you can write:

```
<link rel="stylesheet" type="text/css" href="MyStyles.css">
```

- To establish a relationship to a preferred style sheet, you have to give it a title using the `title` attribute in the `<link>` tag, as follows:

```
<link rel="stylesheet" type="text/css" href=
"MyDefaultStyles.css"title="Default Styles">
```

- To establish a relationship between a document and an alternate style sheet, you can use the `rel` attribute with the value `alternate` style sheet, and then give the style sheet a title, for example:

```
<link rel="alternate stylesheet" type="text/css" href=
"alternate.css" title="MyTitle">
```

There's no limit to the number of `<link>` tags you can include in a document. For example, if you want a document to link to a persistent style sheet, a preferred style sheet, and an optional alternate style sheet, you should include three `<link>` elements in the head section of your document, as follows:

```
<link rel="stylesheet" type="text/css" href="persistent.css">

<link rel="stylesheet" type="text/css" href="preferred.css" title=
"MyTitle">

<link rel="alternate stylesheet" type="text/css" href="alternate.css"
title="MyTitle">
```

Alternate and preferred style sheets must be titled using the `title` attribute. In terms of code, the only difference between a preferred style sheet and a persistent style sheet is that a persistent style sheet cannot be titled.

Accessible Style Sheets

An *accessible style sheet* is any style sheet, typically an alternate style sheet, that provides users with viewing options. These options might include larger text for users who might need it, or a simplified color scheme.

Accessible style sheets can include any number of styles specifically meant to improve the usability of your site. For example, users with vision problems often prefer to read text in a larger font, or a color scheme that provides optimal contrast. Many users who require such style modifications set viewing preferences in their browser.

When users make such changes in their browser settings, it's up to you to determine if their change will have the desired effect. For example, if the font sizes are declared with absolute units of measurement, users will not be able to adjust the size of your text. To ensure that text is accessible, relative units of measurement can be used in the primary style sheet, or an alternate style sheet that uses relative units of measurement should be created.

The styles created in accessible style sheets should be at least partly based on an analysis of your target audience.

How to Create Accessible Style Sheets

When you create an alternate style sheet for purposes of accessibility, you should try to make sure that you meet at least the most common accessibility requirements. Perhaps the most common need among users who require alternate style sheets is larger text. Other users might prefer a simplified color scheme that uses high-contrast colors. Simply by specifying a persistent, preferred, and alternate style sheet, you're already taking a big step toward accessibility.

Guidelines

To ensure that your alternate style sheets successfully integrate accessible styles:

- Use relative units of measurement when specifying font sizes, to ensure that all browsers can scale the size of your text.
- Be consistent with your units of measurement to ensure that the visual relationships between the structures of your text elements are retained; for example, headings larger than paragraphs, subheadings smaller than headings, etc.
- Avoid using colors of similar value, particularly schemes involving red, green, brown, gray, and purple, as color blind users will have a difficult time distinguishing between them.
- Use a high-contrast color scheme. Color schemes involving blue, yellow, white, and black can also help ensure that color blind or other visually impaired users can distinguish between content sections using these colors.

Example:

The style sheet rules with relative units of measurement provide a higher level of accessibility than the style sheet rules containing absolute values.

For example:

```
p, div { font-size: 100%; }
h1 { font-size: 300%; }
h2 { font-size:200%; }
```

The preceding style sheet rule has units of measurement that provide a level of accessibility not provided by absolute values.

When you use an alternate style sheet for accessibility enhancements, it's important that you provide some indication that an alternate style sheet is available, and that this notice is prominently displayed.

ACTIVITY 6-1

Creating and Enabling an Alternate Style Sheet

Activity Time:

10 minutes

Data Files:

- index.html
- large_text.css

Before You Begin:

From the C:\085568Data\alternates\Activity 1\Starter\Project folder, open the index.html file both in Netscape Navigator and Internet Explorer. Also, open its source file in Notepad.

Scenario:

Your client, NewsParrot news service, has informed you that the site must be accessible to users in special-needs situations. They want users to be able to increase the size of text without having to rely on the browser's settings, which many users are not aware of. You decide to solve the problem by creating an alternate style sheet to complement the consistent NewsParrot style sheet.

A developer on your project team has provided you with a JavaScript code that allows users to set their reading preferences directly from the NewsParrot home page, index.html, and sets a cookie on the users' machine so that their preferences are stored for future visits. The developer has also provided instructions for implementing the script:

- Make sure you give any alternate style sheets a title, using the `title` attribute in your `<link>` tag(s).
- Enter the following code as the value of the `href` attribute in the `prefs` link tags:

  javascript:setActiveStyleSheet('*YourTitle*');

What You Do	How You Do It
1. **Create a new link relationship to the existing style sheet, large_text.css.** This version of the page includes a new content box in the upper-right corner. These links will eventually allow users to select their preferred text for reading content in the main section.	a. In the Index.html - Notepad window, **click after the `link` element and press Enter.** b. **Type `<link rel="alternate stylesheet" type="text/css" href="large_text.css">`** c. **Choose File→Save.**

2. Rename the style sheet to Large Text.	a.	Click after `<link rel="alternate stylesheet" type="text/css" href="large_text.css"` and press Spacebar. Type `title="Large Text"`
	b.	Choose File→Save.
	c.	Minimize the Index.html - Notepad window.
3. Select the alternate style sheet in Netscape Navigator.	a.	Restore the Netscape Navigator window and click the Reload button.
	b.	Choose View→Use Style→Large Text.
	c.	Notice that the alternate style sheet contains a larger font size for the main content section.
	d.	Close the Netscape Navigator window.

4. **Make the two link tags in the prefs section activate their indicated style sheet.**

a. **Restore the Index.html - Notepad window.**

b. **Scroll down** to view the `<div id="prefs">` rule.

c. In the first `a` element, **select # and choose Edit→Delete.**

d. **Type `javascript:setActiveStyleSheet⇒('default');`**

e. In the second `a` element, **select # and choose Edit→Delete.**

f. **Type `javascript:setActiveStyleSheet⇒('Large Text');`**

g. **Choose File→Save.**

h. **Close the Index.html - Notepad window.**

i. In the Internet Explorer window, **click the Refresh button** and, on the top-right corner of the window, **click the Large Text link.**

j. **Notice that the font face and font size change.**

k. **Close the Internet Explorer window.**

TOPIC B

Apply User-Defined System Fonts and Colors

You created alternate style sheets and linked pages to them, thereby, accommodating the varying needs of your web audience. Some users set their own computer environments with preferential font and color settings. In this topic, you will create an alternate style sheet that applies a user's system fonts and color styles.

Providing an alternate style sheet that applies a user's system fonts and colors allows you to accommodate users with visual disabilities, or users who prefer to read text in familiar formats and colors. As with other accessibility options, users who view your pages using their own system settings are likely to appreciate being given the option, which can help build site loyalty.

System Fonts and Colors

System fonts and colors are preferences that users can set directly in their computers, so that they can view the contents with fonts and colors that suit their individual needs. There are several predefined system color keywords that can be used with either the `color` or `background-color` property.

The following table lists some of the useful system color keywords and a brief description of their associated system element.

Keyword Value	Description
`Background`	Applies the user's desktop background color.
`ActiveCaption`	Applies the color used in the active window caption.
`WindowText`	Applies the color used for all window text.
`ButtonText`	Applies the color used for button text.
`Window`	Applies the color used for window backgrounds.
`InfoBackground`	Applies the background color used for tooltips.
`InfoText`	Applies the color used for tooltip controls.
`MenuText`	Applies the color used for text in menus.
`Icon`	Applies the color used for all window icons.

System Colors

Some of the predefined keywords and their associated window elements can be explored in the Display Properties dialog box in a Windows-based PC. You just have to right-click anywhere on your desktop and choose Properties. In the Display Properties dialog box, select the Appearance tab, and observe the sample windows provided to preview changes to the system display settings. All aspects of the Windows workspace are customizable through this dialog box.

With the Item drop-down list, users can change the size and color of a Windows element, and the font and text color for text-based options. These system settings can be modified by users to meet their accessibility needs.

The High Contrast schemes are preset color and font settings for users with vision impairment; these are perfect schemes to test your styles with.

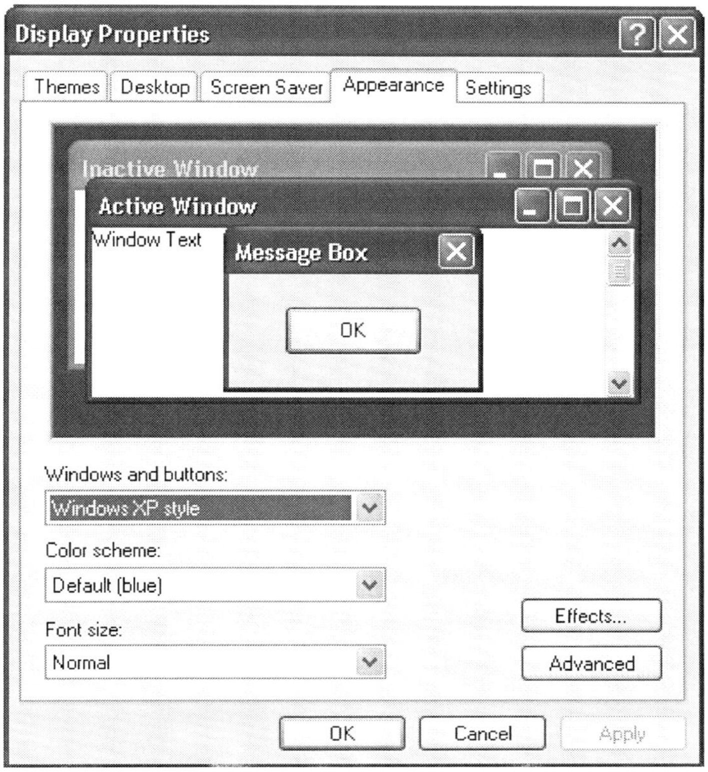

To apply system colors to an alternate style sheet, your rules will be as:

```
body { background-color: Background;

color: WindowText; }

p { background-color: InfoBackground;

color: Infotext; }
```

All system color and font values are case insensitive, but for those values that consist of multiple, non-hyphenated words, using lead caps can help you and other developers read the values. These values are proprietary to Windows.

System Fonts

To declare system fonts, you can use the `font` shorthand, as no other font property is valid for system styles. There is also a more limited palette of keyword choices available with system fonts.

To apply system fonts to an alternate style sheet, your rules might look like this:

```
body { font: menu; }

p { font: caption; }
```

The following table lists the system font keyword values with a description of each.

Keyword Value	Description
`caption`	The font used for captioned controls such as buttons, drop-downs, etc.
`icon`	The font used to label icons.
`menu`	The font used in menus like drop-down lists and menu lists.
`message-box`	The font used in dialog boxes.
`small-caption`	The font used for labeling small controls.
`status-bar`	The font used in window status bars.

How to Apply User-Defined System Fonts and Colors

Procedure Reference: Apply User-Defined System Fonts and Colors

To apply system fonts and colors:

1. Determine which elements or content sections are best suited for system color and font settings.
2. Set both the foreground and background colors for each element if you want to apply system colors.

   Use a system color value reference similar to the preceding table. You can view the complete list of system color values on the official CSS-2 specification, at **http://www.w3.org/TR/REC-CSS2/**.

3. Set your system font values with the `font` shorthand property.
4. Verify and test the changes (on the Windows platform).

   In the Display Properties dialog box, select a few schemes and test each one by applying it on a page and reloading the page in your browser. With each system style change, explore your pages thoroughly to make sure your elements are effectively styled.

ACTIVITY 6-2

Applying System Styles to an Alternate Style Sheet

Activity Time:

5 minutes

Data Files:

- index.html
- system.css

Before You Begin:

From the C:\085568Data\alternates\Activity 2\Starter\Project folder, open the index.html file both in Netscape Navigator and Internet Explorer. Also, open its source file in Notepad.

Scenario:

Your client, NewsParrot news service, wants you to accommodate users who prefer to browse web documents using their own font and color settings. You decide to create another alternate style sheet that applies a user's own system of fonts and colors. Toward this end, you have created an external style sheet named system.css. You need to include this style sheet as an alternative on the NewsParrot home page, index.html.

System styles also work in Internet Explorer, but Internet Explorer (as of version 6.0) does not provide a menu option to choose an alternate style sheet.

What You Do	How You Do It
1. **Create another link to the external style sheet, system.css.** Make sure to give the style sheet a relevant title.	a. In the Index.html - Notepad window, **click after the second link element and press Enter.** b. **Type <link rel="alternate stylesheet" href="system.css" title="Use My System Fonts and Colors" type="text/css">** c. **Choose File→Save and then close the Index.html - Notepad window.**

2. In the system.css file, **apply a system color value to the background of both the headings.**

   a. **Navigate to the My Computer\C:\085568Data\alternates\Activity 2\Starter\Project folder and open the system.css file.**

   b. **Type `h1, h2 {background-color:background;}`**

   c. **Choose File→Save.**

   d. **Minimize the System.css - Notepad window.**

   e. In the Netscape Navigator window, **click the Reload button.**

   f. **Choose View→Use Style→Use My System Fonts And Colors.**

   g. **Minimize the Netscape Navigator window.**

3. **Change the font face for the body text and the heading text using a system font value.**

   a. **Restore the System.css - Notepad window.**

   b. **Click after `h1, h2 {background-color:background;` and type `font:caption;`**

   c. **Click after the `h1, h2` rule and press Enter.**

   d. **Type `body {font:message-box;}`**

   e. **Choose File→Save.**

   f. **Close the System.css - Notepad window.**

   g. **Restore the Netscape Navigator window.**

   h. In the Netscape Navigator window, **click the Reload button.**

   i. **Choose View→Use Style→Use My System Fonts And Colors.**

   j. **Notice that the result varies according to the system fonts and styles you have in use.**

   k. **Close the Netscape Navigator window.**

TOPIC C

Create a Print Style Sheet

You applied user-defined system fonts and colors to your designs, to enhance the accessibility of your websites. When printing a web page, sometimes the text is cut off along the margin, or the color in the page bleeds. In this topic, you will create and enable a style sheet that controls the appearance of your web documents when they are printed.

Sometimes, when you print a web page, you find that the text is cut off along the right margin and is rendered useless, or the color used in the page bleeds and wastes your printer ink. By creating a print style sheet, you can ensure that your site prints optimally without any effort on the part of the user.

Print Style Sheets

A *print style sheet* is a style sheet intended to optimize the appearance of a web document when it's printed.

For example, font sizes specified in pixels work great on screen but are meaningless to a printer. The result can be very different than expected. By creating a separate external style sheet for print, you can ensure that the print result is as reliable and consistent as possible. A print style sheet may be like:

```
/* Print Styles */

body { font-size: 14pt;
       background-color: white;
       color: black; }

h1 { font-size: 24pt; }
h2 { font-size: 20pt; }
h3 { font-size: 16pt; }
```

Consider the example of a print style sheet where all font sizes are declared using points—a unit of print measurement, and therefore, a logical and reliable unit of measurement to use. Also, the page background color is set to white and the text color is set to black. This is the best way for text to appear in a print document.

Once an external style sheet is set up with these print-specific rules, you need to make the browser aware of the rules so that the print styles are applied automatically when a user selects the browser's Print command. To do this, you link the document to the print style sheet using the `<link>` element, and include the `media="print"` attribute and value.

Media Types

A variety of target media types can be specified using the `media` attribute. Most of these media types are not currently supported in the 6.0 generation of browsers, but `screen` and `print` values are well supported. The following table lists the various media types and their description.

Media Type	Description
`all`	Declares that your styles are well-suited for all devices.
`aural`	Declares that your styles are intended for a speech synthesizer or for some other audio device.
`braille`	Declares that your styles are intended for a tactile braille device.
`embossed`	Declares that your styles are intended for a braille printer.
`handheld`	Declares that your styles are intended for a handheld device.
`print`	Declares that your styles are intended for traditional printers.
`projection`	Declares that your styles are intended for a projection presentation device.
`screen`	Declares that your styles are intended for a computer screen.
`tty`	Declares that your styles are intended for TTY devices.
`tv`	Declares that your styles are intended for television.

Specifying Print Style Sheets

Once you have created a print style sheet, all you need to do to enable it is include the `media="print"` attribute and value in your `<link>` tag, as:

```
<link rel="stylesheet" type="text/css" href="print.css" media="print">
```

Users won't have to do any extra work to get an optimized printout of the site's pages. The browser will automatically apply your print style sheet behind the scenes whenever a user selects the browser's Print command.

Print style sheets are automatically applied in Internet Explorer 5 and later, and in Netscape 7.1 and later, but this technique does not work in older browsers.

Display and Visibility

You can determine if an element is displayed on a page using the `display` and `visibility` properties. These properties are typically used with scripts to allow users to toggle between displaying and hiding an element, but you can also use them in your print style sheets to hide page content that's unnecessary in print.

The display Property

The `display` property can be used to remove an element that is irrelevant in print. For example, you could remove a navigation bar or other content that is not relevant to the content the user has selected to print. A script is not required to use the `display` property in print style sheets.

The `display` property accepts several values, but only three of them are well supported even in the 6.0 generation of browsers:

- `none`

  This value makes an element disappear and removes it from the document flow.
- `inline`

  This value sets any element to an inline-level display; it will not create its own line breaks.
- `block`

  This value sets any element to a block-level display; it will create its own line breaks.

To turn off the display of an element and remove it from the document flow, your code would be:

```
element { display: none; }
```

The visibility Property

The `visibility` property can be used to remove an element that is irrelevant in print, but keep the space that it occupies. This allows you to hide elements that aren't important or useful in print but retain your original layout and element spacing. A script is not required to use the `visibility` property in print style sheets.

The `visibility` property accepts two values that are well supported:

- `visible`

  This is the default value; an element is rendered normally on the page.
- `hidden`

  This value makes an element transparent. The element still occupies its normal space on the page, but is not visible.

To turn off the visibility of an element, you would write:

```
element { visibility: hidden; }
```

How to Create a Print Style Sheet

Procedure Reference: Create a Print Style Sheet

To create a print style sheet:

1. Create a style sheet and give it a relevant name.
2. Use the `pt` values for the font sizes and set the page background to white with black text.
3. Link your site's documents to the print style sheet using the `<link>` element with the `media="print"` attribute and value.
4. Test the print style sheet by printing it from both Internet Explorer and Netscape.
5. Make changes to the style sheet rules as needed.

ACTIVITY 6-3

Creating a Print Style Sheet

Activity Time:

5 minutes

Data Files:

- index.html
- print.css

Before You Begin:

From the C:\085568Data\alternates\Activity 3\Starter\Project folder, open the index.html file both in Netscape Navigator and Internet Explorer. Also, open its source file in Notepad.

Scenario:

You need to ensure that visitors to the NewsParrot website can print only the optimized pages. In its current state, printing a page may result in text that's too small to read, depending on the user's printer settings. The darker colors on the site might also result in excess use of printer ink, making the text difficult to read in print. Also, several content sections are unnecessary in the print form, such as navigation bars, images, and other ancillary content.

You need to create a print style sheet that solves these problems, and then test your style sheet by printing a page.

What You Do	How You Do It
1. **Create another link to the external style sheet, print.css.**	a. In the Index.html - Notepad window, **click after the third `link` element and press Enter.**
	b. **Type `<link rel="stylesheet" href="print.css" media="print" type="text/css">`**
	c. **Choose File→Save.**
	d. **Close the Index.html - Notepad window.**

2. In the print.css file, **hide the top section but allow the printing of the NewsParrot logo.**	a. **Navigate to the My Computer\C:\085568Data\alternates\Activity 3\Starter\Project folder and open the Print.css file.** b. **Type `#top{visibility:hidden;}` and press Enter.** c. **Type `#top img{visibility:visible;}` and press Enter.** The band of color across the top of the page will not print, but the space it contains will remain blank. The NewsParrot logo will print, however, to reinforce the company's identity.
3. In the main content section, **set the font color to black and the font size appropriate for print.**	a. **Type `#main{font-size:14pt;color:black;}` and press Enter.** b. **Choose File→Save.**
4. **Disable the display of the Other Headlines section, the navigation boxes, and the Top Story image.**	a. **Type `#headlines, #nav, #nav2, #nav3, #main img {display: none;}`** b. **Choose File→Save.** These elements will not print, and the space they would otherwise occupy will collapse. c. **Close the Print.css - Notepad window.**
5. **Reload the NewsParrot's home page and print the current page.** There should be no change in the way the page is displayed in your browser, since the styles only apply in print.	a. In both the browsers, **choose File→Print.** b. **Verify that the print style commands are successful.** c. **Close both the browsers.**

Lesson 6 Follow-up

In this lesson, you created alternate style sheets and linked web pages to them. By allowing users to choose alternate style sheets, you can enhance the accessibility and functionality of your websites.

1. **How would you implement alternate style sheets in your development projects?**

2. **Find a website that does not provide adequate accessibility enhancements and describe what you would do to improve the site's accessibility.**

Follow-up

In this course, you designed websites using CSS. You can now control all facets of web design, including color, typography, and layout. You can successfully separate all your style information from your document structure, precisely control the appearance and layout of your content sections, integrate all element types into your designs, and create alternate style sheets to enhance the accessibility and functionality of your websites.

What's Next?

Now that you've completed the course *Cascading Style Sheets (Third Edition),* you may find it beneficial to expand your web development skills with Element K's course *Web Design and Usability Techniques.* This course will help you identify elements of effective web design, avoid common design pitfalls, and put into practice some of the vital principles of website design and authoring.

Following that, Element K offers three distinct branches of its web designer curriculum path. If you're interested in using an HTML coding application to help automate some aspects of your web development work, try the courses on *Dreamweaver* or *GoLive*. If you're more interested in creating graphics-intensive websites, you should familiarize yourself with the industry-standard graphics editing tool by taking courses on *Photoshop*. Or, if you're looking to build animation-driven websites, you might want to take the courses on *Flash*, *LiveMotion*, or *Director*.

Finally, no matter what type of web development you're interested in, Element K offers the Web Designer Capstone Series—a line of courses designed to help you assess your skills and start you on the road to creating "portfolio-worthy" work on the web. This Capstone Series consists of three courses: *Plan and Create a Web Site, Create and Integrate Web Graphics,* and *Create and Integrate Web Animation,* all of which are designed to help you assess your knowledge in and practice using a distinctive set of your web design skills.

APPENDIX A

The :first-line and :first-letter Pseudo-Classes

CSS-2 introduced `:first-line` and `:first-letter` pseudo-classes. This allows you to target styles to the first letter in a text element and the entire first line of a text element, respectively. You can apply any text or font properties to the first letter or first line of text in an element.

For example, with the `:first-line` pseudo-class, you can create a *lead cap* style that's common in print publications. For example:

```
p:first-letter { font-size: 300%;
             font-family: cursive;
             color: #009; }
```

The above code will produce the following result:

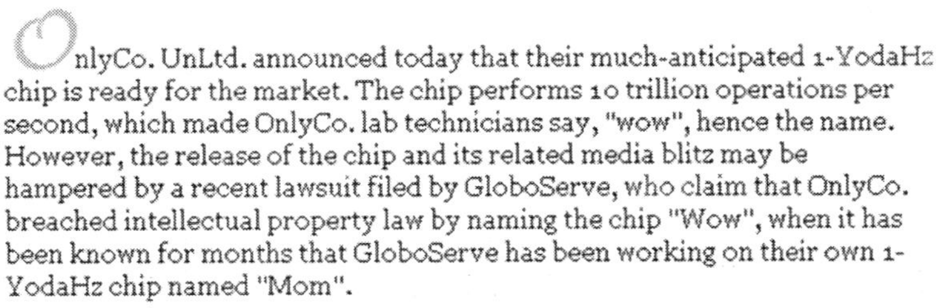

OnlyCo. UnLtd. announced today that their much-anticipated 1-YodaHz chip is ready for the market. The chip performs 10 trillion operations per second, which made OnlyCo. lab technicians say, "wow", hence the name. However, the release of the chip and its related media blitz may be hampered by a recent lawsuit filed by GloboServe, who claim that OnlyCo. breached intellectual property law by naming the chip "Wow", when it has been known for months that GloboServe has been working on their own 1-YodaHz chip named "Mom".

The `:first-line` pseudo-class allows you to attach styles to the entire first line of a text element. For example:

```
p:first-line { font-variant: small-caps;
                             color: #009; }
```

The above code will produce the following result:

ONLYCO. UNLTD. ANNOUNCED TODAY THAT THEIR MUCH-ANTICIPATED 1-YodaHz chip is ready for the market. The chip performs 10 trillion operations per second, which made OnlyCo. lab technicians say, "wow", hence the name. However, the release of the chip and its related media blitz may be hampered by a recent lawsuit filed by GloboServe, who claim that OnlyCo. breached intellectual property law by naming the chip "Wow", when it has been known for months that GloboServe has been working on their own 1-YodaHz chip named "Mom".

The style always applies to the first line of text, no matter how short or long the line is. The first line styles will reflow if the browser window is resized, guaranteeing that your style will always display as you intend.

You can combine pseudo-classes with class selectors, as in `p.ClassName:first-line { your styles }`.

APPENDIX B
The DOCTYPE Switch

The *document type declaration*, or DOCTYPE declaration, declares which version of HTML is used in a document. The HTML *version* refers to the *DTD* in use—the Document Type Definition that defines the rules for the markup. In the 6.0 and later generation of browsers, the version of HTML you declare for a document will determine how it's rendered. There are several DTDs of HTML that you can declare, including older versions of HTML, and HTML frameset for web pages that contain frames.

Forward-compatible web documents use one of the HTML 4.01 and XHTML DOCTYPE declarations, as follows:

- HTML 4.01 Strict:

```
<!DOCTYPE HTML public "-//W3C//DTD HTML 4.01//EN"
"http://www.w3.org/TR/REC-html40/strict.dtd">
```

```
<!DOCTYPE HTML public "-//W3C//DTD HTML 4.01//EN">
```

- HTML 4.01 Transitional:

```
<!DOCTYPE HTML public "-//W3C//DTD HTML 4.01
Transitional//EN">
```

- XHTML 1.0 Strict:

```
<!DOCTYPE HTML PUBLIC "-//W3C//DTD XHTML 1.0 Strict//EN"
"DTD/xhtml1-strict.dtd">
```

```
<!DOCTYPE HTML PUBLIC "-//W3C//DTD XHTML 1.0 Strict//EN">
```

- XHTML 1.0 Transitional:

```
<!DOCTYPE html PUBLIC "-//W3C//DTD XHTML 1.0
Transitional//EN">
```

The DOCTYPE declaration has traditionally been used for validation purposes, but it has taken on a new and more powerful role in the newer, standards-compliant browsers. In Netscape Navigator 7.1, Internet Explorer 5.0 for the Macintosh, and Internet Explorer 6.0 for Windows, you can use the DOCTYPE declaration as a *switch* to enable or disable strict standards compliance. In effect, you tell the browser which *mode* to display your page with—either *backwards-compatible* mode or *quirks* mode for pages designed to older browsers, or the standards-compliant mode.

Internet Explorer 5 (Mac) and 6 (PC) and Netscape Navigator 7.1 all support the `DOCTYPE` switch.

Appendix B

Imagine that you're a webmaster for a large corporation, and you have thousands of documents on your web site. Assume that these documents do not have DOCTYPE declarations, or use transitional or older declarations. The news spreads that the latest browsers have corrected all the wrongly implemented standards in their older browsers. Meanwhile, you and other developers had spent countless hours making your designs work in those older browsers. Your first thought might be, "Well, now we have to go through all those old documents and fix them so they'll display properly in the new browsers." That would obviously be a costly and time consuming endeavor. The DOCTYPE switch precludes the need for any of this extra work. It solves the problem of *legacy* documents in future browsers by keeping the new browsers in the *backwards-compatibility* mode by default.

All the *new* support features of the new browsers are supported by default, no matter what DOCTYPE is in use. Only those elements, attributes, CSS properties, or other features that have been *incorrectly* supported in past browser releases are affected by your DOCTYPE declaration.

The following table describes how standards-compliant browsers will display your document according to the DOCTYPE declaration you use.

DTD	Behavior
No DOCTYPE declaration, or one that is unrecognized or syntactically inaccurate.	If you leave out the DOCTYPE declaration, browsers will render the page in *quirks* mode. So, if you design a page according to strict adherence to the specifications, and then forget to include the appropriate DOCTYPE declaration, your pages might not look the way you intended them to.
HTML 4.01 Transitional	The browser will render the page in *quirks* mode.
HTML 4.01 Strict	The browser will render the page in standards-compliant mode.
XHTML 1.0 Strict	The browser will render the page in standards-compliant mode.

Any declaration of HTML prior to version 4.0, and any frameset declaration, will tell the browser to display the page in quirks mode. Any XML declaration will tell the browser to display the page in standards-compliant mode.

The URL in the DOCTYPE declaration that points to the official DTD on the W3C Web site is an optional feature for all of the DOCTYPE declarations. However, browsers will go into strict mode if a URL is appended to your DOCTYPE declaration—even if you declare the document as transitional and set the URL to the loose DTD.

There are several CSS style interpretations and HTML element and attribute interpretations that are affected by the `DOCTYPE` switch. There are too many to list here, but the following list describes the most common rendering differences.

- *The box model in Internet Explorer, prior to version 6 (PC) and 5 (Macintosh).*

  In these versions of Internet Explorer, an element's specified width incorporates any padding and border widths. According to the CSS specification, any padding and border widths should be added to the specified element width. In standards-compliant mode, Internet Explorer 6 (PC) and 5 (Macintosh) support the box model correctly. In quirks mode, these browsers revert to their old rendering behavior to preserve the layout of existing web documents.

- *Font size keywords in Internet Explorer, prior to version 6 (PC) and 5 (Macintosh).*

In older versions of Internet Explorer, the font-size keyword value `medium` is interpreted incorrectly. According to the specification, this value should be equivalent to the default text size, but `medium` text is larger than default text in these older browsers. In strict mode, Internet Explorer 6 (PC) and 5 (Mac) correct this misinterpretation of the spec; they retain the error in quirks mode.

- *The page canvas.*

  In strict HTML 4.01, the `<html>` element can define the page canvas, in place of the `<body>` element. This wasn't supported until Internet Explorer 5 (Mac) and 6 (PC), and Netscape 6. In standards mode, you can set styles such as background color using `html` as your selector.

Notes

APPENDIX C
Fixing Element Width in IE 5.x

Internet Explorer 5.x for Windows incorrectly supports the CSS box model. Any padding or border widths are incorporated into your specified width. According to the CSS specification, padding and borders should be added to an element's overall declared width. This can significantly affect your intended design. To get around the rendering inconsistency, you can use a strict DOCTYPE declaration to force Internet Explorer 6 and later to support the box model correctly. Internet Explorer 5.x doesn't support the DOCTYPE switch, but there's another way. Tantek Çelik, the lead developer for the Tasman Engine that drives Internet Explorer 5 for the Macintosh, discovered a way to exploit a parsing bug in Internet Explorer 5.x/Windows that allows you to ensure that your element widths will be displayed correctly.

Whenever you declare a width for an element that also has border and/or padding styles:

1. Set the width as you want it to display in Internet Explorer 5.x, by either testing your results in that browser, or by using Internet Explorer 6 in quirks mode. For example:

   ```
   div { border: 5px solid;
         padding: 20px;
         width: 400px; }
   ```

   In this scenario, the element will display with a 400-pixel width. The border and padding values are subsumed by the content area of the element.

2. Enter the following code after your width declaration:

   ```
   div { border: 5px solid;
         padding: 20px;
         width: 400px;
         voice-family: "\"}\"";
         voice-family:inherit; }
   ```

   This code, which uses aural style sheet properties, forces Internet Explorer 5.x/Windows to stop reading the rule.

3. Enter the correct width value, in this case:

   ```
   div { border: 5px solid;
         padding: 20px;
         width: 400px; voice-family: "\"}\"";
         voice-family:inherit;
         width: 450px; }
   ```

Standards-compliant browsers will not be fooled by the workaround, and will apply the second width declaration. This assures that Internet Explorer 5.x/Windows will honor your intended element widths to the same degree that the 6.0 and later generation of browsers do.

For further explanation of this workaround, visit **http://www.tantek.com/CSS/Examples/boxmodelhack.html**.

APPENDIX D
Scroll Bar Colors

With each release of its Internet Explorer browser, Microsoft introduces several proprietary styles that are often incorporated into the next CSS specification. For example, with the release of Internet Explorer 5, Microsoft introduced scroll bar colors, which are not recognized in the CSS-2 specification but might be incorporated into CSS-3. Unless this happens, Internet Explorer will be the only browser that will support scroll bar colors. Either way, you can use them to enhance your design, and they'll do no harm in non-supporting browsers.

There are many other Internet Explorer-specific properties that may one day be integrated into a future CSS specification.

The following table lists all the scroll bar color properties and describes which part of the scroll bar each property targets.

Property	Description
`scrollbar-face-color`	Sets the color of the *surface* of the scroll bar components.
`scrollbar-track-color`	Sets the color of the area *behind* the scroll bar.
`scrollbar-arrow-color`	Sets the color of the scroll bar arrows.
`scrollbar-shadow-color`	Sets the shade color of each scroll bar component.
`scrollbar-darkshadow-color`	Sets the dark shade color of each scroll bar component.
`scrollbar-highlight-color`	Sets the highlight color of each scroll bar component.
`scrollbar-3dlight-color`	Sets the second highlight color of each scroll bar component.
`scrollbar-base-color`	Sets the color for all scroll bar components. It does not affect arrow color. The highlight and shade colors are automatically set according to the color you choose.

These properties are only supported by Internet Explorer 5 and later.

The following figure precisely demonstrates the scroll bar component that each property targets.

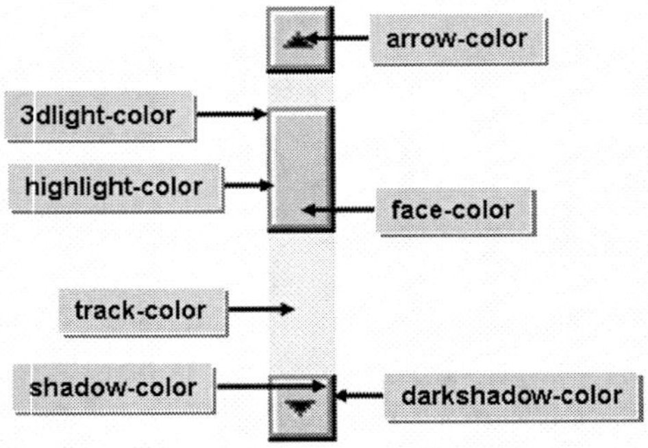

APPENDIX E
Proprietary Cursor Styles

Internet Explorer 6 supports additional cursor styles that are not part of the official CSS-2 specification, but might be integrated into a future CSS specification. The following table lists these cursor styles and describes how each one is meant to be used.

Property, value	Cursor	Description
`cursor: all-scroll`		Intended to indicate that a page or element can scroll in any direction.
`cursor: progress`		Intended to indicate that a process is running in the background.
`cursor: not-allowed`		Intended to indicate that a requested action cannot be carried out.
`cursor: no-drop`		Intended to indicate that a dragged item cannot be dropped at the present cursor location.
`cursor: col-resize`		Intended to indicate that an object or column can be resized horizontally.
`cursor: row-resize`		Intended to indicate that an object or row can be resized vertically.

Property, value	Cursor	Description
`cursor: vertical-text`		Intended to indicate selectable or editable vertical text.

LESSON LABS

Due to classroom setup constraints, some labs cannot be keyed in sequence immediately following their associated lesson. Your instructor will tell you whether your labs can be practiced immediately following the lesson or whether they require separate setup from the main lesson content.

LESSON 1 LAB 1

Applying Color and Typographical Styles Globally

Objective:

Apply color and typographical styles.

Data Files:

- index.html
- enus_085568_01_lab.zip

Before You Begin:

The files necessary to perform this activity are located in the C:\085568Data\color and typography\Lab 1\Starter\grandihost.com folder.

Scenario:

Your client, Grandi-host.com, has reviewed a functional sample of the home page for the site you are designing for them. They have approved most of the style choices you have made and would like you to apply the styles across the remaining pages of the site. You have already created an embedded style sheet to control the styles on the home page, index.html. You need to apply these styles to the remaining pages using a linked style sheet which can also be used to modify the design of all the pages from a single location.

While the client has approved most of the style choices, they have requested a few changes that need to be applied globally. Their requests are as follows:

- Give the heading text the same shade of orange that is applied in the page header.
- Change the heading background color to the dark red color used in the top navigation bar.

- Use a sans-serif font family for all text. Try using Arial, Verdana, and the generic sans-serif family.

1. **Create a new external style sheet named grandihost.css and transfer the styles embedded in index.html to the linked style sheet.**
2. **Link index.html, dedicated.html, advweb.html, ecomm.html, and stdweb.html to the style sheet.**
3. **Apply the requested style changes so that it will affect every page.**

LESSON 2 LAB 1

Modifying Styles on a Specific Page

Objective:
Modify styles on a specific page.

Data Files:
- about.html
- enus_085568_02_lab.zip

Before You Begin:
The files necessary to perform this lesson lab are located in the C:\085568Data\the cascade\Lab 1\Starter\Grandihost.com folder.

Scenario:
Some of the text and links in the About Us page are either not affected by the linked style rules, or the rules that have been applied do not work best in this case. This requires CSS styles that are specific to the About Us page and that are unlike the styles that have been applied across all the pages of the site. Your project team has asked you to make the following style changes to the about.html page:

- In the second paragraph in the center cell, the emphasized word "really" should be in red.
- Decrease the font size of the two paragraphs in the center cell.
- There should be more space on the left and right sides of both the paragraphs.
- In both the paragraphs, increase the readability of the text by adding more space between the lines.

1. **Determine what type of styles or style sheets (linked, embedded, or inline) you should use.**

2. **Determine which selector types will help you best meet the style requirements.**

3. **Apply the required styles using the determined methods and selectors.**

LESSON 3 LAB 1

Formatting Content Sections

Objective:

Format content sections.

Data Files:

- dedicated.html
- enus_085568_03_lab.zip

Before You Begin:

The files necessary to perform this lesson lab are located in the C:\085568Data\box model\Lab 1\Starter\Grandihost.com folder.

Scenario:

While your supervisors like the content on the Dedicated Hosting page, they feel that some changes could be made to improve its presentation and organization. They have discussed it with you and the rest of the project team, and it has been determined that the following modifications will better meet your client's needs:

- Make the text in the top paragraph flow around the right side of the small computer graphic. If necessary, add more space between the graphic and the text that flows around it.
- Increase the amount of space between both paragraphs, as well as the left and right sides of the table cell.
- Create a separate scrollable area of fixed width and height that will allow users to view the dedicated hosting details tables without scrolling the main content.
- Visually separate the scrolling tables from the rest of the page using a border.

1. **Modify the margin and/or padding of the paragraph to meet the style requirements.**

2. In the logical division holding the dedicated hosting information tables, **specify a fixed height that doesn't show all of the table content.**

3. **Add the content overflow style rule that will allow the section to scroll.**

4. **Create a border that separates the scrolling table section from the rest of the page.**

5. **Add a style rule that makes the paragraph text float to the right of the small computer graphic.** Be sure that there is adequate spacing between the floated text and the graphic.

LESSON 4 LAB 1

Creating a Fixed Multi-Column Site Map

Objective:
Create a fixed multi-column site map.

Data Files:
- sitemap.html
- enus_085568_04_lab.zip

Before You Begin:
The files necessary to perform this lesson lab are located in the C:\085568Data\positioning\Lab 1\Starter\Grandihost.com folder.

Scenario:
Your coworker, who has been working on the Grandi-host.com project, has moved to a different project and has asked you to finish the site map for Grandi-host.com. His plan consisted of a layout of ten small content sections in three evenly spaced columns. The site map file (sitemap.html), as shown in the figure, contains the content sections that are not positioned. The mockup that he made in a graphic editing program should give you a general idea of how they should be positioned.

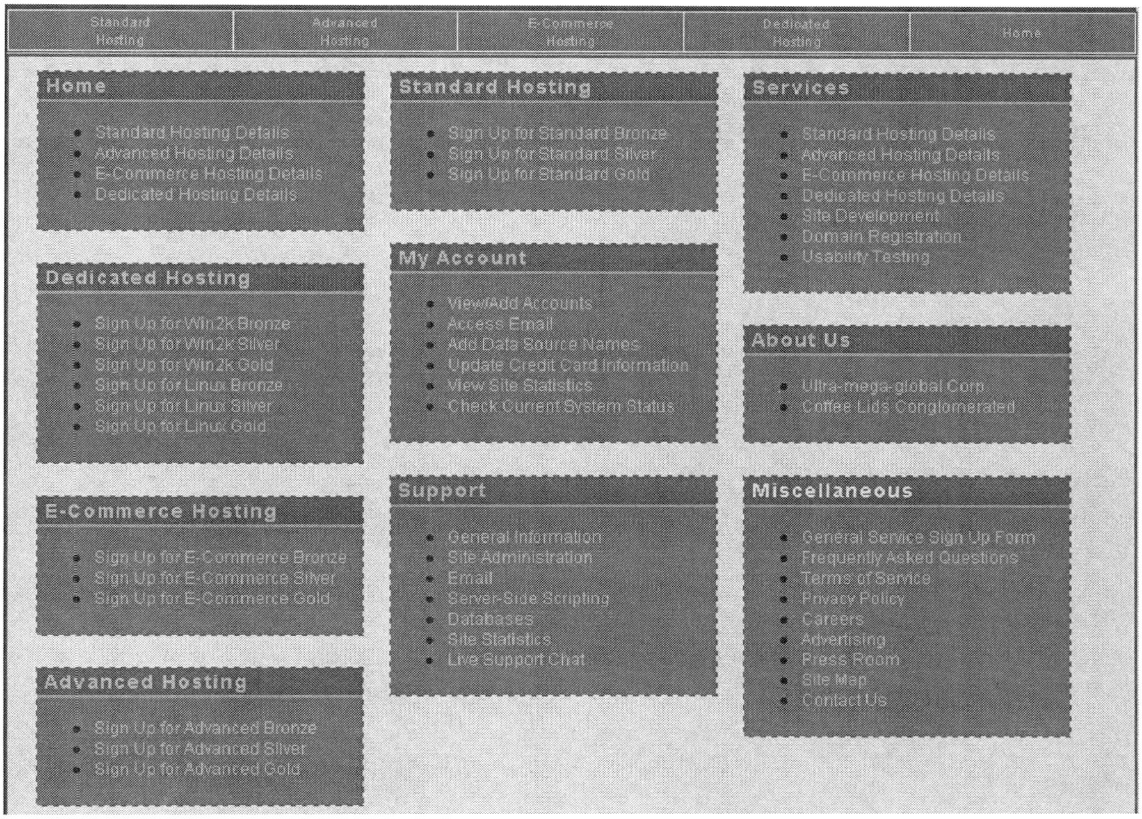

1. **Examine the mockup and the existing code, and then determine a plan to position the columns.**

2. In the embedded style sheet, **enter coordinates for each of the ten content sections.**

3. **Continually enter the coordinates and test the positions of the divisions until a three-column layout is achieved.**

LESSON 5 LAB 1

Enhancing the Existing Site Design

Objective:

Enhance the existing site design.

Data Files:

- index.html
- enus_085568_05_lab.zip

Before You Begin:

The files necessary to perform this lesson lab are located in the C:\085568Data\enhancement\Lab 1\Starter\Grandihost.com folder.

Scenario:

Your project team's creative director has studied the prototypes of the Grandi-host.com site. To add both flair and functionality, she has suggested the following modifications:

- Add link color styles that override the global link color styles in grandihost.css for pages that contain links whose colors conflict with the background color. She specifically makes note of the links contained in the tables with gray backgrounds such as the Frequently Asked Questions page, and the tan links on the About Us, My Account, Support, and Services pages that, in the default link state, aren't visible against the tan background.
- Tie the Support Topics list items on support.html to the Grandi-host.com logo by adding the image sm_earth.gif as graphical bullets (the sm_earth.gif file is located in the Grandihost.com\images folder).
- Use generated content to show a tan asterisk in Netscape before the current page for the Sign Up, My Account, Support, Services, About Us, and FAQ links in the navigation bar on the right hand side of each page.
- Improve the appearance of only the Go button on faq.html by modifying its background color and border. She suggests an orange background and black border.
- If your applied styles remove the default pointer when the mouse pointer hovers above the Go button, specify a cursor to reinforce the fact that it is a button.

---

1. In the embedded style sheet of one of the pages listed in the scenario, **use the existing "topics" or "details" classes to apply colors that are more visible against their background colors for both the default link and visited link states. Apply these same link color styles to any remaining pages that have conflicting colors.**

---

2. In support.html, **create an embedded style that uses sm_earth.gif as a graphical bullet for each item in the bulleted list specified in the scenario.** Use a selector that is dependent on the topics class so that the bullets aren't applied to any other unordered lists on the page.

---

3. In grandihost.css, **add a style rule that will display a tan asterisk before a link with a class named "current."** Be sure to also add the current class to the link on each page that should display after the asterisk when the page is viewed in Netscape.

4. In faq.html, **create a class for the Go button in the Frequently Asked Questions form, and use the class as a dependent selector to modify the button's border and background color.**

5. **Place the mouse pointer over the styled Go button.** If necessary, in the rule you created in the previous step, **specify a different cursor to re-create the browser's default hover behavior.**

LESSON 6 LAB 1

Creating an Accessible Style Sheet and a Print Style Sheet

Objective:

Create an accessible style sheet and a print style sheet.

Data Files:

- enus_085568_06_lab.zip

Before You Begin:

The files necessary to perform this lesson lab are located in the C:\085568Data\alternates\Lab 1\Starter\Grandihost.com folder.

Scenario:

While reviewing the developer's checklist for submitting a site to the usability team for testing, you notice that a part of the requirement is to create alternate style sheets. Specifically, you need to create an accessible style sheet that utilizes the user's chosen system fonts and colors. After reviewing the site, a member of the usability team suggests the following styles:

- Selector: `body`, Property: `background-color`, `font`, Value: `Background`, `status-bar`
- Selector: `div`, Property: `font`, Value: `status-bar`
- Selector: `table`, Property: `background-color`, `color`, Value: `InfoBackground`, `InfoText`

You are also required to create a print style sheet that automatically displays only the most relevant content on a page. It has been decided that the logo and promotional text in the header, the content in the middle table cell, and the content in the right table cell are the most relevant to users. That has led you to make the following style rules:

- Selector: `body`, Property: `background-color`, `color`, `font-size`, Value: `white`, `black`, `14pt`

- Selector: `h4`, Property: `font-size`, Value: `16pt`
- Selector: `#head`, Property: `visibility`, Value: `hidden`
- Selector: `#head img`, Property: `visibility`, Value: `visible`
- Selector: `#topnav`, Property: `visibility`, Value: `hidden`
- Selector: `td.middle`, Property: `width`, Value: `40%`
- Selector: `td.left`, Property: `display`, Value: `none`

1. **Create a new style sheet called sysfontscolors.css.**
2. **Add the styles suggested in the scenario.**
3. **Link the style sheet to a sample page.** Be sure to specify an ***alternate stylesheet*** and a useful title.
4. **Test the stylesheet in Netscape Navigator. Choose View→Use Stylesheet→[Your Link Title] to view the changes.**
5. **Create an additional style sheet called printstyles.css.**
6. **Add the styles suggested in the scenario.**
7. **Test your stylesheet by previewing or by printing the page.**
8. **Copy and paste the `<link>` tags for both the accessible and print style sheets into the remaining pages of the site.**

SOLUTIONS

Lesson 1

Activity 1-2

6. **Would the embedded styles have influence over other pages on the site?**

   No, styles in an embedded style sheet only influence the page in which they are embedded.

Activity 1-3

3. **Of all the colors listed in the scenario, which color cannot be expressed with a shorthand hexadecimal value, and why?**

   The color value `#99CCB3` *can't be expressed with the hexadecimal shorthand because the value of blue is not a matched pair.*

Activity 1-5

2. **Which of these codes represent valid usage of comments?**

   ✓ a) selector { property: value; } /* comment */

   b) selector { property: value; } */ comment /*

   ✓ c) selector { property: value; /* Relevant comment */ property: value; /* Another comment */ }

   d) selector { property: value; /* Relevant comment */ property: value; /* Another comment }*/

   e) selector /* { property: value; } comment /*

3. **How do your comments add to the effectiveness of the code?**

   By indicating which color is at work in each rule, anyone charged with making style revisions in the future won't have to look up the hexadecimal values.

Activity 1-7

3. **If you specify the line height in relative units of measurement like EM units or percentages, will the amount of space change if the browser window is resized?**

   No. Relative units of measurement, when applied to line height, are relative to the size of the font in use.

SOLUTIONS

Activity 1-13

2. **Why don't the other pages on the site pick up the styles in info.html?**

   All the style rules in info.html are in an embedded style sheet, which means that the style rules are applied document-wide only. Embedded style sheet rules cannot influence other documents.

3. **How can you make the styles in info.html apply to all pages on the site?**

   By moving the style sheet rules from the embedded style sheet in info.html to an external style sheet, and then linking all pages to the external style sheet.

8. **What are some advantages of moving the styles to an external style sheet?**

   Answers will vary, but should include:

   - ***Since all the pages share the same color and typography, you only have to specify these related rules once rather than have duplicate styles in an embedded style sheet for each document.***
   - ***Sharing common styles among multiple documents is far more efficient, as it precludes the duplication of styles.***
   - ***The site is now far easier to modify. You can make site-wide style changes from a single location—the external style sheet.***

Activity 2-1

1. **You expected all paragraphs to display with a silver background. Why does one of them display with an orange background color?**

   The paragraph with the `class="nav"` *attribute has an orange background color because it's more specific than the rule applied to all paragraphs.*

2. **What is the *overriding* specificity value for the paragraph with orange background?**

   The specificity value is 11.

3. **You expected the <div> elements to display with a silver background color. Why are both of them orange?**

   Both `<div>` *elements will have an orange background because the last rule, which declares that any* `<div>` *element with the* `"main"` *class has an orange background, has a specificity of 11. This takes precedence over the* `div` *rule and the* `.main` *rule, which have a specificity of 1 and 10, respectively.*

4. **You expected both table rows to have a silver background color. Why is one of them a dark gray?**

   The `tr` *rule declares that all table rows have a silver background, but the* `.head` *rule (specificity of 10) overrides the* `tr` *rule (specificity of 1).*

Activity 2-2

2. **Why are the styles the same for both subheadings?**

   Both headings are defined by the `<h2>` *element, which is attached to a style in the external style sheet.*

3. **How can you change the styles for the first `h2` heading (Nothing New) without affecting the styles for the Other News heading?**

   You can change the styles of first `h2` *heading without affecting the styles of other headings by giving the first subheading a class and applying the new styles with a class selector.*

5. **Are the two subheadings displaying with different styles?**

   Answers will vary, but may include: as long as different values are assigned to the attributes of the headings, subheadings should look different.

7. **Why the NewsParrot text is displayed in orange when there's an existing rule for the `<b>` element that declares black as the color for text?**

   The class rule has a greater specificity, so it overrides the rule for `b`.

8. **Why don't the individual names in each story also display in orange?**

   They don't have the `class` *attribute required to attach the element to the class style.*

Activity 2-4

4. **Can you think of any advantages to using contextual styles over classes?**

   The names you give your classes should be logical, which can help you to understand how the styles are applied. In other words, classes can provide meta information about a style through its name.

5. **How would you make your contextual styles easier to follow when reading or updating a style sheet?**

   You can use comments to indicate what function each contextual style is performing.

Activity 2-5

1. **What attributes or attribute values do these elements have that other like elements in the document do not have?**

   The table holding the contact names is the only one that has an `align` *attribute applied to it. The table cells that contain the navigation links all have a* `height` *attribute set to* `25`.

5. **What are the advantages of this approach to creating styles?**

   Like contextual selectors, you don't have to make any changes to the HTML file to create specifically targeted styles.

Activity 2-6

1. **For the first requirement given in the scenario, should you use the external style sheet or create rules in one or more embedded style sheets?**

   Because the style is only meant for the Staff page, it should be embedded directly in staff.html.

3. **For the second requirement in the scenario, should you use the external style sheet or create rules in one or more embedded style sheets?**

   Because the style is only meant for the Staff page, it should be embedded directly in staff.html.

5. **For the third style requirement in the scenario, should you use the embedded style sheet, the linked style sheet, or both?**

   In this case, you have to use both. First, you need to apply the letter-spacing style to all pages, and then use the embedded style sheet to apply the page-specific background color.

Activity 2-7

3. **Why does the imported style rule for paragraphs override the conflicting style in the linked style sheet?**

   Because the rule in the imported style sheet is imported from within embedded style sheets, so it takes on the same weight as an embedded style sheet. Embedded style sheets are more local than linked style sheets.

4. **If news.css were imported from the linked style sheet parrot.css, how would the paragraphs be displayed?**

   They would display with the larger font size, in accordance with the existing rule in the linked style sheet. Styles in linked style sheets take precedence over rules that are imported from within a linked style sheet.

Activity 2-8

1. **True or False? Inline styles are single instances of a style that are inserted directly into an element via the style attribute.**

   ✓ True

   __ False

3. **What are the possible disadvantages of using inline styles?**

   Answers will vary, but may include:

   - ***Inline styles defeat the primary purpose of CSS—the separation of style and structure.***
   - ***If you ever want to make changes, you have to modify the HTML file directly.***
   - ***Too many inline styles can clutter an HTML document, making it slower to download and more difficult for search engines to index.***

Lesson 3

Activity 3-1

2. **How does setting the page margins to zero help you create precise element margins throughout your pages?**

   Setting the page margins to zero—or any other value to establish consistency across different browsers—can help you to create specific content margins with greater precision because you don't have to consider the different page margins that browsers apply by default.

8. **What has happened to the implicit `0px` value of the bottom margin that is declared for the `<body>` element with the `margin` shorthand property?**

   The `margin-bottom` *value is considered more specific than the implicit value in the shorthand, so the new value overrides the implicit value of the shorthand while retaining its other implicit values for* `margin-left`*,* `margin-right`*, and* `margin-top`*.*

9. **What would the result be if the two properties were reversed in order (if the `margin: 0px` value was specified *after* the more specific `margin-left` value)?**

   The `margin: 0px` *value would override the* `margin-left` *property, even though it's more specific. Preference is given to the conflicting rule that is specified last.*

Activity 3-2

2. **What is the need for setting negative margins?**

   ✓ a) To force an element outside of its container's margin.

   b) To have the same margin settings on all four sides of an element.

   c) To force an element inside of its container's margin.

   d) To override the default value and establish consistency across browsers.

Lesson 4

Activity 4-3

2. **A fixed layout is a layout wherein content sections remain fixed in relation to each other and the page canvas, even when the browser window is resized.**

   _✓_ True

   ___ False

SOLUTIONS

Activity 4-4

1. **Which content sections should have fluid width, and why?**

   To achieve a fluid design, the main content section is best suited for fluid width because it occupies the most space on the page and contains text that can reflow without detracting from readability.

2. **Which content sections are best left with fixed width, and why?**

   The navigation boxes are best left with fixed width because they don't occupy much space on the page.

4. **Why is it necessary to remove the main content section's width?**

   It is necessary because the element's width needs to be flexible. When viewed on a smaller monitor or browser window size, the width of the content needs to adjust to fit that screen. A fixed width prevents this.

5. **Why is it also necessary to remove the positioning properties from the *main* element?**

   In order for each content section to retain its spacing relative to the other elements, the document flow must be recognized. A positioned element does not ***exist*** *in the normal document flow.*

7. **The Top Story section may be displayed in the right spot, but why does the Other Headlines section overlap with the main content section at larger browser window sizes?**

   The overlapping occurs because the Other Headlines section is still absolutely positioned with a `left` *value, which forces the element to display in that position. The main content section is now controlled by the margins, which are relative to the left and right edge of the browser window.*

8. **How can you make the Other Headlines section react to the resizing of the browser window along with the main content section?**

   You can make the Other Headlines section react by declaring its position relative to the right edge of the browser window, rather than the left.

10. **How can you give the page footer a flexible width while keeping a fixed distance between the left edge of the browser window and the left edge of the Headlines section?**

    You can give the page footer a flexible width by removing the positioning properties and replacing them with similar margin values. The footer will retain its vertical position without positioning properties because it and the main content section are the only elements on the page that ***exist*** *in the document flow, so the footer will always be vertically positioned.*

Activity 4-7

1. **Why is the Movies layer displayed on top?**

   The Movies layer is displayed on top because it is the last layer in the document flow. By default, when elements occupy the same position on a page, the last layer in the document is displayed on top.

Lesson 5

Activity 5-2

2. **The cursor: text keyword is used for what purpose?**

   ✓ a) To display the standard icon as the default cursor for an element.

   b) To display the standard icon as the default cursor for text elements.

   c) To display the standard icon as the default cursor for text links.

   d) To display the standard icon as the default cursor for links.

Activity 5-3

1. **What's the difference between using the `a` element as a selector and using the `a:link` selector?**

   Applying styles to the `a` element assigns a general style to links in all of their four states, while the `a: link` selector applies the style to all links that have not been visited.

7. **In your opinion, do these styles enhance the usability of the links and complement the existing design?**

   Answers may vary.

Activity 5-5

3. **Why is the background image hidden behind the logo and link sections?**

   The tiling background image is hidden behind the elements that contain the logo image and the links because they have background colors specified.

Activity 5-7

2. **How can you make only the unordered list item text display in bold and the ordered list text in normal?**

   You can make the unordered list item text display in bold and the ordered list text in normal by overriding the inheritance of the bold style by applying the `font-weight: normal` property to the `<ol>` element.

Notes

GLOSSARY

absolute positioning
A positioning method wherein the elements you arrange on a page are removed from their normal place in the flow of HTML elements.

absolute units
Unit of measurement that specifies a precise length, such as in pixels or inches.

accessible style sheet
Any style sheet, typically an alternate style sheet, that provides users with viewing options.

alternate style sheet
An optional alternative to your site's preferred style sheet that can be selected by the user.

attribute selectors
Selectors that attach styles to an element or elements that have specific attributes or attribute values.

borders
Lines of various styles, colors, and width that display on one or more outside edges of an element's bounding box.

box model
The formatting model of CSS that creates rectangular boxes for the elements in a document.

Cascading Style Sheet
(CSS) The standard presentational markup language for the web.

class selectors
Selectors that allow you to name your own styles, distinguish an element from other like elements, or share styles among multiple different elements.

color names
Predefined keywords that represent a specific color.

contextual selectors
Selectors that target elements within a specified parent-child structure. These are also known as descendant selectors.

declaration
The component of a rule that applies the style to a selected element. It consists of braces that contain the property or series of properties and their associated values.

DHTML
A family of technologies, including HTML, CSS, DOM, and scripts, that enable the creation of dynamic and interactive web pages.

document type (DOCTYPE) declaration
A statement that declares which version of HTML is used in a document.

Document Type Definition (DTD)
The set of rules dictating the structure of a document.

element classes
Classes that are associated with a specific HTML element.

element selectors
In CSS-1, type selectors were referred to as element selectors, while in CSS-2 the terminology changed to type selectors (Also see: type selectors).

embedded style sheets
Style sheets that control the design of the document in which they are embedded.

fixed layout
A layout wherein content sections remain fixed both in relation to each other and the page canvas, even when the browser window is resized.

fixed positioning
A positioning method wherein a positioned element is affixed to the page canvas in the specified location, and will not scroll with other page content.

float
To align an element to either side of an adjacent element.

fluid layout
Layout that accommodates the size of a user's browser. It is also known as flexible layout.

fluid margin
A margin, based on a relative unit of measurement, that increases or decreases in size according to the size of the user's browser window.

font family
Any font face name, such as Times New Roman or Arial, and all of its variations such as bold, italic, etc.

font styles
Styles that relate directly to fonts and their variations, including size and weight.

generated content
Content (text or images) that you specify directly from a style sheet. The content itself is not defined in an HTML document.

generic family
A type of font, such as serif, sans-serif, or monospaced.

hexadecimal values
Base-16 color codes that represent variations in red, green, and blue that combine to create a specific color.

ID selectors
Selectors that target a single element on a page. Styles set with an ID selector must be unique; they cannot be shared among other elements.

independent classes
Classes that are not associated with any specific HTML element.

inheritance
A mechanism in CSS by which elements pick up the styles of their parent elements.

inline styles
Single instances of a style that are inserted directly into an element via the style attribute.

kerning
The amount of space between letters of any given text element.

layers
Elements that are positioned on top of one another.

leading
The amount of space between adjacent lines of text.

link relationship
The relationship between a document and a linked style sheet. You define a link relationship with the `rel` attribute of the `<link>` tag.

link state
The status of a link as defined by user activity. The four link states are default, hover, active, and visited.

linked style sheets
External text files with a .css extension that only contain CSS rules. Linked style sheets can control the design of any number of pages from a central location.

margin
The component of the box model that defines the space between an element's box and its parent element.

modular
The ability of several different style sheets to interact in order to establish a design.

overflow
The content that is left over when an element's specified height is not large enough to contain its content. You can control how the overflowing content is displayed by using the `overflow` property.

padding
Component of the Box model that defines the space between an element's content and its bounding box.

page canvas
The viewing area in which all page elements are contained. The page canvas is defined by the `<body>` element.

persistent style sheet
The style sheet that's always enabled.

positioning
A family of CSS properties that specifically addresses the position of elements on a page. There are three types of positioning: absolute, relative, and fixed.

preferred style sheet
The default style sheet that is disabled when a user selects an alternate style sheet.

print style sheet
A style sheet intended to optimize the appearance of a web document when it's printed.

property
A predefined term that defines the action taken on an element.

pseudo-classes
The means through which the styles for each link state are defined.

pseudo-element
A specification for an element that is only recognized by CSS.

reflow
Describes the behavior of elements that do not have fixed widths. When a browser window changes size, an element without a fixed width will be "redrawn" by the browser so that its dimensions fill up the available space.

relative positioning
A method of positioning elements wherein the elements remain in the document flow.

relative units
Unit of measurement that specifies a length value relative to an inherited or a default value.

RGB format
A method of specifying gradations of red, green, and blue that combine to create a specific color.

rule
A definition of styles for a given element. It consists of a selector, and one or more property-value combinations that make up the rule's declaration.

selector
The component of a rule that selects the element you want to style.

specificity
The amount of "weight" or importance that a given rule has over other rules that might conflict with it. The specificity of a rule is determined by its selector.

stacking order
The order in which overlapping elements, or layers, are displayed.

style sheet
Any rule or series of rules that control the presentation of a document.

text styles
CSS properties that control typographical styles.

type selectors
A selector that attaches a style to a particular HTML element, such as `<p>` or `<div>`. These selectors apply the specified style to all instances of a paragraph or division.

typography
All the styles that deal with fonts, font sizes, and the alignment and spacing of type.

value
An exact specification of a property.

viewport

An term used to describe the area of a browser window in which the pages are rendered.

INDEX

INDEX

Looking for media files?

They are now conveniently located at www.elementk.com/courseware-file-downloads

Downloading is quick and easy:

1. Visit www.elementk.com/courseware-file-downloads
2. In the search field, type in either the part number or the title
3. Of the courseware titles displayed, choose your title by clicking on the name
4. Links to the data files are located in the middle of the screen
5. Follow the instructions on the screen based upon your web browser

Note that there may be other files available for download in addition to the course files.

Approximate download times:

The amount of time it takes to download your data files will vary according to the file's size and your Internet connection speed. A broadband connection is highly recommended. The average time to download a 10 mb file on a broadband connection is less than 1 minute.